Security and Privacy in IoMT

Challenges and Solutions

RIVER PUBLISHERS SERIES IN DIGITAL SECURITY AND FORENSICS

The "River Publishers Series in Security and Digital Forensics" is a series of comprehensive academic and professional books which focus on the theory and applications of Cyber Security, including Data Security, Mobile and Network Security, Cryptography and Digital Forensics. Topics in Prevention and Threat Management are also included in the scope of the book series, as are general business Standards in this domain.

Books published in the series include research monographs, edited volumes, handbooks and textbooks. The books provide professionals, researchers, educators, and advanced students in the field with an invaluable insight into the latest research and developments.

Topics covered in the series include-

- Blockchain for secure transactions
- Cryptography
- Cyber Security
- Data and App Security
- Digital Forensics
- Hardware Security
- IoT Security
- Mobile Security
- Network Security
- Privacy
- Software Security
- Standardization
- Threat Management

For a list of other books in this series, visit www.riverpublishers.com

Security and Privacy in IoMT
Challenges and Solutions

Editors

Deepak Gupta
MAIT, New Delhi, India

Anuj Kumar Singh
Amity University Madhya Pradesh, Gwalior, India

Yu-Dong (Eugene) Zhang
University of Leicester, UK

River Publishers

Routledge
Taylor & Francis Group
NEW YORK AND LONDON

Published 2025 by River Publishers
River Publishers
Broagervej 10, 9260 Gistrup, Denmark
www.riverpublishers.com

Distributed exclusively by Routledge
605 Third Avenue, New York, NY 10017, USA
4 Park Square, Milton Park, Abingdon, Oxon OX14 4RN

Security and Privacy in IoMT / by Deepak Gupta, Anuj Kumar Singh, Yu-Dong (Eugene) Zhang.

Routledge is an imprint of the Taylor & Francis Group, an informa business

ISBN 978-87-7004-167-6 (hardback)
ISBN 978-87-4380-079-8 (paperback)
ISBN 978-87-7004-740-1 (online)
ISBN 978-87-7004-739-5 (master ebook)

DOI: 10.1201/9788770047395

Contents

Preface

Internet of Medical Things, abbreviated as IoMT, is an environment of connected wearable gadgets, sensors, medical instruments, and clinical services. It facilitates numerous healthcare solutions to minimize healthcare expenses, provide prompt medical assistance, and enhance the standards of hospital treatment. The IoMT is revolutionizing the medical sector by providing personalized and targeted treatments and by facilitating seamless communication of medical data. The advances in wireless communication systems, sensor technologies, portable devices, big data analysis, and cloud services mainly drive it. Through technological developments and a combination of analytics that aid in improved diagnosis and therapy, the importance of IoMT in the realm of healthcare is undeniably a win-win situation for patients.

IoMT devices are more trustworthy in monitoring and tracking due to higher accuracy levels, which also assist in minimizing human errors and inaccurate reporting. While these pervasive medical gadgets have many merits, they also pose severe privacy and security risks. Medical systems acquire, process, and perform decision-making on the basis of this sensitive health information. Cyber attackers who exploit the flaws and weaknesses in these IoMT devices might well be able to penetrate the hospital network and also gain unauthorized access to private patient data. Attacks on these IoMT devices can have the potential to endanger the patients' lives and cause serious physical harm.

The security and privacy concerns that patients and medical practitioners confront are being covered in this book. The book identifies a topical subject since IoMT devices are vulnerable to cyberattacks, and a security breach could unlock the door for cybercriminals to penetrate hospital networks. In addition to outlining viable solutions that take into account constrained resources at IoMT end-devices, hybrid network architecture, application characteristics, and communication protocols, the book covers the core concepts of IoMT security and privacy. The book describes both theoretical and practical aspects for those working in security in the IoMT, emphasizing the most significant potential IoT security issues and challenges.

The book is organized into three sections. The first section, which includes four chapters introducing IoMT security, is titled Section 1. Four chapters in Section 2 highlight the latest developments in IoMT security and privacy. Three chapters make up Section 3, which focuses on integrating machine learning and artificial intelligence to secure IoMT.

In-depth information about IoMT is provided in *Chapter 1* of this book, which also examines its uses, architecture, security concerns, and other aspects. Beginning with an overview of the advantages of IoMT in the healthcare sector, the chapter looks at how the integration of intelligent, networked devices facilitates real-time monitoring, remote patient management, and data-driven decision-making. The intricate network of devices, sensors, and communication protocols that form the basis of this revolutionary technology is then revealed through a thorough examination of the IoMT architecture. Lastly, the chapter briefly discusses the crucial subject of IoMT security.

IoMT security issues are examined in *Chapter 2*, which also emphasizes the need for strong security controls to guarantee the IoMT's secure operation. The hazards to patient privacy and health, as well as the security vulnerabilities presented by IoMT, are discussed. We talk about IoMT architecture and the necessity for IoMT security. Furthermore, the chapter highlights potential new study directions. To formally demonstrate the lack of defects and vulnerabilities, *Chapter 3* investigates the relationship between formal methods and security in the literature as it relates to the examination of WBANs in the IoMT sector.

The IoMT laws in various countries like the US Federal Trade Commission (FTC), the FDA, the National Institute of Standards and Technology (NIST), the Health Insurance Portability and Accountability Act (HIPAA), the EU General Data Protection Regulation (GPDR), the Canadian Personal Information Protection and Electronic Documents Act, and the EU Medical Device Regulation (MDR) are discussed in *Chapter 4*. It has been explained that these laws and regulations will support the ethical and lawful use of medical devices in the quickly developing field of healthcare technology, as well as market access, patient safety, and regulatory compliance.

Chapter 5 of the book emphasizes the interdisciplinary nature of the challenges faced in IoBNT, requiring collaboration among fields such as physics, mechanical engineering, chemical engineering, biology, and information technology. It also explains the unification of information security in IoBNT that standardization efforts can greatly aid, but widespread adoption requires user education and awareness. *Chapter 6* explains the modular encryption standard (MES), which is a centrism-tiered paradigm for protecting the confidentiality of healthcare data provided by probability tracking of sensitive information. This chapter also explains a machine learning technique that uses a fuzzy inference system and neural networks to enhance decision-making regarding the risk monitoring strategy of MES. This chapter has also covered methods/tools for analyzing the accuracy and error rate of MES, as well as data collecting, cleaning, analysis, and interpretation of results.

An Arduino-based women's safety gadget for the Internet of Medical Things (IoMT) environment is proposed in *Chapter 7*. The suggested device operates by means of functionality that is triggered by pressing the panic button. The user can start an emergency message in this and include evidence of the situation from the surrounding area. Depending on how critical it is, an emergency message will be sent to the pre-specified members along with the database. Women will have access to safety features with the planned device.

In *Chapter 8*, a case study highlighting the integration of digital twin technology and intelligent transportation system for IoMT has been presented. Using the framework presented in this study, one can design and execute a variety of scenarios in which sensors or the Internet of Everything (IoE) are used to integrate the various parts of a larger Big Data system. Many IoT platform components that enable a dynamic and adaptable setup are explained in this case study. In *Chapter 9*, the advantages and disadvantages of model-agnostic and model-specific approaches to XAI in the medical field are discussed. This article explains the opportunities and risks presented by XAI in healthcare, as well as the necessity of establishing evaluation standards and encouraging moral AI application. The study finds that by bridging the gap between data-driven insights and clinical decision-making, XAI has the potential to improve patient diagnosis and care.

With an emphasis on the integration of cutting-edge AI technologies, *Chapter 10* provides a systematic analysis of the security status of the healthcare system as it stands today. This chapter examines the many methods for securing healthcare systems as well as the uses of AI in this area. Additionally, this chapter examines the difficulties and constraints associated with utilizing AI in healthcare security and suggests avenues for future research. The analysis emphasizes how artificial intelligence (AI) has the potential to improve healthcare system security through monitoring access to sensitive health data, detecting and mitigating cyber risks, and improving authentication procedures. *Chapter 11* investigates the potential solutions for security and privacy issues in IoMT networks using ML-based IDS. Finally, by outlining the challenges and constraints of implementing ML-based IDS at every IoMT layer, the work offers a potential research area.

The book covers every important facet of IoMT and gives readers an overview of current research trends in the field of security and privacy. This book has a unique approach that addresses nearly all aspects of IoMT security.

Editors

Deepak Gupta

Anuj Kumar Singh

Yu-Dong (Eugene) Zhang

List of Figures

List of Tables

List of Contributors

Adebisi, Oluwadare, *Department of Mechatronics Engineering, First Technical University Ibadan, Nigeria; E-mail: oluwadare.adebisi@tech-u.edu.ng*

Adejumobi, Philip, *Department of Electrical and Electronics Engineering, Ladoke Akintola University Ogbomoso, Nigeria E-mail: adejumobiphilip@gmail.com*

Aljohani, Abeer A., *Computer Science Department, Applied College, Taibah University, Saudi Arabia; E-mail: aahjohani@taibahu.edu.sa*

Ayoade, Idowu, *Department of Mechatronics Engineering, First Technical University Ibadan, Nigeria; E-mail: idowu.ayoade@tech-u.edu.ng*

Basak, Sirsha, *Kalinga Institute of Industrial Technology, Deemed to be University, India; E-mail: 2106159@kiit.ac.in*

Belmokadem, Houda, *Information and Communication Technologies Laboratory (LabTIC), National School of Applied Sciences of Tangier, Abdelmalek Essaadi University, Morocco; E-mail: h.belmokadem@uae.ac.ma*

Bhardwaj, Aditya, *School of Computer Science Engineering and Technology, Bennett University, India; E-mail: aditya.bhardwaj@bennett.edu.in*

Bhardwaj, Rajat, *School of Computer Science and Engineering, RV University, India; E-mail: rajatbhardwaj.x@gmail.com*

Bouziane, Imane, *Information and Communication Technologies Laboratory (LabTIC), National School of Applied Sciences of Tangier, Abdelmalek Essaadi University, Morocco; E-mail: imane.bouziane1@etu.uae.ac.ma*

Dureja, Ajay, *Department of Information Technology, Bharati Vidyapeeth's College of Engineering, India; E-mail: ajaydureja@gmail.com*

Dureja, Aman, *Department of Information Technology, Bhagwan Parshuram Institute of Technology (BPIT), India; E-mail: amandureja@gmail.com*

Garg, Ankit, *AIT-CSE, UCER, Chandigarh University, India*

Goyal, Shikha, *Plot No. 2, Yamuna Expressway, Sector 17A, India; E-mail: shikha.goyal@galgotiasuniversity.edu.in*

Gupta, Umesh, *School of Computer Science Engineering and Technology, Bennett University, Gr.Noida, India-201310; E-mail: er.umesh.gupta@gmail.com*

Hasan, Fatima Qasim, *Plot No. 2, Yamuna Expressway, Sector 17A, India; E-mail: fatimaqasim.hasan@galgotiasuniversity.edu.in*

Indra, Gaurav, *Department of IT, Indira Gandhi Delhi Technical University for Women, India; E-mail: gauravindra@igdtuw.ac.in*

Jain, Vishal, *Department of Computer Science and Engineering, School of Engineering and Technology, Sharda University, India; E-mail: drvishal-jain83@gmail.com*

Jothimani, S., *Department of Computer Science and Engineering, Bannari Amman Institute of Technology, Sathyamangalam, India; E-mail: jothimanis.phd@gmail.com*

Karthiga, M., *Department of Computer Science and Engineering, Bannari Amman Institute of Technology, Sathyamangalam, India; E-mail: karthigam@bitsathy.ac.in*

Khalique, Fehmina, *Plot Number 11, Knowledge Park II, India; E-mail: fehmina.khalique@lloydbusinessschool.edu.in*

Kumar, Varun, *Department of Management, Mangalmay Institute of Management and Technology, India; E-mail: varun.management@gmail.com*

Kumar, Ajay, *KIET Group of Institutions, India*

Kumar, Mahesh, *Department of Information Technology, Bharati Vidyapeeth's College of Engineering, India; E-mail: maheshmalkani@gmail.com*

Meena, Vaishali, *Department of IT, Indira Gandhi Delhi Technical University for Women, India; E-mail: vaishali019phd22@igdtuw.ac.in*

Mishra, Sushruta, *Kalinga Institute of Industrial Technology, Deemed to be University, India; E-mail: sushruta.mishrafcs@kiit.ac.in*

Mohapatra, Swastik, *Kalinga Institute of Industrial Technology, Deemed to be University, India; E-mail: 2005137@kiit.ac.in*

Moussaoui, Mohamed, *Information and Communication Technologies Laboratory (LabTIC), National School of Applied Sciences of Tangier, Abdelmalek Essaadi University, Morocco; E-mail: m.moussaoui@uae.ac.ma*

Oladeji, Dolapo, *Department of Mechatronics Engineering, First Technical University Ibadan, Nigeria; E-mail: michaeldolapo21@gmail.com*

Oni, Adedotun, *Department of Biomedical Engineering, First Technical University Ibadan, Nigeria; E-mail: adedotun.oni@tech-u.edu.ng*

Sahoo, Pragynasmita, *Kalinga Institute of Industrial Technology, Deemed to be University, India; E-mail: 2105048@kiit.ac.in*

Sangeethaa, S. N., *Department of Computer Science and Engineering, Bannari Amman Institute of Technology, Sathyamangalam, India; E-mail: dr.snsangeethaa@gmail.com*

Singh, Shweta, *Department of Computer Applications, KIET Group of Institutions, India; E-mail: shweta.vidudi272@gmail.com*

Singh, Anuj Kumar, *Amity University Madhya Pradesh, India; E-mail: anujbtechcs@gmail.com*

Tiwari, Raj Gaurang, *Chitkara University Institute of Engineering and Technology, Chitkara University, India; E-mail: rajgaurang@chitkara.edu.in*

Tripathi, Arun Kumar, *Department of Computer Applications, KIET Group of Institutions, India; E-mail: mailtoaruntripathi@gmail.com*

Vashishtha, Apaar, *Kalinga Institute of Industrial Technology, Deemed to be University, India; E-mail: 20051942@kiit.ac.in*

List of Abbreviations

AAL	Ambient assisted living
ABE	Attribute-based encryption
ADR	Adaptive data rate
AES	Advanced encryption standard
AI	Artificial intelligence
ANN	Artificial neural network
APIs	Application program interfaces
ASL	Arterial spin labeling
ATDR	Adaptive transmission data rate
ATP	Adenosine-triphosphate
AVISPA	Automated validation of internet security protocols and applications
BAKMP	Blockchain-enabled authenticated key management protocol
BAN	Logic Burrows-Abadi-Needham
BAN	Body area network
BCI	Bio-cyber interfaces
BIP	Behavior, Interaction, Priority
BLE	Bluetooth low energy
BR/EDR	Basic rate/enhanced data rate
BS	Base station
BSDMF	Blockchain-assisted secure data management framework
BSN	Body sensor network
CAGR	Compound annual growth rate
CDH	Computational Diffie-Hellman
CDSS	Clinical decision support system
CE	Cloud environment
CNN	Convolutional neural network
CNT	Carbon nano tubes
CPS	Cyber–physical system

CPU	Central processing unit
CRADA	Cooperation Research and Development Agreement
CRT	Chinese remainder theorem
CT	scan Computed tomography scan
DBIs	Deep brain implants
DBN	Deep belief network
DDOS	Distributed denial of service
DDSS	Distributed data storage system
DHTs	Digital health technologies
DICOM	Digital Imaging and Communications in Medicine
DL	Deep learning
DoS	Denial of service
DPIA	Data protection impact assessment
DR	Diabetic retinopathy
DT	Digital twin
EAODV	Enhanced on-demand vector
ECC	Elliptic curve cryptography
ECDSA	Elliptic curve digital signature algorithm
ECGs	Electrocardiograms
EDPDCS	Efficient differentially private data clustering scheme
EEG	Electroencephalogram
EH	Energy harvesting
EHRs	Electronic health records
EM	Electromagnetic
EMG	Electromyogram
e-PHI	Electronically protected health information
EPoSVM	Efficient privacy-preserving outsourced support vector machine
ERED	Electromagnetic radiation emitting device
EU	European Union
EMDR	European Medical Devices Regulation
FDA	Food and Drug Administration
FFD	Full function device
FHIR	Fast Healthcare Interoperability Resources
FMEA	Failure modes and goods analysis
FM-UWB	Frequency modulation UWB

FPR	False positive rate
FTC	Federal Trade Commission
FV	Fisher vector
GAN	Generative adversarial network
GDPR	General Data Protection Regulation
GNR	Graphene nano ribbons
GPDR	General Data Protection Regulation
GPU	Graphics processing unit
HBC	Human body communication
HIDS	Host-based intrusion detection system
HIPAA	Health Insurance Portability and Accountability Act
HIS	Hospital information systems
HL7	Health Level 7
HLPSL	High-Level Protocol Specification Language
HOL	Higher-order logic
HTLBO	Hybrid teaching and learning based optimization
ICDs	Implantable cardioverter-defibrillators
ICT	Information and communication technology
ICU	Intensive care unit
IDC	International Data Corporation
IDS	Intrusion detection system
IEEE	Institute of Electrical and Electronics Engineers
IETF	Internet Engineering Task Force
IF	Intermediate form
IMD	Implantable medical device
IoBDT	Internet Biodegradable Factors
IoBNT	Internet of Bio-Nano Things
IoE	Internet of Everything
IoMT	Internet of Medical Things
IoMT-SAF	IoMT security assessment framework
IoNT	Internet of Nano Things
IoT	Internet of Things
IPFS	Inter planetary file systems
IR-UWB	Impulse radio UWB
ITS	Intelligent transportation system
JSON	JavaScript object notation
KNN	K-nearest neighbor

LACO	Lightweight authentication, access control, and ownership
LIME	Local interpretable model-agnostic explanations
LLC	Logical link control
LoRaWAN	LoRa wide area network
LPWAN	Low-power wide area networking
LSTM	Long short-term memory
MAAKA	Mutual authentication and key agreement
MAC	Media access control
MC	Molecular communication
MDR	Medical Device Regulation
MES	Modular encryption standard
ML	Machine learning
MLP	Multilayer perceptron
MOU	Memorandum of understanding
MQ	Multivariate-quadratic equation
MRI	Magnetic resonance imaging
NB	Narrowband
NB-IoT	Narrowband Internet of Things
NCRB	National Crime Record Bureau
NFC	Near-field communication
NIDS	Network-based intrusion detection system
NIST	National Institute of Standards and Technology
NLP	Natural language processing
OCR	Office for Civil Rights
PACS	Picture archiving and communication systems
PAN	Personal area network
PAT	Physical Authentication Token
PAT	Process Analysis Toolkit
PHA	Process hazard analysis
PHI	Protected health information
PHY	Physical layer
PII	Personal identifiable information
PIPEDA	Personal Information Protection and Electronic Documents Act
PMA	Pre-market approval
PSL	Provably-secure and lightweight
PUFs	Physical unclonable functions
ReLU	Rectified linear unit

RF	Radio frequency
RFD	Reduced function device
RFID	Radio frequency identification
RMA	Risk matrix approach
RNN	Recurrent neural network
SaMD	Software as a Medical Device
SARA	Self-adaptive routing algorithm
SDR	Software-defined radio
SQRA	Semiquantitative risk analysis
SRAC	Selective ring-based access control
sRNA	Short RNA
SVM	Support vector machine
TDD	Targeted drug delivery
TDMA	Time division multiple access
TLS	Transport layer security
UNB	Ultra-narrow band
UWB	Ultra-wideband
VAW	Violence against women
VCU	Virginia Commonwealth University
VPNs	Virtual private networks
WAN	Wide area network
WBAN	Wireless body area network
WCS	Wireless chemical sensor
WMSNs	Wireless medical sensor networks
WPAN	Wireless personal area networking
WPT	Wireless power transfer
XAI	Explainable artificial intelligence
XML	Extensible markup language

1

Introduction to IoMT: Advantages, Limitations, Architecture, Applications, and Security Aspects

Anuj Kumar Singh[1], Ankit Garg[2], and Ajay Kumar[3]

[1]Amity University Madhya Pradesh, India
[2]AIT-CSE, UCER, Chandigarh University, India
[3]KIET Group of Institutions, India
E-mail: anujbtechcs@gmail.com

Abstract

The emergence of the Internet of Medical Things (IoMT) has brought about a significant transformation in the healthcare sector, providing previously unattainable prospects to augment patient care, optimize resource allocation, and elevate healthcare results in general. This book chapter offers a thorough overview of IoMT, exploring its various facets, including benefits, constraints, architecture, uses, and security issues. The chapter starts by outlining the benefits of IoMT in the healthcare industry and examining how the incorporation of intelligent, networked devices enables data-driven decision-making, remote patient management, and real-time monitoring. This is followed by a detailed analysis of IoMT architecture, which reveals the complex web of gadgets, sensors, and communication protocols that serve as the foundation for this game-changing technology. Finally, the chapter touches on the important topic of IoMT security. It looks at the particular cybersecurity issues that linked medical devices present, going over methods to protect private patient information, stop illegal access, and guarantee the integrity of IoMT systems. For researchers, technologists, and healthcare professionals who are interested in learning about the nuances of IoMT, this book chapter provides an insightful and approachable introduction. Readers

DOI: 10.1201/9788770047395-1

will get the knowledge necessary to both mitigate and capitalize on the transformative potential of IoMT by navigating through its many components.

Keywords: IoMT, advantages, limitations, authentication, WBAN, security, attacks.

1.1 Introduction

The Internet of Things, popular as IoT, has been transforming numerous sectors, including the healthcare industry. A specific subset of IoT called the Internet of Medical Things (IoMT) has the potential to completely transform the medical sector by allowing for remote patient health monitoring and management, increasing the effectiveness of healthcare services, and ultimately improving the overall quality of care [1]. In this chapter, we will examine the architecture of IoMT, including its essential components, connectivity options, data management, and possible effects on the industry. Healthcare information technology systems are connected through a network of physical infrastructures, application programs, and clinical devices known as IoMT. To facilitate rapid and flexible analysis of medical data, IoMT, sometimes referred to as IoT in the healthcare industry, enables wireless and remote equipment and devices to connect via the internet safely. Medical personnel can be delivered more rapidly and more efficiently with the help of integrated medical equipment. IoMT advancements have made clinical activities like glucose monitoring and robotic surgery possible. Two of IoMT's main benefits are better treatments and lower expenses. Thanks to IoMT technology, patients may be better and more regularly monitored without having to attend medical facilities, and diagnoses can be made faster and more accurately. With the numerous advantages of IoMT due to technological innovations, there are also a few limitations [2]. The advantages and limitations of IoMT are illustrated in Figure 1.1 and explained below.

1.1.1 Advantages of IoMT

The Internet of Medical Things (IoMT) topic is expanding quickly and includes a vast array of internet-connected medical systems and equipment. These gadgets, which frequently have sophisticated communication capabilities and sensors built in, are revolutionizing the healthcare sector in several ways. Because of its potential to improve patient care, expedite healthcare procedures, and increase the system's overall efficiency, IoMT has attracted

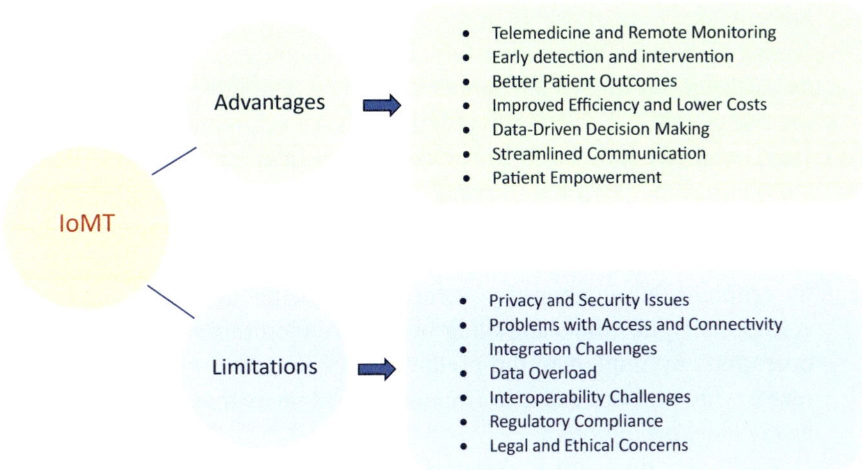

Figure 1.1 Advantages and limitations of IoMT.

a lot of interest and appeal. The prominent advantages of IoMT are listed below [3].

(i) **Telemedicine and remote monitoring:** One of IoMT's biggest benefits is its capacity to provide telemedicine and remote monitoring. The widespread availability of wearable technology and linked sensors has made it possible to monitor patients in real time, even when they are at home. Numerous advantages result from this, including early health issue discovery, fewer hospital visits, and the provision of vital information to healthcare providers so that they may make well-informed decisions regarding patient treatment. Virtual consultations are made possible by telemedicine, which is especially helpful for patients who are unable to attend a medical facility physically.

(ii) **Early detection and intervention:** IoMT devices play a critical role in the early identification and management of health problems. Vital sign monitoring, trend analysis, and alert generation are all possible when a patient's state deviates from the norm. This enables medical professionals to step in early to stop health issues from getting worse and possibly save lives. For instance, wearable technology may identify abnormal cardiac rhythms and notify the user to get help right away.

(iii) **Better patient outcomes:** IoMT devices provide more individualized and data-driven healthcare, which helps to improve patient outcomes. Doctors can review a patient's past medical records to monitor their present state, diagnose them more precisely, and prescribe the best course of therapy. Better long-term health outcomes can also be achieved by tracking and improving patient adherence to treatment programs with the use of IoMT devices' reminders and feedback features.

(iv) **Improved efficiency and lower costs:** The Internet of Medical Things (IoMT) has the potential to greatly improve the efficiency of healthcare delivery by automating data transmission and collection, eliminating the need for manual data entry and paperwork. This can save money by reducing administrative overhead and better allocating resources. Additionally, hospitals and other healthcare facilities can optimize their operations by implementing predictive maintenance on medical equipment, which minimizes downtime and guarantees that vital devices are always in working order.

(v) **Data-driven decision-making:** By producing enormous volumes of data, IoMT facilitates data-driven decision-making. Healthcare practitioners can adjust healthcare protocols, evaluate the efficacy of therapies, and spot patterns and trends using this data. In addition, scientists can utilize this data to carry out research, create novel treatments, and learn more about the long-term health consequences of patient populations.

(vi) **Streamlined communication:** IoMT can help healthcare providers collaborate and communicate more effectively. Physicians, nurses, and other healthcare workers can more easily coordinate patient care and make well-informed decisions when they have access to digital health records, telemedicine platforms, and real-time patient data. As a result, patient care is enhanced, administrative workloads are decreased, and workflow is more efficient.

(vii) **Patient empowerment:** IoMT empowers patients by enabling them to actively participate in their own health management. In addition to setting personal health objectives and getting real-time feedback on their progress, patients can view their health statistics. This results in better health outcomes and motivates patients to take a more active role in their care, which eventually lightens the load on healthcare systems.

1.1.2 Limitations of IoMT

Although IoMT has several benefits, any potential drawbacks and difficulties must be considered to ensure its responsible and secure implementation [4].

(i) **Privacy and security issues:** The possibility of data breaches and privacy violations is one of the biggest drawbacks of IoMT. Hackers may find the large volume of private patient data transferred and stored in the cloud to be an alluring target. In the absence of strong cybersecurity safeguards, unapproved access to medical records could result in identity theft and improper use of patient information [5].

(ii) **Problems with access and connectivity:** Internet of Things devices depend on internet access, which occasionally fails or is prone to interruptions. Losing connectivity could be fatal in emergency scenarios. One of the ongoing challenges is making sure IoMT systems stay connected securely and stably.

(iii) **Integration challenges:** Integrating IoMT technologies with healthcare institutions' current infrastructure might be difficult because they frequently use a wide range of different systems and equipment. Compatibility concerns and the requirement for additional hardware and software might increase the cost and complexity of adopting IoMT solutions.

(iv) **Data overload:** Healthcare providers may find it difficult to handle the massive volume of data produced by IoMT devices. It takes time to sift through the data and find pertinent facts. In addition, there is a chance that medical staff members may have "alert fatigue" from constant notifications, which could result in them ignoring critical signals.

(v) **Interoperability challenges:** Interoperability problems arise when IoMT devices made by various manufacturers do not interact well with one another. Because healthcare practitioners may need to obtain data from numerous sources, this can lead to data fragmentation and make it difficult to deliver comprehensive care.

(vi) **Regulatory compliance:** Adhering to healthcare rules, including the Health Insurance Portability and Accountability Act (HIPAA), in the US is imperative. However, it can be difficult to ensure that IoMT systems follow these rules. For healthcare providers and device makers, noncompliance poses serious risks because it can result in substantial fines and legal ramifications.

(vii) **Legal and ethical concerns:** There are many legal and ethical issues with IoMT. Who, for instance, oversees and owns the patient data that IoMT devices collect? What effects on patient autonomy and consent result from forcing patients to utilize IoMT devices for monitoring? These issues demand in-depth analysis and appropriate legal frameworks.

1.2 Architecture of IoMT

Integrating and connecting medical devices, healthcare systems, and data analytics platforms seamlessly is made possible by the Internet of Medical Things (IoMT) architecture framework [6, 7]. The purpose of its design is to facilitate the safe and seamless gathering, organizing, and evaluation of medical records. This section of the chapter focuses on the architecture of IoMT and will examine its primary components, connectivity options, and data management. These are illustrated in Figure 1.2 and explained below.

1.2.1 Key components of IoMT architecture

The key components of IoMT architecture are devices, sensors, communication protocols, cloud-based data centers, edge devices, gateways, user interfaces, application programs, data analytics, and artificial intelligence.

(i) **Devices and sensors:** The devices and sensors form the foundation of the IoMT architecture. These can include wearable technology like fitness trackers and smart watches, as well as specialized medical equipment like electrocardiogram (ECG) machines, blood pressure monitors, and continuous glucose monitoring. Vital signs, patient activities, and environmental factors are just a few of the data kinds that these sensors gather.

(ii) **Communication protocols:** IoMT uses several different communication protocols to transfer data from devices and sensors to centralized systems. Cellular networks (3G, 4G, and now 5G) and low-power wide area networks (LPWAN) like NB-IoT and LoRaWAN are among the most widely used protocols, as are Bluetooth and Wi-Fi. Range, data rate, power consumption, and the needs of the application are some of the variables that influence the protocol choice.

(iii) **Cloud-based data centers:** Cloud-based data centers play a major role in IoMT for data processing, analytics, and storage. These data centers can handle the massive volumes of data generated by IoMT devices because they are scalable and have strong processing capacity. IoMT applications are made possible by cloud platforms like Microsoft Azure, Google Cloud, and Amazon Web Services (AWS).

(iv) **Edge devices and gateways:** Many IoMT applications begin with data processing and analysis at the edge, which is closer to the location where the data is generated. In this procedure, gateways and edge devices are essential. By doing preliminary data preprocessing, edge devices – which are usually positioned close to the sensors – help minimize the

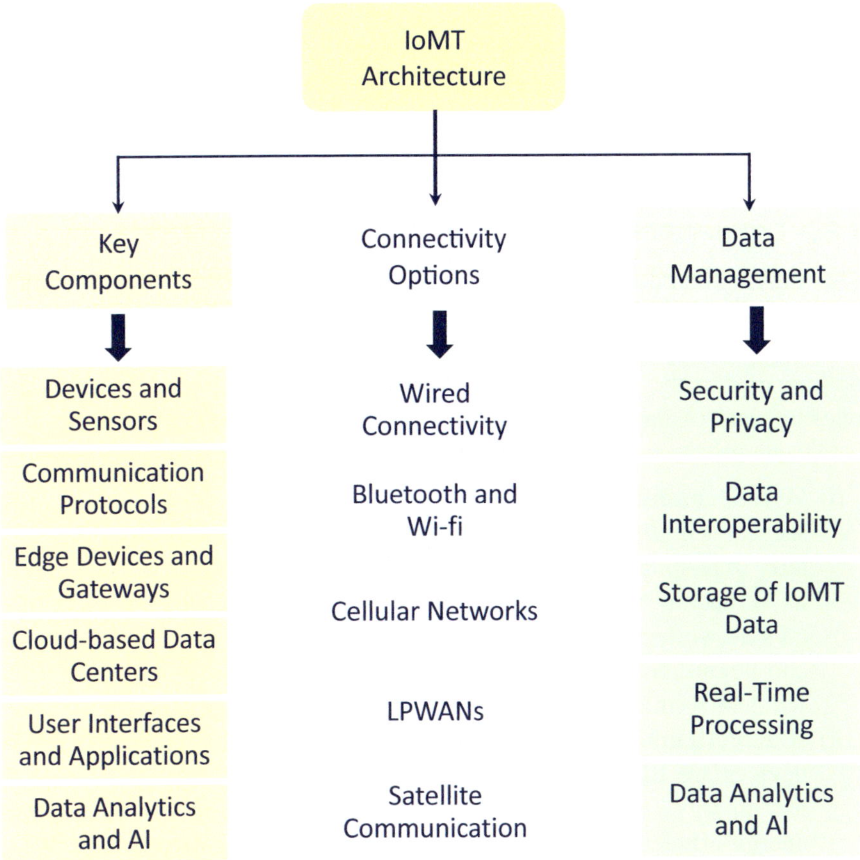

Figure 1.2 Key components, connectivity options, and data management in IoMT.

volume of data transferred to centralized servers. Conversely, gateways gather, combine, and send data from various sensors to the cloud for additional processing.

(v) User interfaces and applications: Healthcare providers, patients, and caregivers can access the data and insights produced by IoMT systems via intuitive applications and user interfaces. Users can stay informed, interact with medical providers, and track their health through mobile apps and web platforms. The user experience using these interfaces is intended to be smooth and intuitive.

(vi) Data analytics and artificial intelligence: IoMT's capacity to produce useful insights from patient data is one of its biggest benefits. This data is processed and interpreted using data analytics and artificial intelligence (AI), giving medical practitioners access to real-time information and predictive analytics. AI systems are capable of identifying patterns, trends, and abnormalities in patient data, which can help with early diagnosis and therapy.

1.2.2 Connectivity options in IoMT

The IoMT architecture depends on several communication technologies, including cellular networks, Bluetooth, Wi-Fi, and specialized medical device communication protocols, to enable data transmission. These connecting options ensure the ability to securely send the gathered health data to the relevant data management systems. The different connectivity options that IoMT can utilize are listed below [8].

(i) **Wired connectivity:** Because cable connectivity is dependable and secure, it is still widely used in some healthcare environments, particularly in hospitals and clinics. Medical equipment such as MRI scanners, ECG machines, and other devices are frequently connected to the hospital's network through wired connections. However, to improve mobility and flexibility in the delivery of healthcare, the trend is moving toward wireless solutions.

(ii) **Bluetooth and Wi-Fi:** The most popular connectivity choices for IoMT devices are Bluetooth and Wi-Fi. For wearable technology, Bluetooth low energy (BLE) is a common protocol that enables short-range, energy-efficient communication. Wi-Fi has greater data transfer rates and a longer range than BLE, making it appropriate for devices used in homes or other inside spaces.

(iii) **Cellular networks:** 3G, 4G, and 5G cellular networks are crucial for Internet of Medical Things (IoMT) devices that require wider coverage regions, such as remote patient monitoring. IoMT stands to benefit greatly from 5G's low latency and high bandwidth, which allow for real-time communication and facilitate telemedicine and other applications.

(iv) **LPWANs:** Low-power wide area networks, or LPWANs, are intended for devices that need low data rates and a long battery life. Smart home healthcare solutions and asset tracking and monitoring are two applications that benefit greatly from the use of technologies like LoRaWAN and narrowband-IoT (NB-IoT).

(v) **Satellite communication:** Satellite communication offers a practical option in isolated or rural locations where traditional connectivity options could be limited. Because they provide worldwide coverage, satellite networks are useful for telemedicine in underdeveloped areas, emergency medical services, and disaster relief.

1.2.3 Data management in IoMT

The IoMT architecture uses cloud infrastructure to store, process, and manage the massive amounts of healthcare data produced by connected devices. Cloud servers, databases, and computing resources offer secure data storage, scalability, and dependability [9]. Healthcare providers and academics can gain useful insights by processing and analyzing the acquired data using machine learning algorithms and data analytics tools.

(i) **Security and privacy of IoMT data:** Security and privacy are critical components of IoMT design since healthcare data is sensitive. Access control procedures, secure authentication, and end-to-end encryption are used to guard against unauthorized access or breaches. Adherence to healthcare laws, such as the Health Insurance Portability and Accountability Act (HIPAA) in the US, is required to protect data security and privacy.

(ii) **Data interoperability:** One of the biggest problems in healthcare is data interoperability. According to IoMT systems, data from several sources, including different devices and electronic health records (EHRs), must be able to be smoothly linked and shared. Achieving interoperability requires the use of standardized data formats, such as fast healthcare interoperability resources (FHIR).

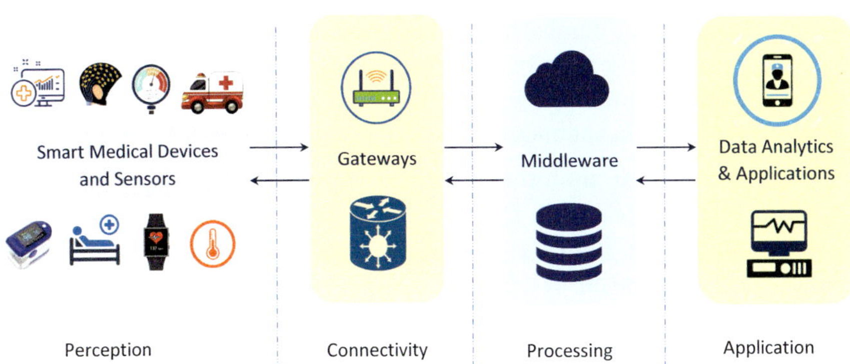

Figure 1.3 Generic architecture of IoMT.

(iii) **Storage of IoMT data:** IoMT devices generate enormous amounts of data; so scalable and reliable storage solutions are needed. Cloud-based storage options are widely used because of their accessibility and flexibility. To prevent data loss, redundancy and backup plans are implemented. Policies for data retention are also established to adhere to legal obligations.

(iv) **Real-time processing of IoMT data:** IoMT systems use real-time data processing capabilities to facilitate real-time monitoring and decision-making. Systems for processing data streams, like Apache Kafka and Apache Flink, handle and analyze data streams as they come in, allowing for quick reactions to important events.

(v) **Data analytics and AI:** Artificial intelligence (AI) and data analytics are essential for extracting valuable insights from the massive volume of patient data. Machine learning models can be trained to recognize trends, anomalies, and predicted patterns in patient health to help with early diagnosis and individualized treatment strategies.

Figure 1.3 shows a generic architecture of IoMT based on the primary components used in IoMT settings, connection types for data transfer, and data management.

1.3 Applications of IoMT

The various uses of IoMT in the healthcare industry are going to be discussed in this section. The introduction of newer gadgets centered around IoMT-based technologies has been held responsible for the transformation of the antiquated healthcare system into a smart and customized system. COVID-19 has increased the number of IoMT-based devices that are now in use. Conversely, a plethora of technologies have been built, especially to combat COVID-19. There are numerous applications of IoMT in the healthcare sector, and the significant ones have been shown in Figure 1.4 [10, 11].

(i) **Remote patient monitoring:** It is one of the main uses of IoMT applications. Real-time monitoring of patients' vital signs and persistent illnesses is made possible by healthcare providers' connected medical equipment, like glucose meters, blood pressure monitors, and wearable fitness trackers. To enable prompt response and lessen the need for frequent in-person visits, this data is provided to healthcare providers. Healthcare systems can manage resources more effectively while providing patients with more individualized treatment.

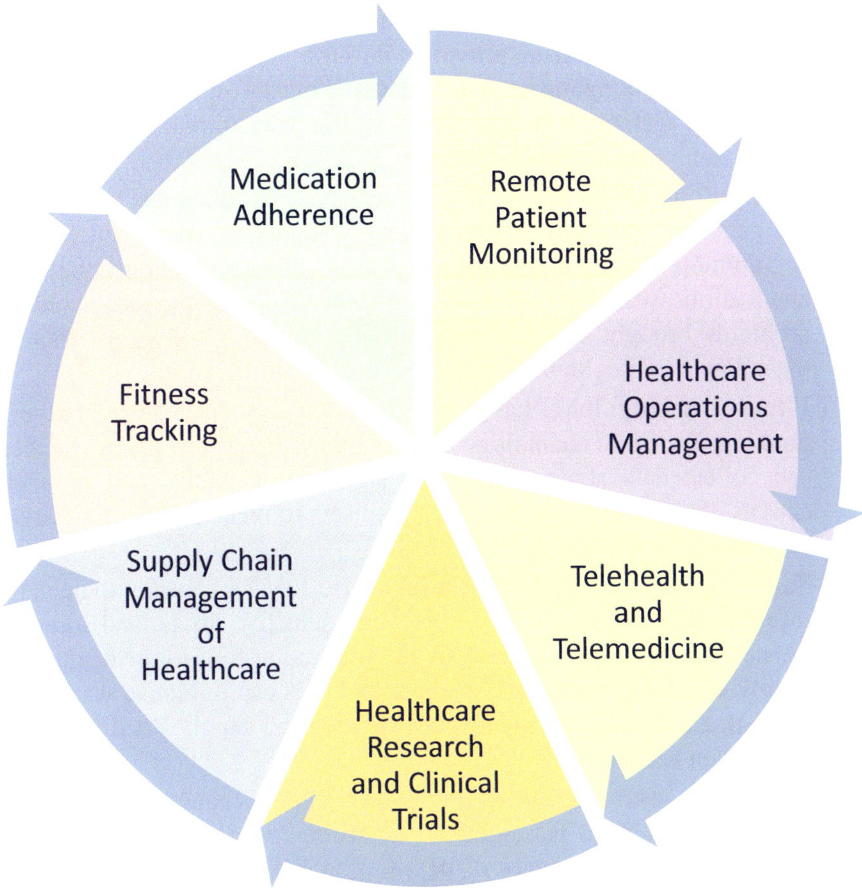

Figure 1.4 Applications of IoMT.

(ii) Healthcare operations management: IoMT can improve hospital operations by checking the whereabouts and condition of medical equipment and keeping an eye on patients' vital signs while they are there. Wait times can be decreased, resources can be allocated more effectively, and overall patient care may be improved using this data. Tracking the transmission of diseases within healthcare institutions and keeping an eye on hand hygiene also aids in infection control.

(iii) Telehealth and telemedicine: The combination of IoMT with telemedicine and telehealth services has increased access to healthcare, especially in rural or economically deprived regions. It is easier to manage chronic diseases and get prompt medical advice when patients can speak with healthcare providers through video chats and have their vital signs remotely monitored. Because it makes remote treatment and counseling services possible, IoMT is also very important for mental health.

(iv) **Medication adherence:** IoMT can increase drug adherence by tracking dose trends and delivering reminders. Patients' medicine intake can be monitored using smart pill dispensers and medication adherence applications, which can send out alerts when a dose is missed. Avoiding problems brought on by non-adherence not only assists patients in managing their health but also lowers healthcare expenses.

(v) **Fitness tracking:** IoMT has greatly impacted personal health and fitness tracking. Wearable technology such as fitness bands and smart watches can collect data about users' vital signs, sleep habits, and physical activity. This knowledge better equips users to make proactive lifestyle decisions and enhance their health.

(vi) **Supply chain management of healthcare:** IoMT's capacity to manage inventories, keep an eye on temperature-sensitive drugs, and forecast the need for medical supplies can all be advantageous to the healthcare supply chain. By doing this, medical facilities can minimize waste and guarantee patient safety by having the required supplies and drugs on hand when needed.

(vii) **Healthcare research and clinical trials:** IoMT is beneficial to clinical studies and medical research. In real-world settings, participants can provide enormous volumes of data to connected devices and sensors, which can produce more thorough and precise results. Researchers can use this data to test novel medicines, gain a better understanding of diseases, and enhance healthcare procedures.

1.4 Security Aspects of IoMT

Despite IoMT's involvement in a large-scale service deployment in the healthcare sector, the resource constraints' nature of IoMT devices and sensors expose them to severe security and privacy risks. The entire healthcare ecosystem is at risk due to these vulnerabilities, which could endanger human lives in addition to being devastating for IoMT. Threat channels for IoMT have become more diverse, complex, and scalable over time, making it harder to identify and offer strong defenses against these attacks [12]. The four

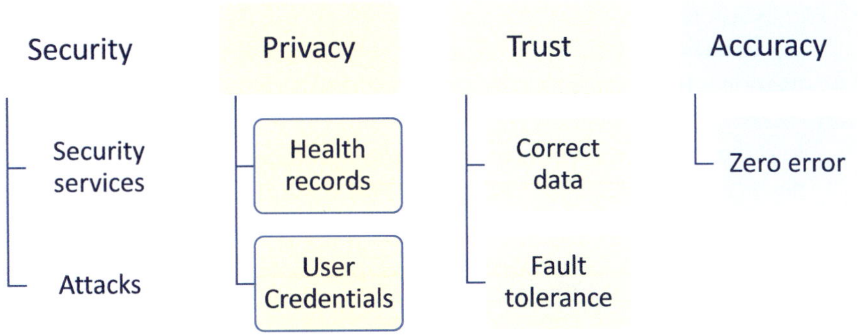

Figure 1.5 IoMT safety aspects.

fundamental pillars to ensure the safety of IoMT are security, privacy, trust, and accuracy, as shown in Figure 1.5.

(i) Security:

Because most IoMT devices have insufficient security measures, which can be attributed to design flaws or insufficient secure authentication mechanisms that a skilled attacker easily circumvents, an attacker can intercept and seize both inbound and outbound data and information across IoMT. Because of the inability to detect and prevent such attacks, it is also feasible to get unauthorized access without being detected. This could lead to malicious code being injected, devices becoming infected with malware, or the attacker obtaining additional access. Ensuring and maintaining the safety of medical equipment, networks, and the medical cyber–physical system requires healthcare product manufacturers to prioritize security [13]. Reducing the primary IoMT security threats requires defense against both passive and active attacks.

(ii) Privacy:

Due to the possibility of collecting and disclosing private and sensitive medical data, passive assaults like traffic monitoring raise privacy concerns. This is a very serious risk since it allows an adversary to learn about a patient's specific medical conditions and history, endangering the patient's life. Attacks on hospitals can lead to identity theft, which violates patients' privacy. In practically all of these real-world attacks, patients' privacy was violated via the disclosure of sensitive or private information.

(iii) Trust:

A breach of a patient's privacy creates serious trust difficulties. Those in professions like doctors, nurses, and office workers are starting to question the notion that technology will eventually replace people. People dread the idea that a clinical robot, device, or gadget is watching them and their issues.

(iv) Accuracy:

IoMT data accuracy is very important. Medical robots have lost a great deal of their precision and diagnostic capacity due to unintentional mistakes. Numerous incidences demonstrating how medical robots execute activities with inadequate accuracy and precision have been reported; these incidents result in incorrect prescriptions and patient misdiagnoses.

1.4.1 Security requirements for IoMT

Confidentiality, availability, and integrity are the three main security requirements for every system, according to the National Institute of Standards and Technology (NIST) [14, 15]. More security features and functionalities, however, must be met in real-world scenarios. An IoMT system must meet the following security requirements in addition to the fundamental ones listed by NIST: forward security, data freshness, scalability, authentication, non-repudiation, authorization, and auditability [16]. Figure 1.6 displays the entire set of security properties needed by the IoMT system.

- **Confidentiality:** No unauthorized entity is going to receive access to data coming from IoMT devices.
- **Integrity:** The data coming from IoMT devices must not be modified while in transit.
- **Availability:** Authorized users can access the medical data from the devices at any time.
- **Forward security:** Even when a long-term session key is compromised, the prior communications are not accessible to the attacker.
- **Authorization:** It is a right granted to an entity that gives them access to data from IoMT devices [5].
- **Authentication:** The authorized user needs to be verified before they may access the IoMT device and data [6].
- **Auditability:** IoMT systems must be capable of reviewing and analyzing security-related operations and records to assess the effectiveness of system controls, make sure that established security protocols and policies are followed, identify potential security breaches, and recommend any adjustments that may be required for defensive measures.

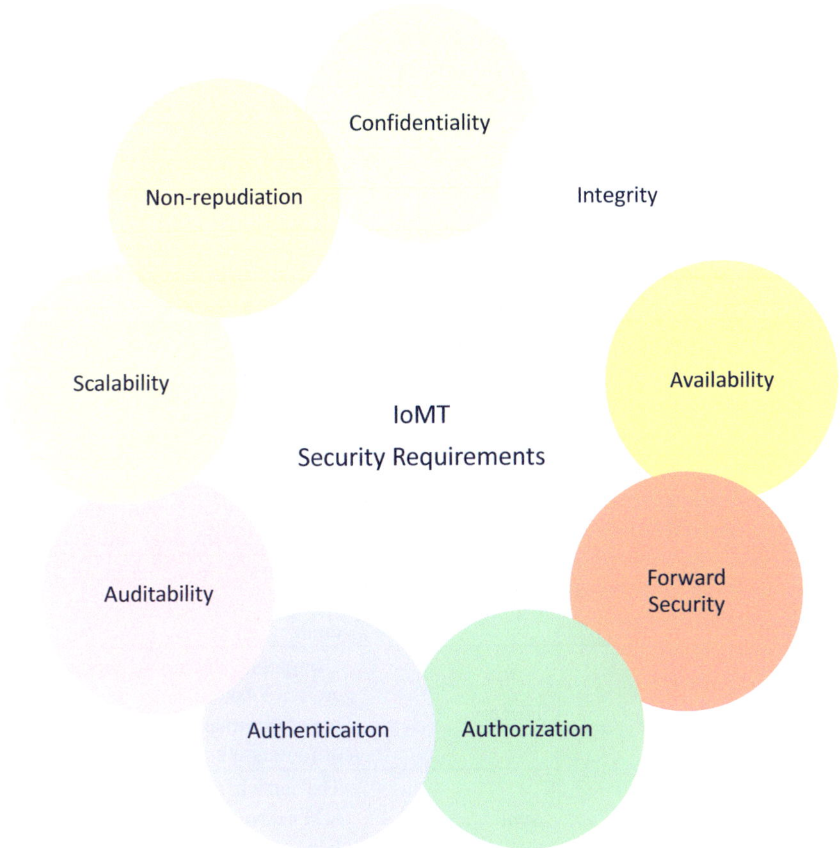

Figure 1.6 Security requirements of IoMT [4].

- **Scalability:** The IoMT system must be capable of integrating extra devices.
- **Non-repudiation:** The user and IoMT device cannot deny the data once it has been transmitted or received.

1.4.2 Attacks on IoMT

After examining the attacks that were tried on the IoMT system, it was found that these attacks can be classified as follows: attacks on data confidentiality, attacks on authorization, attacks on integrity, attacks on authentication, and attacks on availability [17]. Table 1.1 provides insight into this type of attack classification.

Table 1.1 Classification of attacks in IoMT.

Attack category	Specific attack	Elucidation
Attacks on confidentiality	Eavesdropping	In order to collect confidential information, the attacker discreetly listens to communication media.
	Traffic analysis	The attacker uses the patterns in the transmission to deduce details about the private information.
	Impersonation	An attacker mimics the identity of a trustworthy entity in order to access the IoMT data.
Attacks on integrity	Man-in-the-middle	The attacker has the power to alter data and interrupt the user and IoMT device during their discussion.
	Physical	An attacker with physical access to an IoMT device could change the device's functionality and structure.
	Malware	An attacker could harm an IoMT device by installing malicious codes on it.
Attacks on authentication	Forgery	Using this technique, the attacker creates a fake identity and transfers bogus information with the intention of fooling other entities.
	Sybil	The attacker accesses a genuine IoMT device by using multiple false IDs.
	Device cloning	An attacker can create a large number of clones by gathering confidential information from a legal device [21].
	Masquerading	An attacker poses as an authorized user to gain access to IoMT data.
Attacks on authorization	Social engineering	An adversary may trick the IoMT edge network into believing they are credible in order to obtain access to users' medical devices [22].
	Malware	Attackers may infect linked IoMT devices, compromising them [23].
Attacks on availability	Denial of service	Once the attacker sends the bogus queries, the IoMT system becomes unavailable [24].

An extensive array of possible threats becomes available to the IoMT ecosystem as it grows to encompass a diverse range of connected devices and applications. In order to prevent unwanted access to and tampering with private medical data, authentication is an essential security precaution. Many attacks, such as brute force, man-in-the-middle, and credential stuffing, pose a major threat to the security of authentication systems in IoMT [18, 19]. To increase the security of IoMT networks and prevent future breaches, strong authentication protocols, multi-factor authentication systems, and encryption techniques must be implemented to address these challenges. To keep an IoMT infrastructure secure and resilient, it must also be maintained. This involves fast upgrades to handle new threats, frequent security audits, and continuous monitoring [20].

1.5 Conclusion

IoMT's potential to transform healthcare delivery by providing practitioners with real-time data, enabling remote patient management, and encouraging data-driven decision-making has been demonstrated by the benefits of its exploration. The comprehensive examination of IoMT architecture provided readers with a profound comprehension of the structural complexities of this revolutionary technology by illuminating the networked network of gadgets, sensors, and communication protocols that support it. The chapter also addressed the crucial topic of security in IoMT, acknowledging the particular cybersecurity difficulties brought on by medical equipment that is networked. Through an exploration of methods to safeguard patient data, stop illegal access, and maintain system integrity, it emphasized how crucial a strong security framework is to achieving the full potential of IoMT. This chapter provides a well-informed and approachable introduction to IoMT for academics, technologists, and healthcare professionals. Through navigating the many IoMT components, readers get the knowledge necessary to fully realize the transformative potential of this technology as well as the ability to negotiate and lessen the problems that come with putting it into practice.

References

[1] Monteiro, A. C. B., França, R. P., Arthur, R., & Iano, Y. (2023). An overview of the Internet of medical things (IoMT): Applications, benefits, and challenges. Security and Privacy Issues in Internet of Medical Things, 83-98.

[2] Yaacoub, J. P. A., Noura, M., Noura, H. N., Salman, O., Yaacoub, E., Couturier, R., & Chehab, A. (2020). Securing internet of medical things systems: Limitations, issues and recommendations. Future Generation Computer Systems, 105, 581-606.

[3] https://digitalhealth.folio3.com/blog/benefits-of-iomt/ (Last accessed: 16 Nov 2023).

[4] Alex Shpachuk, https://empeek.com/how-the-internet-of-medical-things-solves-the-challenges-in-medical-device-industry/ (Last accessed: 16 Nov 2023).

[5] Singh, Anuj Kumar, and B. D. K. Patro. "Performance Comparison of Signcryption Schemes–A Step towards Designing Lightweight Cryptographic Mechanism." International Journal of Engineering and Technology (IJET) 9, no. 2 (2017).

[6] Awotunde, J. B., Ijaz, M. F., Bhoi, A. K., AbdulRaheem, M., Oladipo, I. D., & Barsocchi, P. (2022). Edge-IoMT-based enabled architecture for smart healthcare system. In 5G IoT and Edge Computing for Smart Healthcare (pp. 1-27). Academic Press.

[7] Srivastava, J., Routray, S., Ahmad, S., & Waris, M. M. (2022). Internet of Medical Things (IoMT)-based smart healthcare system: Trends and progress. Computational Intelligence and Neuroscience, 2022.

[8] Koutras, D., Stergiopoulos, G., Dasaklis, T., Kotzanikolaou, P., Glynos, D., & Douligeris, C. (2020). Security in IoMT communications: A survey. Sensors, 20(17), 4828.

[9] Abbas, A., Alroobaea, R., Krichen, M., Rubaiee, S., Vimal, S., & Almansour, F. M. (2021). Blockchain-assisted secured data management framework for health information analysis based on Internet of Medical Things. Personal and ubiquitous computing, 1-14.

[10] Joyia, G. J., Liaqat, R. M., Farooq, A., & Rehman, S. (2017). Internet of medical things (IoMT): Applications, benefits and future challenges in healthcare domain. J. Commun., 12(4), 240-247.

[11] Bharati, S., Podder, P., Mondal, M. R. H., & Paul, P. K. (2021). Applications and challenges of cloud integrated IoMT. Cognitive Internet of Medical Things for Smart Healthcare: Services and Applications, 67-85.

[12] Singh, A. K., Garg, A., & Nayyar, A. (2023). Blockchain for security and privacy in healthcare informatics. Innovations in Healthcare Informatics: From Interoperability to Data Analysis, IET, 41, 157.

[13] Singh, A. K., & Patro, B. D. K. (2021). Security Attacks on RFID and their Countermeasures. In Computer Communication, Networking and IoT: Proceedings of ICICC 2020 (pp. 509-518). Springer Singapore.

[14] Singh, A. K., Nayyar, A., & Garg, A. (2023). A secure elliptic curve-based anonymous authentication and key establishment mechanism for IoT and cloud. Multimedia Tools and Applications, 82(15), 22525-22576.

[15] Garg, A., Singh, A. K., & Garg, M. (2023). Role of Internet of Things and artificial intelligence for healthcare informatics: an overview. Innovations in Healthcare Informatics: From Interoperability to Data Analysis, IET, 41, 107.

[16] Hireche, R., Mansouri, H., & Pathan, A. S. K. (2022). Security and privacy management in Internet of Medical Things (IoMT): A synthesis. Journal of Cybersecurity and Privacy, 2(3), 640-661.

[17] Lopez Martinez, A., Gil Pérez, M., & Ruiz-Martínez, A. (2023). A Comprehensive Review of the State-of-the-Art on Security and Privacy Issues in Healthcare. ACM Computing Surveys, 55(12), 1-38.

[18] Garg, A., & Singh, A. K. (2022). Internet of Things (IoT): Security, Cybercrimes, and Digital Forensics. In Internet of Things and Cyber Physical Systems (pp. 23-50). CRC Press.

[19] Garg, A., & Singh, A. K. (2021). Applications of Internet of Things (IoT) in Green Computing. Intelligence of Things: AI-IoT Based Critical-Applications and Innovations, 1-34.

[20] Hasan, M. K., Ghazal, T. M., Saeed, R. A., Pandey, B., Gohel, H., Eshmawi, A. A., ... & Alkhassawneh, H. M. (2022). A review on security threats, vulnerabilities, and counter measures of 5G enabled Internet-of-Medical-Things. IET Communications, 16(5), 421-432.

[21] Singh, A. K., & Patro, D. B. (2019). A novel security protocol for wireless sensor networks based on elliptic curve Signcryption. International Journal of Computer Networks & Communications (IJCNC) Vol, 11.

[22] Singh, A. K., & Patro, B. D. K. (2020). Signcryption-based security framework for low computing power devices. Recent Advances in Computer Science and Communications (Formerly: Recent Patents on Computer Science), 13(5), 845-857.

[23] Singh, A. K., & Kumar, S. (2024). An efficient and secure CLAKA protocol for blockchain-aided wireless body area networks. Expert Systems with Applications, 242, 122740.

[24] Singh, A. K., & Kumar, S. (2023). Performance Analysis of ECC-Based Security Solutions for Internet of Medical Things. In International Conference on Data Analytics & Management (pp. 337-347). Singapore: Springer Nature Singapore.

2

Security of Internet of Medical Things: Techniques, Challenges, and Potential Solutions

Oluwadare Adebisi[1], Idowu Ayoade[1], Philip Adejumobi[2], Adedotun Oni[3], and Dolapo Oladeji[1]

[1]Department of Mechatronics Engineering,
First Technical University Ibadan, Nigeria
[2]Department of Electrical and Electronics Engineering,
Ladoke Akintola University Ogbomoso, Nigeria
[3]Department of Biomedical Engineering,
First Technical University Ibadan, Nigeria
E-mail: oluwadare.adebisi@tech-u.edu.ng; idowu.ayoade@tech-u.edu.ng; adejumobiphilip@gmail.com; adedotun.oni@tech-u.edu.ng; michaeldolapo21@gmail.com

Abstract

The Internet of Medical Things (IoMT) is a fast-growing field with the potential to revolutionize the provision of healthcare services. It consists of an intelligent medical devices network that enables remote and wireless appliances to communicate and easily evaluate clinical data online. The Internet of Medical Things enhances the healthcare system by providing real-time information, remote monitoring of patients, and improved patient experience. Recently, IoMT networks have become increasingly susceptible to cyber-attacks, which could have detrimental effects on patient safety and data security. Each internet-connected device poses a potential security risk, and numerous threats could result in a data breach. Security breaches against IoT devices could result in patient treatment delays, inaccessible medical records, and ransomware attacks. This chapter investigates the security challenges associated with the IoMT and highlights the necessity for effective security measures to ensure its secure functioning. The security threats posed by the

DOI: 10.1201/9788770047395-2

IoMT and the associated risks to patient health and privacy are examined. The need for IoMT security and IoMT architecture are discussed. Additionally, the chapter identifies prospective new directions for future research. It is essential that healthcare professionals are aware of the security risks posed by the IoMT and that organizations make the necessary efforts to guarantee safe and secure operations.

Keywords: Internet of Medical Things, security, privacy of data, encryption, authentication, IoMT devices, sensor.

2.1 Introduction

The Internet of Medical Things (IoMT) consists of medical devices and various applications that connect with healthcare information systems for communication via online computer networks [1]. It is an interconnected network of medical devices, sensors, software, and systems that collect, transmit, and analyze healthcare data. The rapid rise of IoMT involves monitoring environmental variables with high-tech hardware and software platforms, communication channels, and the development of cutting-edge data analytic tools [2]. Generally, IoT has three layers: the physical layer, the network layer, and the application layer. The data are gathered in the physical layer. The network layer transforms the data into a suitable form while the end users use the device at the application layer [1]. The application layer is subdivided into an application support platform sublayer for information sharing and industry-specific applications for smart transportation, smart healthcare, and smart energy management [2, 3].

IoMT, with the application of data analytics and artificial intelligence, has brought much positivity to the medical healthcare system by enabling real-time date medical information. IoT gained attention because of its ability to connect people, devices, and sensors. It improves productivity through pro-activeness in various aspects of life, especially medicine, which was what oriented the idea of the Internet of Medical Things (IoMT). IoMT replaces "precision medicine" by helping to simplify the general medical approach to care and treatment plans with respect to each patient's genetic profile, environmental factors, and lifestyle. Furthermore, it helps in the provision of rich, personalized data in preventive medicine and diagnosis for accurate treatment pathways [4]. Positively, IoMT increases the health of the population and reduces medical errors with preventive care strategies. Its magnanimous effect has affected special medical domains like nursing, rehabilitation, ambient assisted living (AAL), and medicine. The aspects of medicine that have recently received more medical attention are neurology, cardiology, psychiatry, and psychology. It also has an impactful effect on the accuracy of accident diagnosis with high data transmission [5].

Furthermore, IoMT reduces unnecessary hospital re-admission and promotes an outpatient approach to receiving medical treatment, thereby tracking and monitoring the diagnosis and controlling disease spread in the body. Examples are smart wearable devices and the use of robotics and drones. Another important gap IoMT fills is in record keeping and follow-up of medical history. Although the advancement of IoMT improves the remote monitoring of patients, the wireless communication between remote patients and medical doctors can easily be modified, which poses a serious problem for patient privacy in open wireless channels. There is still a general need for improvements in various aspects of medicine, especially in the aspect of precision medicine for intensive care, which has been predicted to yield much more effectiveness in 2050 [6].

2.1.1 Contribution

In this chapter, we present the security challenges related to the IoMT and highlight the necessity for security measures. We discuss the effectiveness of current security measures and potential areas for improvement. The chapter also describes the present techniques focused on securing IoMT networks and identifies prospective new directions for future research. This work will expose professionals to the security risks posed by the IoMT and help organizations make appropriate decisions to ensure safe and secure operations.

2.1.2 Organization of the chapter

The chapter is organized as follows: Section 2.1 is the general introduction. Sections 2.2 and 2.3 explain the need for IoMT security and IoMT architecture, respectively. Section 2.4 describes methods of sensor data collection and transfer. Sections 2.5 and 2.6 discuss IoMT communication protocols and security threats posed by IoMT, respectively. Section 2.7 presents techniques for securing the IoMT network. Finally, Section 2.8 gives a conclusion and future research direction on IoMT security.

2.2 Need for IoMT Security

The basic factors initiating insecurity issues in the use of IoT generally include lack of cost, constant power supply, memory size, and inaccessibility to IoT in some environments [7]. In the healthcare system, the Internet of Things (IoT) plays a significant role as it is embedded in the sensor and actuator, placed on the patient's body to track or monitor the physiological parameters of a patient. It also helps transfer information directly to the physician, with or without direct contact with a hospital. With the rise in the cost of health treatment across the globe, many individuals would consider adopting the Internet of Medical Things (IoMT) [6]. In an era of successful IoMT adoption, the pressing challenge that can't be put aside will be the issue of privacy and security. Authentication is one of the major reasons why privacy and security should be considered. Access to the personal health records of each patient must be protected against non-authorized persons; only nurses and physicians should have access to health records. Communication between patients and hospitals should be 100% secure; their integrity could buy the confidence of the patient to rely on the IoMT device during data exchange. Furthermore, the location and identity of the patient with the device should be kept private in real time without interference [8].

2.3 IoMT Architecture

The architecture of IoMT involves various components working together to enable the seamless integration of medical devices and healthcare systems [9]. Figure 2.1 illustrates the IoMT architecture available currently. It is noteworthy that specific implementations may vary. Here is a general overview of the IoMT architecture:

2.3.1 Medical devices and sensors

IoMT architecture starts with a wide range of medical devices and sensors that collect patient data. These devices can include wearable devices, implantable devices, remote monitoring systems, vital sign monitors, imaging equipment, and more [10]. They capture various health-related parameters such as heart rate, blood pressure, glucose levels, temperature, and so on. Medical devices and sensors play a vital role in the architecture of the Internet of Medical Things (IoMT) [11]. It forms the foundation of the IoMT ecosystem, collecting essential healthcare data and enabling remote monitoring, diagnostics, and personalized care. Below is a primer on medical devices and sensors in the context of IoMT architecture.

Medical devices and sensors form the frontline of the IoMT architecture, acting as the primary data acquisition tools in healthcare settings [12].

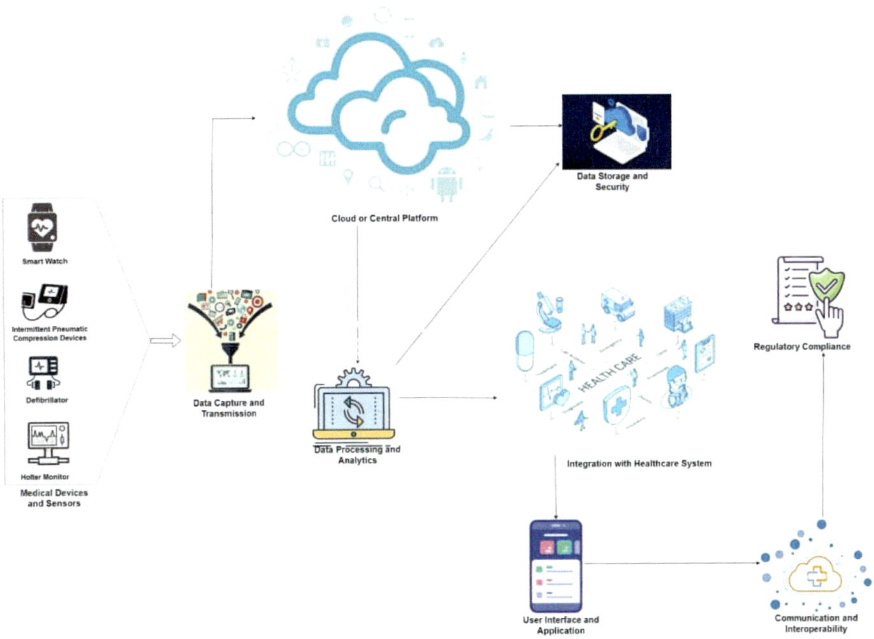

Figure 2.1 Internet of Medical Things architecture.

These devices encompass a wide range of technologies, including wearable devices, implantable devices, remote monitoring systems, vital sign monitors, imaging equipment, and more. These devices are equipped with various sensors that capture and measure important physiological parameters such as heart rate, blood pressure, glucose levels, temperature, oxygen saturation, and movement patterns [13]. They can also collect data from specific medical procedures, such as electrocardiograms (ECGs), electroencephalograms (EEGs), or imaging scans.

The collected data from medical devices and sensors is transmitted to a central platform or cloud-based infrastructure, where it is securely stored and processed [14]. The data transmission can occur through wired or wireless connectivity options, such as Wi-Fi, Bluetooth, cellular networks, or specialized medical device communication protocols. The integration of medical devices and sensors into the IoMT architecture enables real-time monitoring, continuous data collection, and remote patient management [15]. This facilitates early detection of health issues, improves diagnosis accuracy, enhances treatment effectiveness, and allows for proactive interventions and personalized care plans.

Furthermore, the data obtained from medical devices and sensors can be analyzed using advanced algorithms and analytics tools; such tools provide analysis and valuable insights, identify patterns, and support clinical decision-making [16]. Machine learning and artificial intelligence techniques can be applied to derive meaningful insights, predict health outcomes, and enable more precise and personalized healthcare interventions [14, 17]. Interoperability is a key aspect of medical devices and sensors within the IoMT architecture. Standardized communication protocols, such as Health Level 7 (HL7), Digital Imaging and Communications in Medicine (DICOM), and Fast Healthcare Interoperability Resources I (FHIR), ensure seamless integration and interoperability with other devices, systems, and healthcare applications [18]. This enables the exchange of data among different stakeholders, including healthcare providers, patients, and electronic health record systems.

Overall, medical devices and sensors are the fundamental components of the IoMT architecture [19, 20], enabling the capture, transmission, and analysis of healthcare data. They empower healthcare professionals with valuable information, improve patient monitoring and care, and pave the way for more efficient, accurate, and patient-centric healthcare delivery.

2.3.2 Data capture and transmission

The data collected by medical devices and sensors is typically transmitted to a central platform or a cloud-based infrastructure. This transmission can occur through wired or wireless connectivity options, such as Wi-Fi, Bluetooth, cellular networks, or specialized medical device communication protocols. Data capture and transmission play a critical role in the IoMT architecture [21]. They involve the collection, transfer, and delivery of healthcare data from various medical devices and sensors to central platforms or cloud-based infrastructures.

(a) Data capture:

- **Medical devices:** Medical devices and sensors, including wearable devices, implantable devices, vital sign monitors, imaging equipment, and more, capture a wide range of health-related data. These devices are equipped with sensors that measure physiological parameters such as heart rate, blood pressure, glucose levels, temperature, oxygen saturation, and movement patterns [22].
- **Sensor technologies:** Different sensor technologies capture specific types of data. For instance, electrocardiogram (ECG) sensors

capture electrical signals from the heart, while imaging devices capture detailed visual information from medical scans [23].

- **Real-time monitoring:** Many medical devices support real-time monitoring, enabling continuous data capture and immediate feedback on a patient's health status. This real-time data capture is particularly useful for critical care scenarios or remote patient monitoring [24].

(b) Data transmission:

- **Wired and wireless connectivity:** Medical devices and sensors transmit the captured data to a central platform or cloud-based infrastructure using wired or wireless connectivity options. Wired connections may include Ethernet or USB cables, while wireless connections can utilize Wi-Fi, Bluetooth, Zigbee, cellular networks, or specialized medical device communication protocols.
- **Standards and protocols:** Standardized communication protocols play a crucial role in data transmission within the IoMT architecture. Protocols such as Health Level 7 (HL7) [25, 26], Digital Imaging and Communications in Medicine (DICOM) [27, 28], and Fast Healthcare Interoperability Resources (FHIR) [29, 30] ensure interoperability and data exchange among different devices and systems.
- **Security and privacy:** Data transmission in IoMT must be secure to protect patient privacy and prevent unauthorized access. Encryption techniques, secure authentication methods, and data integrity checks are employed to ensure the confidentiality and integrity of the transmitted data. Compliance with healthcare regulations, such as the Health Insurance Portability and Accountability Act (HIPAA) in the United States and the General Data Protection Regulation (GDPR) in the European Union, is essential [31].

(c) Data delivery and storage:

- **Cloud-based infrastructure:** Once the data is transmitted, it is delivered to a cloud-based infrastructure or central platform. This infrastructure provides the necessary computing resources, storage capacity, and data management capabilities for handling the large volume of healthcare data generated by the IoMT ecosystem [32].
- **Scalability and resilience:** The cloud-based infrastructure ensures scalability to handle increasing data volumes and the ability to accommodate multiple devices simultaneously. Redundancy

measures, such as data replication and backup systems, are implemented to ensure data resilience and minimize the risk of data loss.

(d) Real-time and batch processing:

- **Real-time processing:** Some IoMT applications require real-time data processing, where the captured information is analyzed immediately to trigger alerts, notifications, or interventions. Real-time processing is crucial in situations where rapid decision-making is necessary, such as detecting abnormal vital signs or providing real-time feedback during remote consultations [33].
- **Batch processing:** In other cases, data captured by medical devices is processed in batches. The collected data is stored and processed periodically, enabling comprehensive analysis, long-term monitoring, and the generation of historical trends. Batch processing is commonly used for research purposes, population health management, and retrospective analysis.

(e) Integration with healthcare systems:

- **Electronic health records (EHRs) and healthcare systems:** The processed data from the IoMT architecture can be integrated with existing healthcare systems, including electronic health record systems (EHRs), hospital information systems (HIS), and other healthcare applications [34]. This integration enables seamless data sharing and exchange.

2.3.3 Cloud or central platform

The captured medical data is sent to a cloud-based infrastructure or a central platform where it is stored, processed, and analyzed. This platform provides the necessary computing resources, storage capacity, and data management capabilities for handling the large volume of healthcare data generated by the IoMT ecosystem. The cloud or central platform is a fundamental component of the Internet of Medical Things (IoMT) architecture [21]. It serves as a centralized hub where healthcare data from medical devices and sensors is stored, processed, analyzed, and made accessible to healthcare professionals, patients, and other authorized stakeholders. Here is a detailed note on the cloud or central platform in relation to IoMT architecture:

(a) Storage and data management:

- **Scalable infrastructure:** The cloud or central platform provides a scalable infrastructure capable of handling the massive volume of healthcare data generated by IoMT devices and sensors. It offers storage capacity to accommodate diverse data types, including text, images, videos, and sensor readings, ensuring data persistence and availability.

- **Data organization:** The platform incorporates efficient data management mechanisms to organize and categorize healthcare data, enabling easy retrieval, search, and retrieval of specific patient records or data subsets.
- **Data integration:** The cloud or central platform facilitates the integration of data from various sources, such as medical devices, electronic health record systems (EHRs), and healthcare applications. This integration allows for a holistic view of patient data, facilitating comprehensive analysis and informed decision-making.

(b) Data security and privacy:

- **Encryption and access controls:** Robust security measures, including encryption techniques and access controls, are implemented to protect the privacy and confidentiality of patient data [35]. Access to sensitive healthcare information is strictly regulated, ensuring that only authorized individuals can access, view, or modify the data [36].
- **Compliance with regulations:** The cloud or central platform adheres to healthcare regulations and data protection laws, such as the Health Insurance Portability and Accountability Act (HIPAA) in the United States, the General Data Protection Regulation (GDPR) in the European Union, and other regional or national regulations specific to the deployment location [7].

(c) Computing resources and processing:

- **High-performance computing:** The cloud or central platform provides high-performance computing capabilities, enabling efficient processing and analysis of healthcare data [37]. This facilitates real-time or near-real-time data processing, predictive analytics, and complex algorithmic calculations.
- **Machine learning and AI:** Advanced technologies such as machine learning and artificial intelligence can be leveraged on the cloud platform to derive valuable insights, detect patterns, and enable predictive analytics from the collected healthcare data. These techniques help in disease diagnosis, risk assessment, and treatment optimization [27].

(d) Analytics and decision support:

- **Data analysis and insights:** The cloud or central platform incorporates analytics tools and algorithms to process and analyze healthcare data. This analysis can reveal trends, identify anomalies, and generate insights that can support clinical decision-making, population health management, and research initiatives [37].
- **Real-time monitoring and alerts:** The platform enables real-time monitoring of patient data, allowing healthcare professionals to receive alerts or notifications based on predefined thresholds or abnormal data patterns [38]. This feature assists in timely intervention, remote patient management, and proactive healthcare delivery.

(e) Integration with healthcare systems and applications:

- **Interoperability:** The cloud or central platform ensures interoperability by integrating with existing healthcare systems and applications. This integration facilitates seamless data exchange and interoperability with electronic health record systems (EHRs), hospital information systems (HIS), telemedicine platforms, and other healthcare applications [39].
- **User interfaces and applications:** The platform provides user interfaces, such as web-based portals or mobile applications, to enable healthcare professionals, patients, and caregivers to interact with the IoMT ecosystem. These interfaces offer real-time access to patient data, analytics, alerts, and notifications, enhancing the efficiency and quality of healthcare delivery.

The cloud or central platform serves as the backbone of the IoMT architecture, offering a secure, scalable, and integrated environment for storing, processing, and analyzing healthcare data [40]. It empowers healthcare professionals with valuable information, enables patient-centric care, and supports evidence-based decision-making.

2.3.4 Data storage and security

The cloud or central platform stores medical data securely, ensuring the privacy and confidentiality of patient information. Robust data storage and security mechanisms, including encryption, access controls, and backup systems, are implemented to safeguard sensitive health data from unauthorized access or breaches. Data storage and security are crucial aspects of the

Internet of Medical Things (IoMT) architecture [31]. They ensure the safe and reliable storage of healthcare data generated by medical devices and sensors while protecting patient privacy and complying with relevant regulations. Here is a short note on data storage and security in relation to IoMT architecture:

(a) Data storage:

- **Centralized storage:** IoMT architecture utilizes centralized storage systems, such as cloud-based infrastructures or central platforms, to store the vast amount of healthcare data collected from medical devices and sensors.
- **Scalability:** The storage systems are designed to handle the increasing volume of data generated by IoMT devices. They provide scalability, allowing for the storage of diverse data types, including text, images, videos, and sensor readings.
- **Data organization:** Effective data organization mechanisms are implemented to structure and categorize healthcare data. This enables easy retrieval and efficient management of patient records or specific data subsets.
- **Integration:** The storage systems facilitate the integration of data from various sources, such as medical devices, electronic health record systems (EHRs), and healthcare applications. This integration allows for a comprehensive view of patient data, supporting better analysis and decision-making.

(b) Data security:

- **Encryption:** Robust encryption techniques protect the confidentiality and integrity of healthcare data. Encryption ensures that data transmitted between devices, sensors, and storage systems remains secure, minimizing the risk of unauthorized access or data breaches [7, 35].
- **Access controls:** Strict access controls are implemented to regulate who can access, view, or modify healthcare data. Multi-factor authentication, role-based access control, and user permissions help enforce authorized access and prevent unauthorized individuals from tampering with sensitive information.
- **Data anonymization:** To further protect patient privacy, data anonymization techniques may be applied. Personally identifiable information (PII) is removed or transformed to ensure that the stored data cannot be directly linked to specific individuals.

- **Data backup and recovery:** Regular data backups and reliable recovery mechanisms are implemented to protect against data loss. Redundancy measures, such as data replication and backup systems, are in place to ensure data availability and resilience in the event of system failures or disasters.
- **Regulatory compliance:** Data storage systems in the IoMT architecture adhere to relevant healthcare regulations and data protection laws, such as HIPAA (Health Insurance Portability and Accountability Act) in the United States, GDPR (General Data Protection Regulation) in the European Union, and other regional or national regulations specific to the deployment location.

Data storage and security in IoMT architecture are essential for maintaining the confidentiality, integrity, and availability of healthcare data [38, 41, 42]. By ensuring secure storage and access to patient information, these measures contribute to patient trust, enable accurate analysis, and support effective decision-making in healthcare settings.

2.3.5 Data processing and analytics

Once the data reaches the cloud or central platform, it can be processed and analyzed using various algorithms and analytics tools. This enables healthcare professionals to gain insights, identify patterns, and make informed decisions based on the collected data. Advanced techniques such as machine learning and artificial intelligence can be employed to derive meaningful insights and predictive analytics from the data.

Data processing and analytics are vital components of the architecture of the Internet of Medical Things (IoMT). They involve the extraction of valuable insights and meaningful information from the vast amounts of healthcare data collected by medical devices and sensors. Here is a short note on data processing and analytics in relation to IoMT architecture:

(a) Real-time processing:
IoMT devices generate a continuous stream of data, and real-time processing allows for immediate analysis and response. Algorithms and computational models are applied to the incoming data to identify patterns, anomalies, or critical events. Real-time processing is particularly valuable in scenarios where quick decision-making is crucial, such as detecting abnormal vital signs, identifying potential emergencies, or providing timely feedback during remote consultations [43].

(b) Batch processing:
Batch processing involves analyzing data collected over a specific period or in batches. The collected data is stored and processed periodically, enabling comprehensive analysis, long-term monitoring, and retrospective investigations. Batch processing allows for in-depth analysis and the identification of trends, correlations, and patterns over extended periods [44]. It supports research initiatives, population health management, and retrospective analysis.

(c) Machine learning and artificial intelligence (AI):
Machine learning and AI techniques are employed to derive valuable insights from IoMT data. These technologies enable the identification of complex patterns, predictive modeling, and the development of intelligent algorithms [14]. Machine learning algorithms can learn from historical data to make predictions, detect anomalies, and assist in diagnosis and treatment decisions. AI techniques enable intelligent decision support systems, personalization of care plans, and the automation of routine tasks [45].

(d) Data analytics:
Data analytics tools and techniques extract meaningful information from the collected healthcare data. Descriptive, diagnostic, predictive, and prescriptive analytic methods gain insights and support decision-making. Descriptive analytics summarizes and visualizes data, providing an overview of historical patterns and trends. Diagnostic analytics helps identify the causes behind specific events or outcomes [46]. Predictive analytics forecasts future health conditions or events, while prescriptive analytics suggests optimal actions or interventions.

(e) Clinical decision support:
Data processing and analytics support clinical decision-making by providing healthcare professionals with evidence-based insights. By analyzing patient data, algorithms can assist in risk assessment, treatment optimization, and personalized care planning. Clinical decision support systems integrate data from various sources, including IoMT devices, electronic health records (EHRs), and medical literature databases [37]. These systems assist healthcare professionals in making informed decisions, improving patient outcomes, and reducing medical errors.

Data processing and analytics within the IoMT architecture enable healthcare providers to leverage the wealth of healthcare data for improved diagnosis, treatment, and patient management. By uncovering hidden patterns and insights, these processes enhance the understanding of health conditions, support evidence-based care, and drive innovations in the field of healthcare.

2.3.6 Integration with healthcare systems

The processed data from the IoMT architecture can be integrated with existing healthcare systems, including electronic health records (EHRs), hospital information systems (HIS), telemedicine platforms, and other healthcare applications. This integration allows for a seamless exchange of data and facilitates better coordination and decision-making among healthcare providers. Integration with healthcare systems is a crucial aspect of the Internet of Medical Things (IoMT) architecture [30]. It enables seamless data exchange, interoperability, and collaboration among different healthcare applications, electronic health record systems (EHRs), and medical devices. Here is a short note on integration with healthcare systems in relation to IoMT architecture:

(a) Interoperability:
IoMT architecture aims to achieve interoperability, ensuring that diverse healthcare systems and devices can communicate and exchange data effectively. Interoperability allows for the seamless integration of data from different sources, promoting a comprehensive view of patient information. Health Level 7 (HL7) standards, Fast Healthcare Interoperability Resources (FHIR), and other standardized protocols facilitate interoperability by defining common data formats, messaging standards, and APIs for data exchange [25].

(b) Electronic health record (EHR) integration:
Integration with EHR systems enables the incorporation of IoMT-generated data into the patient's medical record. This integration provides a consolidated view of the patient's health information, including data from medical devices, laboratory tests, medications, and clinical notes. IoMT data integration with EHRs enhances the accuracy and completeness of patient records, improves care coordination among healthcare providers, and supports evidence-based decision-making.

(c) Telemedicine and remote patient monitoring:
IoMT integration with telemedicine platforms allows for remote consultations and virtual care. Patient data captured by medical devices and sensors can be securely transmitted to healthcare professionals, enabling remote monitoring and real-time telehealth services. Remote patient monitoring systems collect vital signs, symptoms, and other

health-related data, which are then transmitted to healthcare providers for analysis and intervention. Integration with telemedicine platforms ensures seamless communication between patients and healthcare professionals [47].

(d) Hospital information systems (HIS) integration:
Integration with hospital information systems enables IoMT data to be incorporated into broader healthcare workflows within hospitals and medical facilities. IoMT data can be seamlessly integrated with HIS, enabling access by clinicians, nurses, and other healthcare professionals. Integration with HIS allows for efficient care coordination, timely access to patient information, and improved operational efficiency [48]. IoMT-generated data can be used for patient triage, scheduling, resource allocation, and outcome analysis.

(e) Analytics and decision support:
Integration with analytics platforms and decision support systems allows for comprehensive analysis of IoMT-generated data. Advanced analytics techniques can be applied to gain insights, detect patterns, and support clinical decision-making. By integrating IoMT data with analytics systems, healthcare providers can leverage predictive modeling, machine learning algorithms, and artificial intelligence to improve patient outcomes, identify high-risk individuals, and optimize treatment plans [38].
Integration with healthcare systems in the IoMT architecture enables seamless data exchange, enhances care coordination, and supports evidence-based decision-making. By integrating IoMT-generated data with existing healthcare infrastructure, providers can harness the full potential of connected devices and sensors, leading to more efficient and effective healthcare delivery.

2.3.7 User interfaces and applications

User interfaces and applications are developed to enable healthcare professionals and patients to interact with the IoMT ecosystem. These interfaces can be web-based portals, mobile applications, or specialized software that provide real-time access to patient data, analytics, alerts, and notifications. User interfaces and applications play a vital role in the Internet of Medical Things (IoMT) architecture by enabling healthcare professionals, patients, and caregivers to interact with the IoMT ecosystem. They provide intuitive interfaces and applications that facilitate data visualization, remote monitoring, and access to healthcare services. Here is a short note on user interfaces and applications in relation to IoMT architecture:

(a) Web-based portals:
Web-based portals serve as user interfaces that allow healthcare professionals and authorized personnel to access and interact with IoMT-generated data. These portals provide a centralized platform for data visualization, analytics, and decision support. Healthcare providers can review patient data, monitor vital signs, and access historical records through intuitive web interfaces. These interfaces enable efficient navigation, search, and interpretation of the data collected from medical devices and sensors.

(b) Mobile applications:
Mobile applications extend the accessibility of IoMT-generated data to healthcare professionals, patients, and caregivers. These applications provide a convenient and user-friendly interface, allowing users to access their health information on smartphones or tablets. Mobile applications enable remote monitoring of vital signs, medication reminders, and real-time alerts. Patients can view their health data, track progress, and actively participate in their care plans. Healthcare professionals can monitor patients remotely and provide virtual consultations or telemedicine services.

(c) Wearable device interfaces:
Wearable devices, such as smart watches and fitness trackers, often serve as interfaces in the IoMT ecosystem. They allow individuals to monitor their health and wellness by collecting data on vital signs, activity levels, and sleep patterns. These devices provide real-time feedback and notifications, encouraging users to adopt healthy behaviors and make informed decisions about their well-being. The collected data can be synchronized with mobile applications or web-based portals for further analysis and integration with healthcare systems.

(d) Integration with electronic health records (EHRs):
User interfaces and applications in the IoMT architecture integrate with EHR systems to ensure seamless access and exchange of data. Healthcare professionals can view IoMT-generated data within the context of the patient's comprehensive medical record. Integration with EHRs allows for a holistic view of patient data, supporting accurate diagnoses, treatment plans, and care coordination [49]. Users can access historical data, review medication lists, and view test results, promoting continuity of care.

(e) Remote monitoring and alerts:
User interfaces and applications provide remote monitoring capabilities, enabling healthcare professionals to track patients' health status and receive alerts based on predefined thresholds or abnormal data patterns. Real-time alerts and notifications help identify potential emergencies, ensure timely intervention, and facilitate proactive healthcare delivery. Healthcare providers can remotely monitor patients' conditions, adjust treatment plans, and provide personalized care [50]. User interfaces and applications in the IoMT architecture enhance the accessibility and usability of healthcare data generated by medical devices and sensors. They empower healthcare professionals and individuals to make informed decisions, monitor health status, and actively participate in their healthcare journey. These interfaces promote collaboration, patient engagement, and the delivery of personalized and timely care.

2.3.8 Communication and interoperability

IoMT architecture requires standardized communication protocols and interoperability frameworks to ensure seamless integration and communication among various devices, systems, and applications. Standards like HL7 (Health Level 7), DICOM (Digital Imaging and Communications in Medicine), and FHIR (Fast Healthcare Interoperability Resources) play a crucial role in achieving interoperability in healthcare environments [26, 30]. Communication and interoperability are fundamental elements of the Internet of Medical Things (IoMT) architecture. They enable seamless data exchange and collaboration among various devices, systems, and stakeholders within the healthcare ecosystem. Here is a short note on communication and interoperability in relation to IoMT architecture:

(a) Device-to-device communication:
IoMT devices and sensors need to communicate with each other to enable data sharing and coordination. They establish direct or indirect communication channels to exchange data, synchronize operations, and enable collaborative functionality. Device-to-device communication facilitates interoperability between different types of medical devices, such as wearable devices, monitoring equipment, and therapeutic devices. This enables comprehensive health monitoring, data aggregation, and coordinated care.

(b) Device-to-system communication:
IoMT devices need to communicate with larger systems, such as electronic health record (EHR) systems, hospital information systems (HIS), or centralized platforms, to integrate data and support broader healthcare workflows. Device-to-system communication enables seamless data transmission from medical devices and sensors to the respective healthcare systems. It allows for the incorporation of real-time or periodic data into patient records, decision support systems, and analytics platforms.

(c) Standardized protocols and interfaces:
To ensure interoperability, standardized protocols and interfaces are employed within the IoMT architecture. These protocols define common data formats, messaging standards, and communication methods to enable seamless data exchange and integration. Health Level 7 (HL7), Fast Healthcare Interoperability Resources (FHIR) [30], and other interoperability standards provide a common framework for communication and data sharing among different IoMT devices, systems, and applications.

(d) Secure data transmission:
Communication in the IoMT architecture emphasizes the importance of secure data transmission. Robust encryption techniques and secure communication protocols are employed to protect the confidentiality, integrity, and privacy of healthcare data during transmission. Secure communication protocols, such as transport layer security (TLS) or virtual private networks (VPNs), ensure that data transmitted between devices, systems, and platforms remains protected from unauthorized access, interception, or tampering.

(e) Interoperability with healthcare ecosystem:
Communication and interoperability in the IoMT architecture extend beyond device-level integration. They also involve interoperability with other components of the healthcare ecosystem, such as EHR systems, telemedicine platforms, and external healthcare providers. Interoperability allows for seamless data exchange, care coordination, and collaboration among different stakeholders, promoting continuity of care, better clinical decision-making, and improved patient outcomes [51, 52].
Communication and interoperability are vital for the success of IoMT architecture. They enable devices, systems, and stakeholders to communicate effectively, exchange data, and work together to deliver efficient, coordinated, and patient-centric healthcare services. By establishing

robust communication channels and adhering to interoperability standards, the IoMT architecture can unlock the full potential of connected devices, enhance data-driven insights, and improve healthcare delivery.

2.3.9 Regulatory compliance

IoMT architecture must comply with relevant healthcare regulations and data protection laws, such as HIPAA (Health Insurance Portability and Accountability Act) in the United States, GDPR (General Data Protection Regulation) in the European Union, and other local regulations specific to the country or region where the IoMT solution is deployed. Regulatory compliance is a critical aspect of the architecture of the Internet of Medical Things (IoMT). It ensures that the design, development, deployment, and operation of IoMT solutions adhere to the regulations and standards set forth by governing bodies in the healthcare industry [53]. Here is a short note on regulatory compliance in relation to IoMT architecture:

(a) Safety and effectiveness:
Regulatory compliance ensures that IoMT devices, sensors, and systems meet the necessary safety and effectiveness requirements. It involves rigorous testing, certification, and adherence to quality standards to minimize risks to patients and healthcare professionals. Compliance with safety standards helps ensure that IoMT devices function properly, accurately collect data, and do not pose a threat to patient safety. Similarly, effectiveness requirements ensure that the devices perform as intended and deliver the expected clinical outcomes.

(b) Privacy and data security:
Regulatory compliance in the IoMT architecture addresses privacy and data security concerns. It requires implementing measures to protect the confidentiality, integrity, and availability of patient data collected and transmitted by IoMT devices. Compliance with data protection regulations, such as the General Data Protection Regulation (GDPR) or the Health Insurance Portability and Accountability Act (HIPAA), ensures that patient information is handled securely, access is restricted to authorized individuals, and appropriate consent mechanisms are in place [32].

(c) Medical device regulations:
IoMT devices and sensors that are classified as medical devices must comply with medical device regulations specific to the region in which they are deployed. These regulations typically outline requirements

related to safety, performance, labeling, documentation, and post-market surveillance. Compliance with medical device regulations, such as the European Union's Medical Device Regulation (MDR) or the U.S. Food and Drug Administration (FDA) regulations, ensures that IoMT devices meet the necessary standards for quality, safety, and performance.

(d) Interoperability and standardization:
Regulatory compliance also encourages interoperability and standardization within the IoMT architecture. It promotes adherence to industry standards and protocols to facilitate seamless communication and data exchange between different devices, systems, and applications. Compliance with interoperability standards ensures that IoMT solutions can work together effectively, enabling data interoperability, system integration, and care coordination.

(e) Post-market surveillance and reporting:
Regulatory compliance requires ongoing monitoring of IoMT devices and systems once they are deployed in the market. Manufacturers and operators are responsible for post-market surveillance, including monitoring adverse events, conducting risk assessments, and reporting incidents to regulatory authorities. Compliance with post-market surveillance requirements helps identify potential issues, address safety concerns, and continuously improve the safety and performance of IoMT devices and systems.

Regulatory compliance in the IoMT architecture is essential to safeguard patient safety, protect data privacy, and ensure the effectiveness and quality of healthcare solutions. By adhering to relevant regulations and standards, IoMT stakeholders can instill trust, mitigate risks, and contribute to the advancement of safe and secure connected healthcare. It is important to note that this is a high-level overview of the IoMT architecture, and actual implementations may have variations depending on specific use cases, technologies, and regulatory requirements.

2.4 Methods of Sensor Data Collection and Transfer

In the Internet of Medical Things (IoMT), sensor data collection and transfer are crucial processes that enable the gathering and transmission of health-related information from various medical devices and sensors. Figure 2.2 illustrates the methods of sensor data transfer.

Here are some common methods used for sensor data collection and transfer in the IoMT.

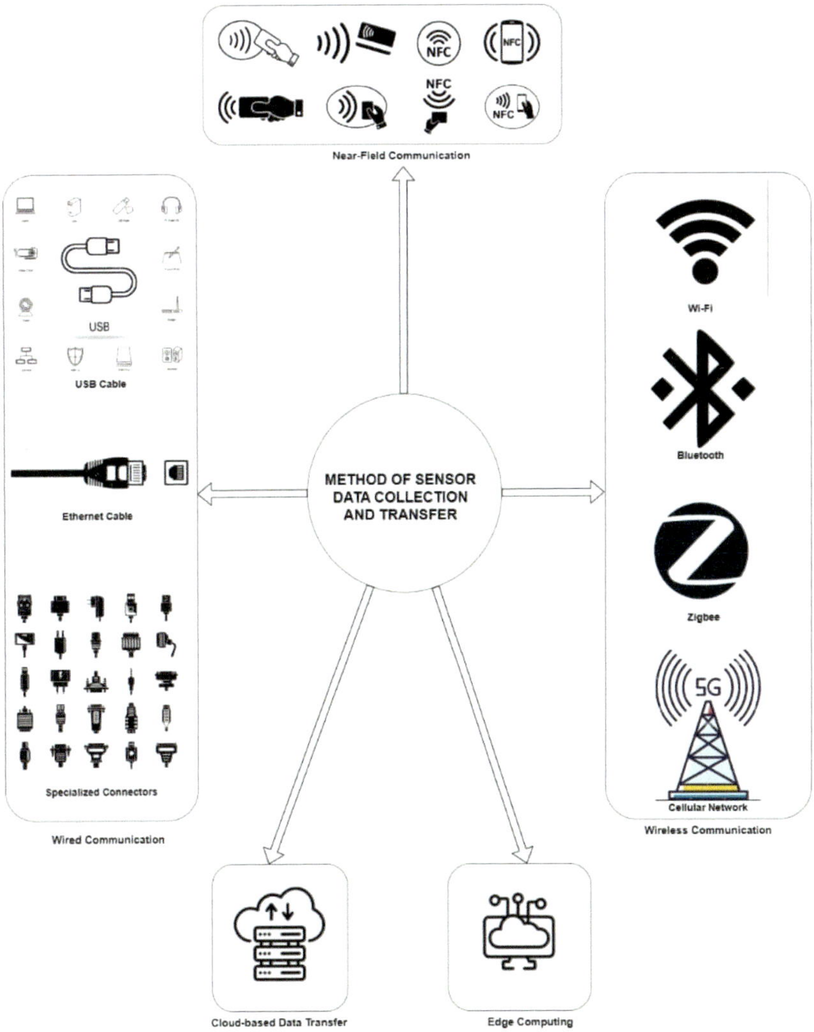

Figure 2.2 Methods of sensor data collection and transfer.

2.4.1 Wired connection

Many medical devices and sensors are directly connected to data collection and processing systems using wired connections. These connections can include USB cables, Ethernet cables, or specialized connectors. Wired connections offer a reliable and secure means of data transfer, ensuring high-speed and accurate transmission. They are commonly used in hospital settings or when devices are near data collection systems.

2.4.2 Wireless communication

Wireless communication methods are extensively utilized for sensor data collection and transfer in the IoMT.

Wi-Fi: Medical devices can be connected to local Wi-Fi networks, allowing for wireless data transmission to centralized systems or cloud platforms. Wi-Fi provides good coverage and higher bandwidth for data transfer [13].

Bluetooth: Bluetooth technology enables short-range wireless communication between medical devices and nearby smartphones, tablets, or gateway devices. It is commonly used for wearable devices and remote patient monitoring applications [34].

Zigbee: Zigbee is a low-power wireless communication standard ideal for remote monitoring and sensor networks. It enables data transfer over longer distances and is commonly used in home healthcare environments [54].

Cellular networks: Medical devices can use cellular networks, such as 3G, 4G, or 5G, to transmit data to remote servers or healthcare systems. This method allows for broader coverage and continuous connectivity, making it suitable for telemedicine and remote patient monitoring applications [42].

2.4.3 Near-field communication (NFC)

NFC is a short-range wireless communication technology that allows two devices to exchange data when they are near each other. NFC is commonly used for contactless payments and identification, but it can also be utilized for secure and convenient data transfer between medical devices and mobile devices.

2.4.4 Cloud-based data transfer

Sensor data can be transmitted to cloud-based platforms or services for storage, processing, and analysis. This method leverages the Internet to securely transmit data from medical devices to cloud servers. Cloud-based data transfer enables remote access to data, facilitates real-time monitoring, and supports advanced analytics. It also allows for seamless integration with other healthcare systems and applications.

2.4.5 Edge computing

In edge computing, sensor data is processed and analyzed locally at the edge devices or gateways before being transmitted to centralized systems. This approach reduces latency, conserves network bandwidth, and enables real-time decision-making [16]. Edge computing is particularly useful in scenarios where real-time insights or immediate action is required, such as critical care environments or remote locations with limited network connectivity.

These methods of sensor data collection and transfer in the IoMT provide diverse options for transmitting health-related information. The choice of method depends on factors such as the nature of the medical device, the required data transfer speed, the range of connectivity, and the specific application or use case.

2.5 IoMT Communication Protocols

IoMT (Internet of Medical Things) communication protocols play a vital role in enabling seamless and secure data exchange between medical devices, sensors, and healthcare systems. These protocols define the rules and standards for transmitting, receiving, and interpreting data in the IoMT ecosystem. Figure 2.3 illustrates the IoMT communication protocols available in the medical technology industry.

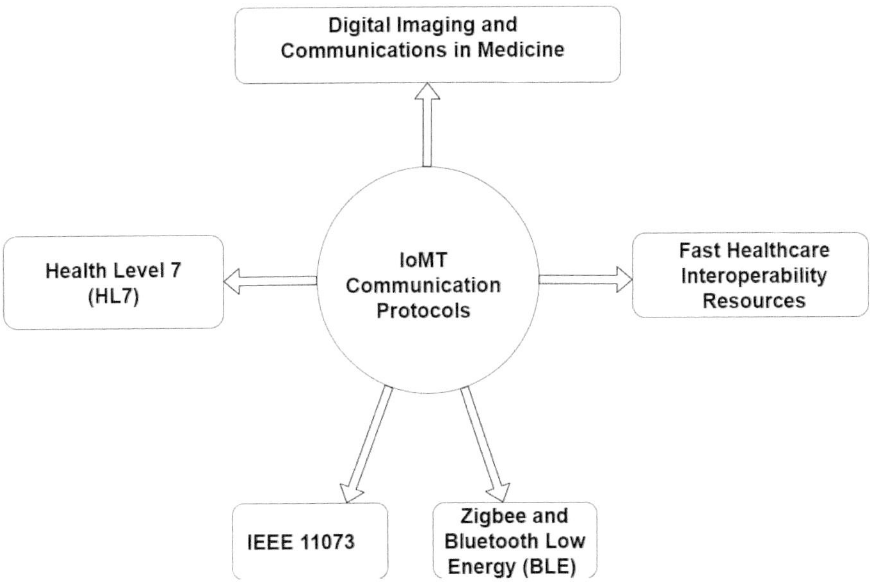

Figure 2.3 IoMT communication protocols available in the medical technology industry.

Explained below are some of the IoMT communication protocols available in the medical technology industry:

(a) Health Level 7 (HL7):
HL7 is one of the most widely adopted communication protocols in healthcare. It provides a standardized framework for exchanging clinical and administrative data between different healthcare systems. HL7 defines message formats, syntax, and protocols for transmitting information such as patient demographics, laboratory results, imaging data, and clinical notes [25, 26]. It enables interoperability and seamless integration of IoMT data into electronic health record (EHR) systems and other healthcare applications.

(b) Fast Healthcare Interoperability Resources (FHIR):
FHIR is an emerging standard developed by the healthcare industry to facilitate interoperability and data exchange in a more modern and web-friendly way. FHIR uses a RESTful web services approach and employs standard data formats (e.g., JSON, XML, etc.) to transmit health-related data. It allows for easier integration with web and mobile applications, enabling developers to build IoMT solutions that can interact with different healthcare systems and devices [29].

(c) Digital Imaging and Communications in Medicine (DICOM):
DICOM is a widely used standard for the exchange, storage, and management of medical imaging data, including radiological images, ultrasound scans, and more. DICOM specifies communication protocols and data formats that enable seamless interoperability between medical imaging devices (such as MRI, CT, and X-ray machines) and picture archiving and communication systems (PACS). It ensures that medical images can be captured, stored, transmitted, and viewed consistently across different platforms and healthcare settings [55].

(d) IEEE 11073:
IEEE 11073 is a set of standards specifically designed for medical device communication and interoperability. IEEE 11073 defines a framework and messaging protocols for exchanging data between medical devices, sensors, and healthcare systems. It covers various aspects, including device identification, data formats, measurement data transmission, and device-to-device interoperability. This protocol enables the seamless integration of IoMT devices into the broader healthcare ecosystem.

(e) Zigbee and Bluetooth low energy (BLE):
Zigbee and BLE are wireless communication protocols commonly used in the IoMT ecosystem, especially for remote monitoring and home

healthcare applications. Zigbee is a low-power, low-data-rate protocol that allows devices to communicate over short distances, making it suitable for sensor networks and remote monitoring solutions. BLE is a power-efficient wireless communication protocol that enables devices to exchange data over short ranges. It is commonly used in wearable devices, health trackers, and mobile health applications.

The selection of a protocol depends on factors such as the type of data being transmitted, the range of communication, power requirements, interoperability needs, and the specific use case or application in the healthcare environment. Choosing the appropriate protocol ensures efficient, secure, and standardized communication within the IoMT ecosystem.

2.6 Security Threats Posed by the IoMT and Associated Risks to Patient Health and Privacy

Medical systems generally gather and process sensitive data on patients' health conditions that would contribute to the decision-making for proper treatment [56]. Patient security and privacy are key areas of focus in the IoMT system [1]. IoMT is susceptible to security threats that could pose a risk to the privacy and health of patients. The security threat could lead to the risk of patient life. Any attack against any of the devices directly connected to a patient affects its performance. Any exploitation of software or medical devices could lead to the exposure of patients' data and thus violate data privacy in the medical field [57]. Another effect of security threat is loss of reputation on the part of the device or software manufacturer; an attack on the software or device could lead to brand value and integrity loss, thereby violating the privacy rules. Financial loss is another effect on the security of the IoMT system [6]. Any damage on IoMT networks by attacks would require the process of damage control and recovery plans. These processes would lead to an extra financial budget for the affected healthcare organization. The identified security threats to the IoMT network are:

Confidentiality threat: Confidentiality ensures that patients' information is protected against unauthorized disclosures. However, confidentiality threat ensures that a patient's confidential medical information that was shared with the personal physician or medical practitioners could be intruded upon, thereby using the medical information against a patient [36]. Examples of confidential threats are eavesdropping, data interception, packet capturing, wiretapping, and dumpster diving. Eavesdropping is an attack that is used to amass information from biomedical sensors. Eavesdropping could either be passive or active. In active eavesdropping, an attacker sends multiple friendly queries to collect information, while in passive eavesdropping, an attacker listens to the transmitted message to detect information. In other instances, attackers could locate and intercept targeted hardware for the collection of sensitive and vital patient information during transmission [1]. In the absence of an efficient authentication measure, the enemy could intercept and eavesdrop on incoming and outgoing data to acquire important data [58]. The data could also be read and altered [59]. This compromises data availability, integrity, and confidentiality and can lead to medication misadministration and patient death. Disclosure of this data to unauthorized persons may compromise patient privacy [8].

Privacy threats: Privacy ensures that patients' private data is secured against any move to illegally exploit them. Patients do not want their medical information to leak. Examples of privacy threats are traffic analysis and identity tracking. [6] The leakage of the data could hurt patients' lives.

Data integrity and message authentication threat: Integrity refers to a system's fidelity. A lack of integrity can occur when critical data is interrupted. Data integrity is a key requirement for an efficient healthcare system [8, 60].

System availability attacks: Availability is the capability of medical devices and servers to be ready for use when the service is required. It is a critical part of the system, especially when it is necessary to monitor the patient [61]. For example, in an availability attack, an attacker can bypass network security by blocking the computing resources of a wearable device or a computer by sending a substantial number of network packets that frequently seem to be genuine. DoS attacks deny authorized nurses and doctors access to medical records; they also prevent patients from getting medication, thereby disrupting the accessibility of a given medical IoMT device or system [62, 63].

System authentication threat: Authentication is necessary to confirm the identity of the user. Examples of system authentication threats are man-in-the-middle, masquerading, cracking, replay, dictionary, brute force, and rainbow table. Such an attack can be active or passive. If an attack only interrupts and reads the medical information, it is known as an active attack. The passive attack involves the modification of the data without any permission [64].

Malware threat: IoMT devices are susceptible to diverse types of malware attacks such as botnets, worms and viruses, spyware, remote access trojans, rootkits, ransomware, backdoors, and spyware [51]. Malware attacks exploit both known and unknown vulnerabilities to automatically spread across the network [65]. Once the malware successfully gains access through a backdoor, attackers can restrict access to the IoMT system. Also, an attacker can use software or firmware to run destructive programs, destroy medical records, and compromise the reliability, privacy, and accuracy of IoMT systems. In healthcare security, the prevention of malware attacks is of the uppermost priority, as it can introduce damage to IoMT systems [66].

Cyberattack threats: Cyberattacks are a wide spectrum of attacks that take advantage of software vulnerabilities and connected devices in the IoT system. Examples of cyberattacks on the IoMT system include data theft, cyber spying, denial-of-service attacks, and malware distribution. Cyberattacks can take several different forms, such as destruction of information, unauthorized access, removal of content, network hacking, disruptions to medical services, and loss of patient data [2, 67]. IoMT devices can be prone to cyberattacks if they are either poorly secured or not secured at all against possible adversaries [63]. The resultant effect poses a negative effect on the overall security of the IoMT system as well as patient safety. This could lead to damage to the information systems and computer networks, financial losses, threat to patient privacy [64], and even death of patients [51]. Botnet attack is the collection of internet-connected devices that leak sensitive information [58], carry out security breaches, and give botnet attackers control over IoMT devices [68].

2.7 Techniques for Securing IoMT Networks

IoMT is confronted by several security and privacy problems, such as confidentiality, authentication, health-related data integrity, and many more, which make this technology susceptible to diverse attacks [63]. Presently, numerous security techniques have been projected to improve the IoMT security network.

- **Intrusion detection technology:** This is a modern technology that is used to detect security problems and network attacks in IoMT. In this technology, threat intelligence, security policies, log monitoring, signature-based rules, prevention systems, device monitoring, network traffic irregularities, and vulnerability management are implemented to identify security attacks in IoMT-based networks.

- **Blockchain technology:** This technology was first presented in the year 2008 by Satoshi Nakamoto [69]; it comprises grip information. It is a distributed and decentralized structure that permits transparent and protected communications among untrusted devices in the absence of a third party. In IoMT security, blockchain is used to construct a decentralized device network that is capable of firmly swapping transactions and information [54]. However, each user's identity is saved as a secret. Medical devices and patients are registered initially, and authenticated submission to the blockchain network is made. Then, the authenticity and authority of the registered medical devices and patients are harmonized. Lastly, information is circulated in the blockchain to permit secured communication of data among diverse users.
- **Authentication technique:** The authentication technique is the foremost in the building of an efficient IoMT system for securing patients' data privacy [1]. Authentication is a significant security mechanism for the design of IoMT architecture. The most secure type of security is mutual authentication. The server and client must first authenticate one another before the transfer of secured data [70]. Hackers must first gain entry into the IoMT system before the attack can be launched. This technique safeguards communication within the IoMT network by approving the rights and identities of the user before giving authorization for the resources in the network. Authorization and authentication structure play a very vital part in certifying the safety of sensitive healthcare data against eavesdropping [1]. However, the traditional authentication method, such as physical layer key generation mechanisms, can be affected by complexity, high latency, and failure to adapt in complex dynamic environments such as IoMT systems. Consequently, during security management operations, a leak could occur in the generated keys. Automatic authentication threats can be prevented by the provision of authentication over a challenge-response protocol for both server and client at every step. Also, in the creation of authentication that provides privacy and accuracy to users, the server should be responsible for providing authorization and privacy for each user, and the authenticated user should be matched independently.
- **Cryptographic technique:** Cryptographic techniques improve the reliability and security of IoMT devices [62]. Conventional cryptography mechanisms can improve the security level and offer protection against security challenges. This could lead to high overhead in both communication and computation [57]. Lightweight security techniques

such as lightweight hybrid anomaly detection, lightweight cryptography, lightweight cryptographic algorithms, and lightweight multi-factor authentication are potentially feasible options to implement stronger authentication in IoMT frameworks due to hardware restraints [63]. Lightweight authentication algorithms are becoming increasingly common [70]. Encryption techniques such as Diffie–Hellman and elliptic curve cryptography (ECC) can be employed to create text data and provide a defense against malicious threats.

- **Machine learning (ML):** Machine learning techniques have been employed to develop detection methods for the classification of cyberattacks targeting the IoMT network and to detect unusual network activities. ML and deep learning can be used to develop effective attack detection systems in IoMT, and they are also applicable to attack forecasting. In general, machine learning participates in securing IoMT systems through the use of important data to provide self-adaptation authentication. Machine-learning-based models can provide security, management, and secure authentication for IoMT networks [63].

2.8 Conclusion and Future Research Direction on IoMT Security

Nowadays, attackers use modern hacking methods and updated attacking strategies to avoid security measures by examining the network routers and firewall configurations to get access to vital information. A secured data transmission certifies that the system did not reveal any information regarding the identity and the patient's medical data. The development of digital signature techniques to prevent access to important data by unauthorized personnel and its consequences will go a long way in securing IoMT networks. The development of a robust system is essential to prevent threats and attacks on IoMT devices. Lightweight authentication, as well as the blockchain method, provides better security measures when compared to traditional algorithms [1]. Future research may examine the features of IoMT devices and how they affect patient data confidentiality [71].

References

[1] T. Vaiyapuri, A. Binbusayyis, and V. Varadarajan, "Security, privacy and trust in IoMT enabled smart healthcare system: a systematic review of current and future trends," Int. J. Adv. Comput. Sci. Appl., vol. 12, no. 2, 2021.

[2] O. A. Adebisi, S. A. Ajagbe, J. A. Ojo, and M. A. Oladipupo, "Computer Techniques for Medical Image Classification: A Review," Intell. Healthc. Infrastructure, Algorithms Manag., pp. 19–36, 2022.

[3] M. K. Hasan et al., "A review on security threats, vulnerabilities, and countermeasures of 5G enabled Internet-of-Medical-Things," IET Commun., vol. 16, no. 5, pp. 421–432, 2022.

[4] X. Huang and S. Nazir, "Evaluating security of internet of medical things using the analytic network process method," Secur. Commun. Networks, vol. 2020, pp. 1–14, 2020.

[5] S. S. Rani, J. A. Alzubi, S. K. Lakshmanaprabu, D. Gupta, and R. Manikandan, "Optimal users based secure data transmission on the internet of healthcare things (IoHT) with lightweight block ciphers," Multimed. Tools Appl., vol. 79, pp. 35405–35424, 2020.

[6] P. Khatiwada and B. Yang, "An Overview on Security and Privacy of Data in IoMT Devices: Performance Metrics, Merits, Demerits, and Challenges," pHealth 2022, pp. 126–136, 2022.

[7] F. Alsubaei, A. Abuhussein, V. Shandilya, and S. Shiva, "IoMT-SAF: Internet of medical things security assessment framework," Internet of Things, vol. 8, p. 100123, 2019.

[8] D. Koutras, G. Stergiopoulos, T. Dasaklis, P. Kotzanikolaou, D. Glynos, and C. Douligeris, "Security in IoMT communications: A survey," Sensors, vol. 20, no. 17, p. 4828, 2020.

[9] A. Gatouillat, Y. Badr, B. Massot, and E. Sejdić, "Internet of medical things: A review of recent contributions dealing with cyber-physical systems in medicine," IEEE internet things J., vol. 5, no. 5, pp. 3810–3822, 2018.

[10] F. Qureshi and S. Krishnan, "Wearable hardware design for the internet of medical things (IoMT)," Sensors, vol. 18, no. 11, p. 3812, 2018.

[11] S. Vishnu, S. R. J. Ramson, and R. Jegan, "Internet of medical things (IoMT)-An overview," in 2020 5th International Conference on devices, circuits, and systems (ICDCS), 2020, pp. 101–104.

[12] S. Jain et al., "Internet of medical things (IoMT)-integrated biosensors for point-of-care testing of infectious diseases," Biosens. Bioelectron., vol. 179, p. 113074, 2021.

[13] G. Gardašević, K. Katzis, D. Bajić, and L. Berbakov, "Emerging wireless sensor networks and Internet of Things technologies—Foundations of smart healthcare," Sensors, vol. 20, no. 13, p. 3619, 2020.

[14] P. Manickam et al., "Artificial intelligence (AI) and internet of medical things (IoMT) assisted biomedical systems for intelligent healthcare," Biosensors, vol. 12, no. 8, p. 562, 2022.

[15] M. Irfan and N. Ahmad, "Internet of medical things: Architectural model, motivational factors and impediments," in 2018 15th learning and technology conference (L&T), 2018, pp. 6–13.
[16] L. Sun, X. Jiang, H. Ren, and Y. Guo, "Edge-cloud computing and artificial intelligence in internet of medical things: architecture, technology and application," IEEE Access, vol. 8, pp. 101079–101092, 2020.
[17] R. J. S. Raj, S. J. Shobana, I. V. Pustokhina, D. A. Pustokhin, D. Gupta, and K. Shankar, "Optimal feature selection-based medical image classification using deep learning model in internet of medical things," IEEE Access, vol. 8, pp. 58006–58017, 2020.
[18] G. Manogaran, N. Chilamkurti, and C.-H. Hsu, "Emerging trends, issues, and challenges in Internet of Medical Things and wireless networks," Pers. Ubiquitous Comput., vol. 22, pp. 879–882, 2018.
[19] G. Thamilarasu, A. Odesile, and A. Hoang, "An intrusion detection system for internet of medical things," IEEE Access, vol. 8, pp. 181560–181576, 2020.
[20] G. J. Joyia, R. M. Liaqat, A. Farooq, and S. Rehman, "Internet of medical things (IoMT): Applications, benefits and future challenges in the healthcare domain.," J. Commun., vol. 12, no. 4, pp. 240–247, 2017.
[21] B. Farahani, F. Firouzi, and K. Chakrabarty, "Healthcare iot," Intell. Internet Things From Device to Fog Cloud, pp. 515–545, 2020.
[22] S. M. Nagarajan, G. G. Deverajan, U. Kumaran, M. Thirunavukkarasan, M. D. Alshehri, and S. Alkhalaf, "Secure data transmission in internet of medical things using RES-256 algorithm," IEEE Trans. Ind. Informatics, vol. 18, no. 12, pp. 8876–8884, 2021.
[23] P. P. Ray, D. Dash, and N. Kumar, "Sensors for internet of medical things: State-of-the-art, security and privacy issues, challenges and future directions," Comput. Commun., vol. 160, pp. 111–131, 2020.
[24] K. Wei, L. Zhang, Y. Guo, and X. Jiang, "Health monitoring based on internet of medical things: architecture, enabling technologies, and applications," IEEE Access, vol. 8, pp. 27468–27478, 2020.
[25] K. Plathong and B. Surakratanasakul, "A study of integration Internet of Things with health level 7 protocol for real-time healthcare monitoring by using cloud computing," in 2017 10th Biomedical Engineering International Conference (BMEiCON), 2017, pp. 1–5.
[26] J. S. Hooda, E. Dogdu, and R. Sunderraman, "Health Level-7 compliant clinical patient records system," in Proceedings of the 2004 ACM symposium on Applied computing, 2004, pp. 259–263.

[27] Y. Xu et al., "Deep learning-enhanced internet of medical things to analyze brain ct scans of hemorrhagic stroke patients: a new approach," IEEE Sens. J., vol. 21, no. 22, pp. 24941–24951, 2020.

[28] T. Han et al., "Internet of medical things—based on deep learning techniques for segmentation of lung and stroke regions in CT scans," IEEE Access, vol. 8, pp. 71117–71135, 2020.

[29] M. L. Braunstein, "Patient—Physician collaboration on FHIR (Fast Healthcare Interoperability Resources)," in 2015 International Conference on Collaboration Technologies and Systems (CTS), 2015, pp. 501–503.

[30] C. N. Vorisek et al., "Fast healthcare interoperability resources (FHIR) for interoperability in health research: systematic review," JMIR Med. informatics, vol. 10, no. 7, p. e35724, 2022.

[31] F. Chen et al., "An infrastructure framework for privacy protection of community medical internet of things: Transmission protection, storage protection and access control," World Wide Web, vol. 21, pp. 33–57, 2018.

[32] M. Mushtaq, M. A. Shah, and A. Ghafoor, "The internet of medical things (iomt): Security threats and issues affecting digital economy," 2021.

[33] T. Zhang et al., "A joint deep learning and internet of medical things driven framework for elderly patients," IEEE Access, vol. 8, pp. 75822–75832, 2020.

[34] M. Papaioannou et al., "A survey on security threats and countermeasures in internet of medical things (IoMT)," Trans. Emerg. Telecommun. Technol., vol. 33, no. 6, p. e4049, 2022.

[35] Y. Ding et al., "DeepEDN: A deep-learning-based image encryption and decryption network for internet of medical things," IEEE Internet Things J., vol. 8, no. 3, pp. 1504–1518, 2020.

[36] C. Kotronis et al., "Evaluating Internet of Medical Things (IoMT)-based systems from a human-centric perspective," Internet of Things, vol. 8, p. 100125, 2019.

[37] R. Blazek, L. Hrosova, and J. Collier, "Internet of medical things-based clinical decision support systems, smart healthcare wearable devices, and machine learning algorithms in COVID-19 prevention, screening, detection, diagnosis, and treatment," Am. J. Med. Res., vol. 9, no. 1, pp. 65–80, 2022.

[38] S. Shreya, K. Chatterjee, and A. Singh, "A smart secure healthcare monitoring system with Internet of Medical Things," Comput. Electr. Eng., vol. 101, p. 107969, 2022.

[39] R. Dwivedi, D. Mehrotra, and S. Chandra, "Potential of Internet of Medical Things (IoMT) applications in building a smart healthcare system: A systematic review," J. oral Biol. craniofacial Res., vol. 12, no. 2, pp. 302–318, 2022.

[40] E. Balestrieri et al., "The architecture of an innovative smart T-shirt based on the Internet of Medical Things paradigm," in 2019 IEEE International symposium on medical measurements and applications (MeMeA), 2019, pp. 1–6.

[41] X. Li, H.-N. Dai, Q. Wang, M. Imran, D. Li, and M. A. Imran, "Securing internet of medical things with friendly-jamming schemes," Comput. Commun., vol. 160, pp. 431–442, 2020.

[42] O. Salem, K. Alsubhi, A. Shaafi, M. Gheryani, A. Mehaoua, and R. Boutaba, "Man-in-the-Middle attack mitigation in internet of medical things," IEEE Trans. Ind. Informatics, vol. 18, no. 3, pp. 2053–2062, 2021.

[43] H. Z. Almarzouki, H. Alsulami, A. Rizwan, M. S. Basingab, H. Bukhari, and M. Shabaz, "An internet of medical things-based model for real-time monitoring and averting stroke sensors," J. Healthc. Eng., vol. 2021, 2021.

[44] J. Han, Y. Li, J. Liu, and M. Zhao, "An efficient lucas sequence-based batch auditing scheme for the internet of medical things," IEEE Access, vol. 7, pp. 10077–10092, 2018.

[45] J. Liu, J. Ma, J. Li, M. Huang, N. Sadiq, and Y. Ai, "Robust watermarking algorithm for medical volume data in internet of medical things," IEEE Access, vol. 8, pp. 93939–93961, 2020.

[46] Y. Zhang, Y. Zhang, X. Zhao, Z. Zhang, and H. Chen, "Design and data analysis of sports information acquisition system based on internet of medical things," IEEE Access, vol. 8, pp. 84792–84805, 2020.

[47] J. Sawyer, "Wearable Internet of Medical Things sensor devices, artificial intelligence-driven smart healthcare services, and personalized clinical care in COVID-19 telemedicine," Am. J. Med. Res., vol. 7, no. 2, pp. 71–77, 2020.

[48] M. Wazid, J. Singh, A. K. Das, S. Shetty, M. K. Khan, and J. J. P. C. Rodrigues, "ASCP-IoMT: AI-enabled lightweight secure communication protocol for internet of medical things," IEEE Access, vol. 10, pp. 57990–58004, 2022.

[49] J. N. S. Rubí and P. R. de L. Gondim, "Interoperable Internet of Medical Things platform for e-Health applications," Int. J. Distrib. Sens. Networks, vol. 16, no. 1, p. 1550147719889591, 2020.

[50] K. Kakhi, R. Alizadehsani, H. M. D. Kabir, A. Khosravi, S. Nahavandi, and U. R. Acharya, "The internet of medical things and artificial intelligence: trends, challenges, and opportunities," Biocybern. Biomed. Eng., 2022.

[51] J.-P. A. Yaacoub et al., "Securing internet of medical things systems: Limitations, issues and recommendations," Futur. Gener. Comput. Syst., vol. 105, pp. 581–606, 2020.

[52] I. Ayoade, A. Adedigba, O. A. Adeyemi, O. A. Adeaga, and O. Akanbi, "Trends and prospects of digital twin technologies: A review," Quantum J. Eng. Sci. Technol., vol. 3, no. 4, pp. 11–24, 2022.

[53] S. Razdan and S. Sharma, "Internet of medical things (IoMT): overview, emerging technologies, and case studies," IETE Tech. Rev., vol. 39, no. 4, pp. 775–788, 2022.

[54] Solanki, A., Singh, A.K., & Tanwar, S. (Eds.). (2023). Blockchain Technology for IoE: Security and Privacy Perspectives (1st ed.). CRC Press. https://doi.org/10.1201/9781003366010.

[55] X. Gong, W. Chen, and J. Chen, "A low-rank tensor dictionary learning method for hyperspectral image denoising," IEEE Trans. Signal Process., vol. 68, pp. 1168–1180, 2020.

[56] F. Ullah et al., "Cyber security threats detection in internet of things using deep learning approach," IEEE access, vol. 7, pp. 124379–124389, 2019.

[57] S. S. Ahamad and A.-S. Khan Pathan, "A formally verified authentication protocol in secure framework for mobile healthcare during COVID-19-like pandemic," Conn. Sci., vol. 33, no. 3, pp. 532–554, 2021.

[58] A.K.Singh, A Solanki, A Nayyar, and B Qureshi, "Elliptic curve signcryption-based mutual authentication protocol for smart cards," Applied Sciences, vol 10 (22), 8291, 2020.

[59] S. P. RM et al., "An effective feature engineering for DNN using hybrid PCA-GWO for intrusion detection in IoMT architecture," Comput. Commun., vol. 160, pp. 139–149, 2020.

[60] P. G. Shambharkar and N. Sharma, "Artificial Intelligence driven Intrusion Detection Framework for the Internet of Medical Things," 2023.

[61] S. Rai, M. Sood, and A. Kaur, "Is perinatal asphyxia associated with an increase in serum bilirubin in neonates? A case-control study," J. Fam. Med. Prim. Care, vol. 11, no. 7, pp. 3840–3843, 2022.

[62] M. Narang, A. Jatain, and N. Punetha, “A study on Cyber-attack detection in IoMT using Machine Learning Techniques,” Available SSRN 4387775, 2023.

[63] D. S. Gupta, N. Mazumdar, A. Nag, and J. P. Singh, “Secure data authentication and access control protocol for industrial healthcare system,” J. Ambient Intell. Humaniz. Comput., pp. 1–12, 2023.

[64] P. Theodorou, P. Kydonakis, M. Botzori, and C. Skanavis, “Augmented reality proves to be a breakthrough in Environmental Education,” Prot. Restor. Environ., vol. 7, pp. 219–228, 2018.

[65] A. Karthick Kumar, K. Vadivukkarasi, R. Dayana, and P. Malarvezhi, “Botnet Attacks Detection Using Embedded Feature Selection Methods for Secure IOMT Environment,” in Pervasive Computing and Social Networking: Proceedings of ICPCSN 2022, Springer, 2022, pp. 585–599.

[66] Y. Benslimane, K. Benahmed, and H. Benslimane, “Security mechanisms for 6LoWPAN network in context of internet of things: A Survey,” in Renewable Energy for Smart and Sustainable Cities: Artificial Intelligence in Renewable Energetic Systems 2, 2019, pp. 49–69.

[67] J. B. Awotunde, A. K. Bhoi, R. G. Jimoh, S. A. Ajagbe, F. E. Ayo, and O. A. Adebisi, “Internet of Things Based Enabled Convolutional Neural Networks in Healthcare,” in IoT-enabled Convolutional Neural Networks: Techniques and Applications, River Publishers, 2023, pp. 329–357.

[68] R. A. Alsemmeari, M. Y. Dahab, A. A. Alsulami, B. Alturki, and S. Algarni, “Resilient Security Framework Using TNN and Blockchain for IoMT,” Electronics, vol. 12, no. 10, p. 2252, 2023.

[69] M. Mettler, “Blockchain technology in healthcare: The revolution starts here,” in 2016 IEEE 18th international conference on e-health networking, applications and services (Healthcom), 2016, pp. 1–3.

[70] A. Alrawais, A. Alhothaily, C. Hu, and X. Cheng, “Fog computing for the internet of things: Security and privacy issues,” IEEE Internet Comput., vol. 21, no. 2, pp. 34–42, 2017.

[71] S. M. Pournaghi, M. Bayat, and Y. Farjami, “MedSBA: a novel and secure scheme to share medical data based on blockchain technology and attribute-based encryption,” J. Ambient Intell. Humaniz. Comput., vol. 11, pp. 4613–4641, 2020.

3

Formal Methods-based Security for the Internet of Medical Things (IoMT)

Imane Bouziane, Houda Belmokadem, and Mohamed Moussaoui

Information and Communication Technologies Laboratory (LabTIC), National School of Applied Sciences of Tangier, Abdelmalek Essaadi University, Morocco
E-mail: imane.bouziane1@etu.uae.ac.ma; h.belmokadem@uae.ac.ma; m.moussaoui@uae.ac.ma

Abstract

Security is of utmost importance in wireless body area networks, also referred to as WBANs, within the domain of IoMT (Internet of Medical Things), considering the crucial significance of the data involved, which primarily consists of sensitive medical information of patients. WBANs play a crucial role in healthcare applications by enabling the collection and transmission of physiological data from wearable or implantable medical devices. For this reason, ensuring the security of this data is paramount to protect patient confidentiality, prevent unauthorized access, and maintain the trustworthiness of healthcare systems.

In this context, formal verification emerges as a highly effective method for not only identifying potential vulnerabilities but also providing security guarantees for WBANs in the IoMT domain. In contrast to testing techniques that reveal problems but cannot prove their absence, formal verification involves mathematically analyzing the behavior and properties of a system, such as a WBAN protocol, using rigorous and systematic techniques. By subjecting WBANs to formal verification, researchers can detect design flaws, uncover potential security weaknesses, and validate the effectiveness of security measures.

DOI: 10.1201/9788770047395-3

This chapter seeks to explore the intersection of formal methods and security in literature. It considers the analysis of WBANs within the IoMT domain to prove the absence of flaws and vulnerabilities formally.

Keywords: Internet of Medical Things (IoT), IoMT security, formal methods, model checking, theorem proving, WBANs.

3.1 Introduction

The term "Internet of Things" or IoT pertains to the connectivity of diverse smart computing devices embedded in everyday objects that enable them to exchange data over the internet. In today's context, IoT encompasses a broad spectrum of applications that have become integral parts of our daily lives, including areas such as business, logistics, environments, social gaming robots, and city information systems.

However, the medical and healthcare industry stands out as one of the vital areas in which IoT technology is applied. The Internet of Medical Things (IoMT) [1, 2] integrates the principles of broader IoT within healthcare, focusing on allowing healthcare providers to collect and analyze up-to-date patient data, track medication adherence, remotely monitor patients, and enhance overall patient outcomes. With its ability to facilitate various healthcare applications, IoMT stands at the forefront of the healthcare revolution, promising transformative impacts across the facets of the industry. Its rapid expansion suggests that it will be of paramount significance in revolutionizing medical care by reducing healthcare costs, improving medical treatment quality, and enabling timely medical responses.

A forecast from the International Data Corporation (IDC) estimates that by 2025, there will be over 41.6 billion connected IoT devices around the globe, generating 79.4 zettabytes (ZB) of data. However, this massive wave of new gadgets, more and more sophisticated and infinitely complex, comes with costs. Indeed, as more physical devices connect to the internet, handling sensitive data of our lives, safety, and security are essential and seem to be among the most significant challenges of the IoT. The repercussions of unsecured IoT systems can be catastrophic. Especially since, on the one hand, the open nature of the internet easily exposes connected devices to attacks and exploitation, eventually risking user or smart object security. On the other hand, because the Internet of Things (IoT) market is growing rapidly across industries, IoT devices are designed for demand fulfillment rather than application security.

The lack of security-focused design in cyber–physical devices, including IoMT, leaves them susceptible to cyber threats. Unfortunately, IoMT devices have more severe implications than other cyber–physical systems (CPS) due to their association with patient risks. Cybercriminals often target the vulnerabilities in IoMT devices to gain access to sensitive personal and healthcare information. Any compromise of IoMT devices could endanger the safety of patients.

To secure IoT devices – including IoMT – at an early stage, it is therefore crucial to detect potential vulnerabilities and weaknesses during the design phase. Without IoT security, any connected device, from a smart home camera to an implantable medical device, can be hacked and accessed via the internet by anyone anywhere.

Formal verification refers to the procedure of affirming or refuting the accuracy of a system in relation to a specified formal specification or property. Just as a builder relies on a blueprint, designers rely on critical system specifications describing how it should and should not work, but often, the specifications and the system do not match, causing flaws that lead to failures, malfunctions, or cyberattacks. With formal verification, the specifications and design are analyzed to prove that everything is preserved in translation and that the designed system does only what it is supposed to do. To do this, the design and specifications are translated into mathematical representations, which are then checked against each other by mathematical proof; if they do not align, the cause is isolated for correction. Thus, this method can be an effective technique for not just detecting potential vulnerabilities but also providing security guarantees for an IoT device.

Theorem proving and model checking are the two most common approaches for automatic formal verification, and both can be used early in the design process.

Theorem proving primarily relies on high-order logic and mathematical frameworks to build formulas that correlate to system behavior. Usually, theorem provers formalize design and expected requirements as algebraic axioms or theorems to facilitate a proof of correctness. Given a model of the implementation (or an abstraction of it) and a formula representing a property in a specification language, model checking consists of algorithmically verifying if the formula is satisfied by the model. It analyzes the state-space of a system's model automatically and completely in accordance with a specified specification. Even while most tools are intended for model checking, some also offer the option of manual assistance, serving as theorem provers as a result.

In contrast to testing techniques that reveal problems but cannot prove their absence, formal verification employs mathematical approaches to explore all possible design behaviors. It can provide total coverage, which is comparable to simulating all possible scenarios.

Formal methods effectively establish the correctness of both hardware and software systems in a wide range of fields, including cyber–physical systems, software development, robotics, and embedded system design. Many other research areas could benefit from their application.

Because of their uniqueness, diversity, and complexity, IoMT systems present a sizable attack surface that has yet to be thoroughly explored and tested. This can potentially have serious consequences for both patients and healthcare providers. Therefore, developing a robust formal security model can serve as a means to conduct security proofs, comparisons, and evaluations of different IoMT systems.

Although security properties apply to many protocols, this chapter will only focus on the security of IoMT-based wireless body area networks (WBANs) by presenting the application of formal approaches, including tools, techniques, and languages, to prove the security of WBAN protocols.

The chapter will be organized as follows. In Section 3.2, we begin with a general introduction to formal verification methods. Section 3.3 discusses the architecture of a remote health monitoring system. Section 3.4 describes the most used communication protocols in the IoMT domain, such as WBANs. Finally, in Section 3.5, we discuss the tools and methods used to detect weaknesses and vulnerabilities in WBANs.

3.2 Formal Verification

Errors are human; they certainly are not desirable, but in certain critical areas, they are inadmissible and unacceptable. Therac-25 is a well-known incident of a software error that had disastrous results. Between 1985 and 1987, six cancer patients died as a result of overexposure to radiation due to a software error in the machine's controller. Another software and hardware error that caused a huge loss of money is the Arian V rocket bug: an error in one of the software modules led to the explosion of the rocket Arian V in June 1996. These examples show that testing is insufficient. Developing formal methods of exhaustive verification is, therefore, a crucial point and an area of research that is constantly evolving. Software systems that are of critical importance are becoming increasingly significant in all aspects of society. These systems need to be built with extraordinary skill, with a significant amount of effort taking advantage of the most cutting-edge thinking about software and technologies themselves in order to give mathematical guarantees of correctness and safety. Formal methods provide mathematical proofs ensuring the reliability and absence of malfunction of a system or software. It offers techniques that make it possible to convince that a system conforms to its specifications and that it satisfies safety properties. Their applications are multiple in the industrial field. The formal verification process begins with the specification of requirements to verify them [3].

3.2.1 Specification languages

Several languages are proposed for requirements analysis and systems design. Specification languages are characterized by their syntax and their semantics. They are [4] generally based on mathematical notations, allowing automatic verification of specified requirements.

In the model-oriented approach, languages allow the specification of different views of the system. We can cite state machines, timed automata [5], Petri nets [6, 7], Z [8], and the B method [9].

In the property-oriented approach, the requirements are described with logical axioms, usually concentrated on temporal computational logic. Among these languages are Coq [10] or temporal logics [11], such as CTL [12].

In the specific case of communication protocols, Burrows, Abadi, and Needham have developed a formal framework for specifying and verifying them. It uses a logic based on formal rules, called BAN logic [13], to express security properties, such as authentication, confidentiality, and integrity, in the context of message exchanges between secure entities.

Suppose the specification's role is to rewrite what we need clearly and precisely. The verification role is to verify that the requirements resulting from the specification are respected throughout the development cycle. Its purpose is to detect the errors introduced in each stage of development. Verification answers the question, "Are we making the product correctly?"

Definition [14]: Verification consists of confirmation by tangible proof that the requirements specified have been met.

3.2.2 Formal verification methods

Within the existing body of literature, two primary methodologies are commonly discussed when it comes to the utilization of formal techniques in design: model checking and theorem verification.

- **Model checking**
  Model checking [15, 16] is an automatic method, generally implemented by a computer tool called the "Model-Checker." It consists of automatically checking the properties specified on a system. The system is usually expressed in a formal model using model-oriented languages, mainly state machines, and the properties to be checked are written in a properties-oriented language such as LTL or CTL. Then, according to the specifications system and properties, the Model-Checker explores the state-space. It checks the satisfaction of the specified property in each state. If this property is violated, the Model-Checker provides a counterexample showing the trace of the error, that is, the sequence of states that violate the property (Figure 3.1).
  However, for large systems, this exhaustive exploration of states can make verification fail if the capacity of machines (computers) is insufficient. This problem is known as the state-space explosion. To avoid

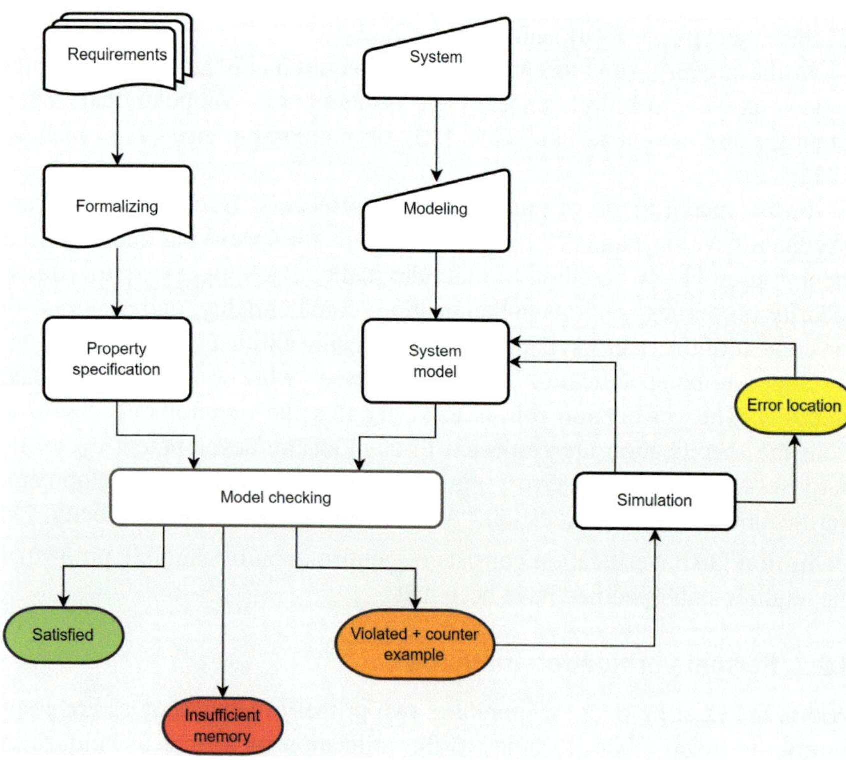

Figure 3.1 Model checking.

this problem, several techniques are proposed in the literature, such as BDD, SAT, abstraction, and bi-simulation [17]. Among the model-checker tools, UPPAAL [18] is a tool that is used for timed systems. SPIN [19] is used for the verification of concurrent systems. Romeo [20] is a model-checker used to ensure the correctness of Petri net models of real-time systems. PAT [21], which stands for Process Analysis Toolkit, is widely employed in both academic and industrial settings to verify and validate concurrent and distributed systems. It supports various modeling languages, including process algebra and Petri nets, allowing users to describe system behavior and properties formally and mathematically.

- **Theorem proving**
  Axiomatic languages are mathematical logic closely based on Hoare's logic and are generally verified by theorem proving [22]. This logic was defined by the British researcher Tony Hoare [23], who introduced logical formalism, which allows reasoning and proves the correctness of computer programs. Intuitively, this logic gives semantics to the effect of a computer program's instruction on the state of its variables. These languages also define rules for procedures, jumps, pointers, and the concurrency aspect.
  Theorem proving is a formal method that uses axiomatic language to specify the system and its expected properties (requirements). The state-space explosion problem does not limit this technique, but it is only partially automatic. This depends on the expressiveness of the logical language used. Event-B [24] is an example of the proving theorem method based on first-order logic. Event-B employs events to model system behavior and relies on refinement techniques to gradually introduce more details into the system model.
  For first-order logic, the proof is automated by default: this is the case, for example, from the ACL2 theorem prover [25] or Rodin Tool [24]. However, if the logic is more expressive, such as higher-order logic (HOL), the automation of the proof is partial, like Isabelle/HOL [26].
  Figure 3.2 illustrates the theorem proving technique. It involves two steps: formalizing the system and determining the expected properties to produce a set of reasoning (proof obligations) to demonstrate with a proof assistant tool. These proofs can be done automatically or semi-automatically with human interaction. If they cannot be checked, it is essential to modify the formalism specification.

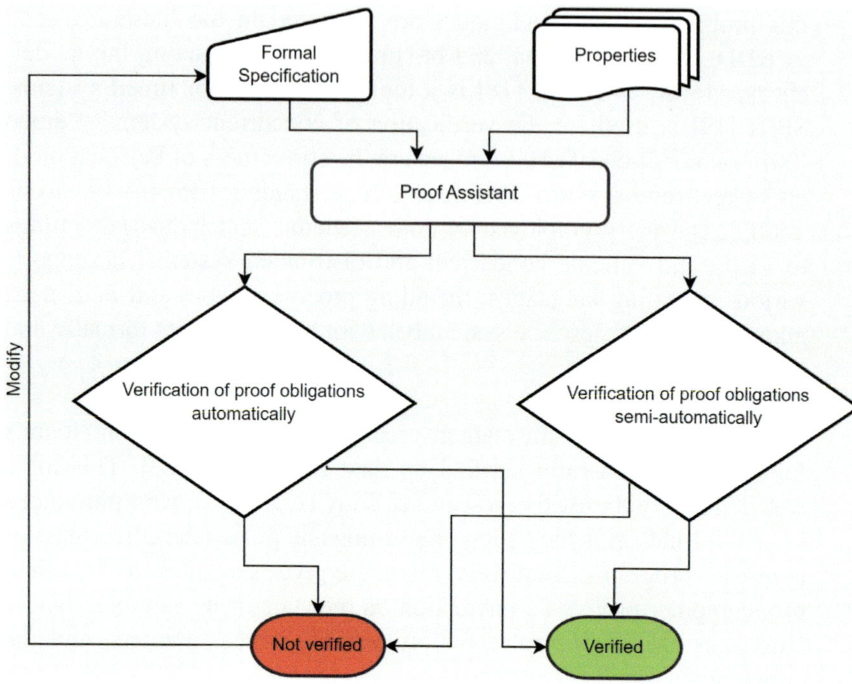

Figure 3.2 Theorem proving.

3.3 Remote Health Monitoring Systems

Figure 3.3 shows the architecture of a remote health monitoring system based on WBAN networks. It is divided into five subsystems:

- The body area network (BAN)
- The personal area network (PAN)
- The access network
- The wide area network (WAN)
- The end user of the healthcare monitoring application

The BAN network consists of a network of intelligent biomedical sensors that are implanted or worn by the patient. They collect data, interact with each other, and communicate important information to the collection node via a short-range wireless connection. The collection node has more hardware resources and allows for the collection and storage of information from the sensors. A BAN network rarely operates independently. The collection node and environmental sensors and devices deployed around the patient

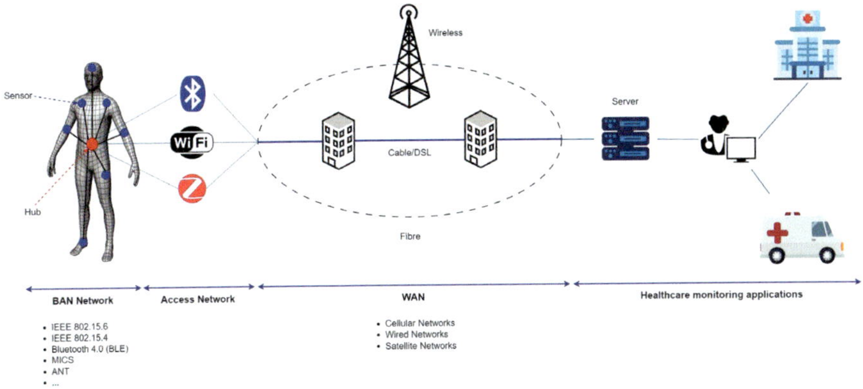

Figure 3.3 The architecture of a remote health monitoring system based on WBAN networks.

form a PAN network connected to the WAN network. The access point is responsible for establishing the connection between the BAN network and the PAN network on the one hand and the extended WAN networks on the other hand. The PAN network can also be used as an access network to the network, forming a mesh network that allows for wider coverage at a lower cost. The WAN networks can be cellular networks, wired communication networks, or satellite networks. The end user represents the medical team (doctors, nurses, etc.) or the analysis and surveillance center. The collected medical data will allow real-time monitoring of patients' health problems and their location. These data are interpreted, and necessary actions are triggered. Sensors are employed to track diverse physiological indicators, including but not limited to heart rate, pulse, oxygen saturation (SpO_2), respiratory rate, body temperature, electrocardiogram (ECG), electromyogram (EMG), electroencephalogram (EEG), blood pressure, glucose levels, and more.

There are different types of possible communications between elements in a BAN network depending on the position of each element. Thus, an element is referred to as an "implant" when it is surgically inserted into the body. It is termed "body surface" when it is positioned on the outer layer of the body. Lastly, it is classified as "external" when it is located in close proximity to the body, within a maximum distance of 5 m. Four types of BAN channel models are distinguished according to these connections. Figure 3.4 shows these different types of connections. We distinguish the CM1 channel for communications between implants, the CM2 channel for communication between an implant and a body surface or external element (up to 5 m), and

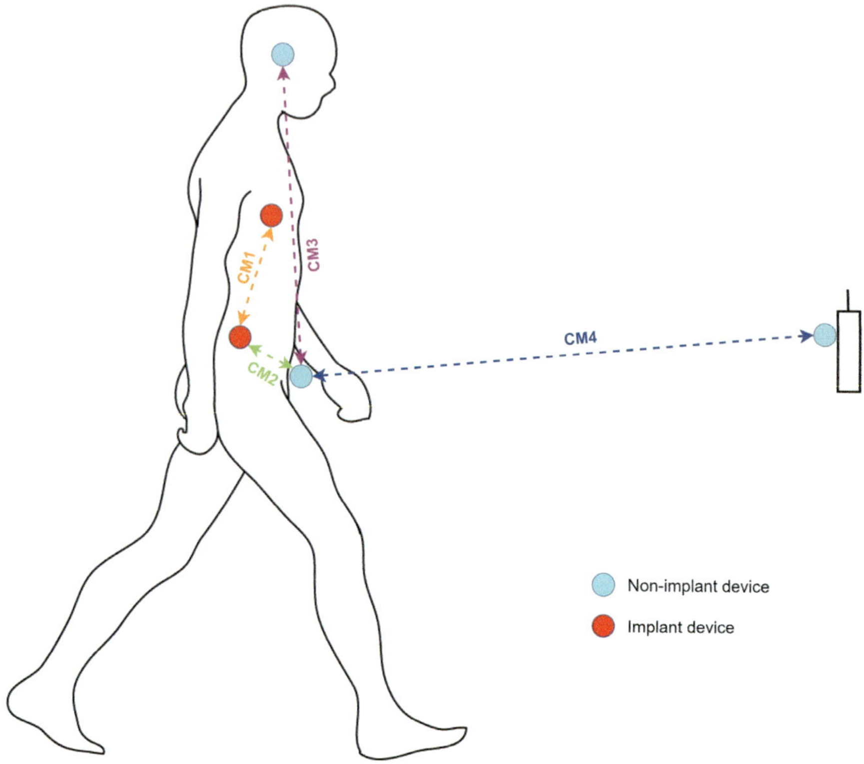

Figure 3.4 Possible communications between elements in the BAN.

the CM3 channel for two elements on the body surface (with or without direct line of sight), and finally CM4 channel for a body surface element and an external element (with or without direct line of sight).

3.4 Communication Protocols in the IoMT

It is challenging to develop a low-power architecture and implement communication protocols in IoMT devices. Power consumption, data rate, network, and network security are just a few of the factors that influence the communication type used in an IoMT application.

To overcome resource constraints and optimize performance, new technologies and communication protocols have been designed or modified to meet those specific requirements [27–30].

Considering the significance of power consumption in the design of IoT networks, there is a preference for low-power wireless network technologies. These technologies can typically be categorized into two primary clusters: low-power wide area networking (LPWAN) and wireless personal area networking (WPAN).

Each communication protocol has a particular technical background and an associated interest area. The following subsections discuss some common IoT protocol solutions for the IoT domain that were used in this study.

3.4.1 Short-range wireless communication

This section describes three protocols for short-range wireless communications with low power consumption: WBAN, Bluetooth, and ZigBee, which refer to IEEE 802.15.6, IEEE 802.15.1, 802.15.4, and proprietary-based standards, respectively. The IEEE organization defines only the physical and MAC layers of the network stack. A group of companies known as an alliance maintains specifications to implement each protocol feature.

- **WBAN IEEE 802.15.6** The IEEE 802.15.6 standard was published by the Institute of Electrical and Electronics Engineers (IEEE) in February 2012 (Figure 3.5). This standard facilitates communication both internally within the human body and externally within the human body. It also outlines three different alternatives for the physical layer (PHY) to meet the specific requirements of medical uses, accompanied by compatible operational modes for the media access control (MAC) layer, as well as robust encryption and authentication mechanisms for low-level data. Narrowband, ultra-wideband (UWB), and human body communications (HBC) are all distinct physical layer specifications in the IEEE 802.15.6 standard. The narrowband (NB) physical layer is commonly considered the optimal choice for medical applications. The device operates over multiple frequency ranges. This feature enables the installation of data rates that may be adjusted from 100 to 1000 Kbps.
  The IEEE 802.15.6 UWB employs two different technological methods: impulse radio UWB (IR-UWB) and frequency modulation UWB (FM-UWB). Within the realm of wireless communication, the distinction between IR-UWB and FM-UWB often revolves around their perceived necessity and optional use within various applications. IR-UWB is considered mandatory, while FM-UWB is perceived as optional. With a channel bandwidth of 499.2 MHz, the UWB channelization specifies

three low-band (3–5 GHz) physical channels and eight high-band (6–10 GHz) physical channels.

Human body communication (HBC) is an innovative method that utilizes the human body as a medium for the transmission of communications using electric fields rather than the more conventional electromagnetic waves. Devices can communicate with each other even without a wireless connection or radio link. The IEEE 802.15.6-HBC uses a 5.25-MHz bandwidth and a frequency range of 21 MHz. The data rate that is supported exhibits a range of variability, spanning from 164 kilobits per second to 1.3125 megabits per second. In the "1-hop" or "2-hop" neighborhoods, respectively, the star topology is the only one supported in the IEEE 802.15.6 standard. In all operating bands, the "1-hop" star topology can be applicable. However, it should be noted that a "2-hop" (extended star) architecture is not supported in IEEE 802.15.6 networks running the MICS band.

- **Bluetooth**

  Bluetooth is a short-range radio communication technology that operates in the ISM free frequency band (2.4–2.483 GHz) and is specifically designed to simplify data sharing between devices at a low cost. Bluetooth version 1.1 is the first wireless personal area network (WPAN) communication standard, approved by the IEEE in 2002 under the denomination of IEEE 802.15.1-2002 [31]. In addition to conserving IEEE protocol specifications, this standard includes the establishment of a logical link control (LLC) interface of the IEEE 802 standards. Bluetooth has evolved gradually and continuously through versions 1.0, 1.2, 2.0, 2.1, 3.0, 4.0, 4.1, and 4.2, and we are now at version 5. In 2010, Bluetooth 4.0 supported two variants of Bluetooth technology: Bluetooth classic BR/EDR (basic rate/enhanced data rate) and Bluetooth

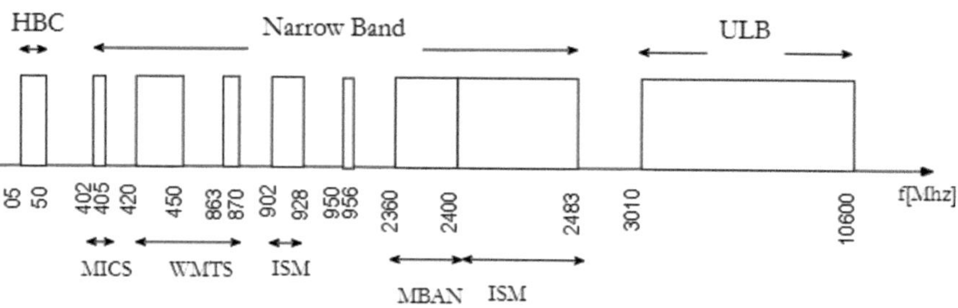

Figure 3.5 The IEEE 802.15.6 standard frequency bands.

"low energy" (BLE) [32]. These two technologies can operate independently or in complementarity. To overcome the incompatibility and establish communication between BR/EDR and BLE, dual mode (Bluetooth Smart Ready) nodes implement BR/EDR and BLE protocol stacks. Bluetooth systems can provide either a point-to-point or a point-to-multipoint connection. The channel is shared among multiple Bluetooth nodes in a point-to-multipoint connection. A piconet is composed of two or more nodes that share the same channel. One node serves as the piconet's master, while the other(s) serve as slaves(s). In the piconet, up to seven enslaved people can be active. However, Bluetooth "low energy" (BLE) was initially designed to support star topology networks exclusively. This feature, however, would restrict BLE's usability in critical IoT application scenarios where a star topology network cannot guarantee coverage for all targeted devices. Each enslaved person communicates with one master through a separate physical channel. The enslaved person cannot play the roles of enslaver and enslaved person at the same time and can only be in one "piconet." Figure 3.6 shows an example of a Bluetooth "low energy" topology (BLE).

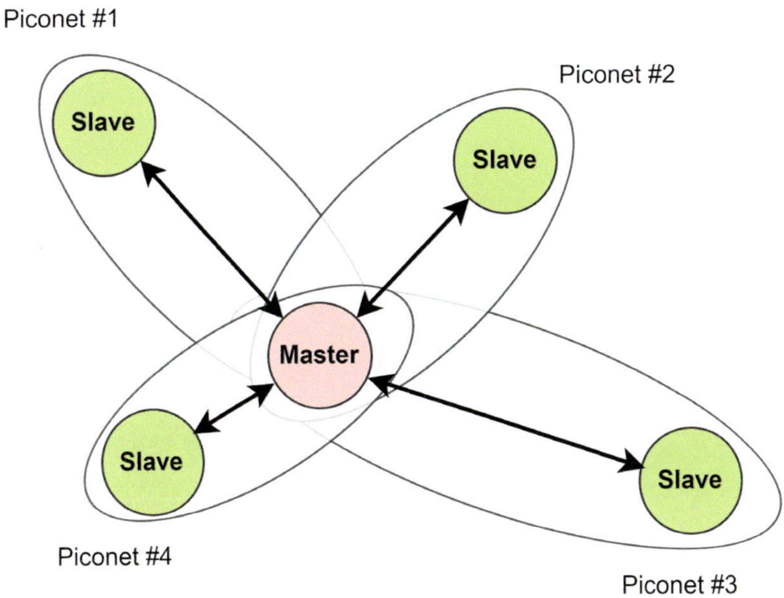

Figure 3.6 Example of a Bluetooth "low energy" topology (BLE).

Moreover, the Internet Engineering Task Force (IETF) has established an adaptation layer to support IPv6 via BLE, allowing BLE devices to connect to the IoT [33]. In 2017, the Bluetooth Core Specification version 5.0 was released, which included the "Bluetooth Smart Mesh" protocol. Bluetooth 5.0 outperforms Bluetooth 4.2 in terms of transmission speed, range, and broadcasting capacity by a factor of two, four, and eight, respectively [34].

- **ZigBee IEEE 802.15.4**

The first IEEE 802.15.4 standard was published in 2003 [35]. It aims to offer wireless communications over short distances that are low-cost and low-power (LR-WPAN), especially to fulfill the requirements for low data rates, low energy usage, and cost efficiency. The standard's lower layers (physical layer and data layer) serve as the foundation for other standards such as ZigBee®, 6LoWPAN, ISA100.11a, WirelessHART®, and MiWi®, which add their upper layers, including the network and application layers. The updated IEEE 802.15.4-2006 specification includes a MAC sub-layer and four physical layers [36]. The specifications define 27 communication channels: 16 channels for the 2.4–2.4835 GHz band, 10 channels for the 902–928 MHz band, and one channel for the 868–868.6 MHz band. The data rates are relatively

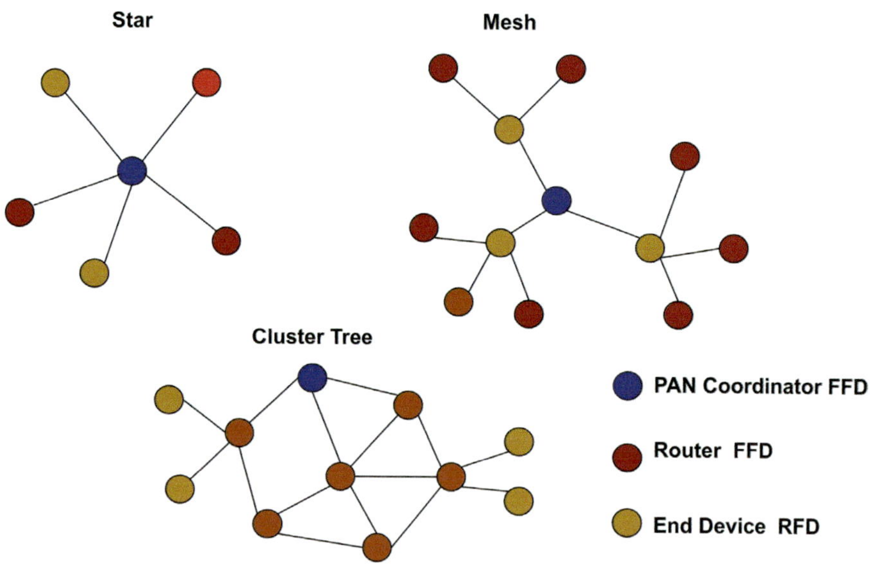

Figure 3.7 Topologies supported by the IEEE 802.15.4 standard.

low, varying from 20 to 250 kbit/s, and depend on the selected frequency bandwidth and physical layer. The IEEE 802.15.4 standard defines two basic types of devices that can be connected to the network: full function device (FFD) and reduced function device (RFD). The FFD device implements the full protocol set; it can act as a network coordinator, router, or simple device. The reduced function device (RFD) is designed to be extremely simple with minimal resources and communication necessities; as a result, it can only communicate with FFDs and cannot ever act as a coordinator. Figure 3.7 shows the three possible topologies of an IEEE 802.15.4 network (star, mesh, and cluster tree).

3.4.2 Low-power wide area network (LPWAN)

Low-power wide area networking (LPWAN) is a technology that transmits data over large distances with a low bit rate [37]. It was specifically designed for applications that have a low daily communication volume. The most widely used technologies are SigFox, LoRaWAN, and NB-IoT.

- **LoRa wide area network (LoRaWAN)**
  The LoRaWAN specification is managed by the LoRa Alliance, a non-profit organization that also provides a certification process to guarantee interoperability.
  The LoRaWAN standard specifies three key components: the physical layer (PHY), the link layer, and the network architecture [38]. Figure 3.8 illustrates LoRaWAN technology.
  LoRaWAN communicates exclusively in sub-gigahertz frequency bands, and its specifications vary by region according to regulatory requirements. Modulated radio frequency (RF) signals are sent directly from devices to one or more LoRaWAN gateways, which then relay the data to the LoRaWAN network server over the internet. The server in charge of the network filters out duplicate data before sending them to the correct application server. The LoRaWAN protocol employs the ALOHA MAC mode to manage collisions. The network's topology is a star, with client devices connecting directly to network servers via the gateway. LoRaWAN's bit rate varies from 300 to 50 kbps depending on the bandwidth used and the spreading factor. The network server contains a key component of LoRa technology known as adaptive data rate (ADR). The ADR offers data rate adaptation and optimization for static end devices.

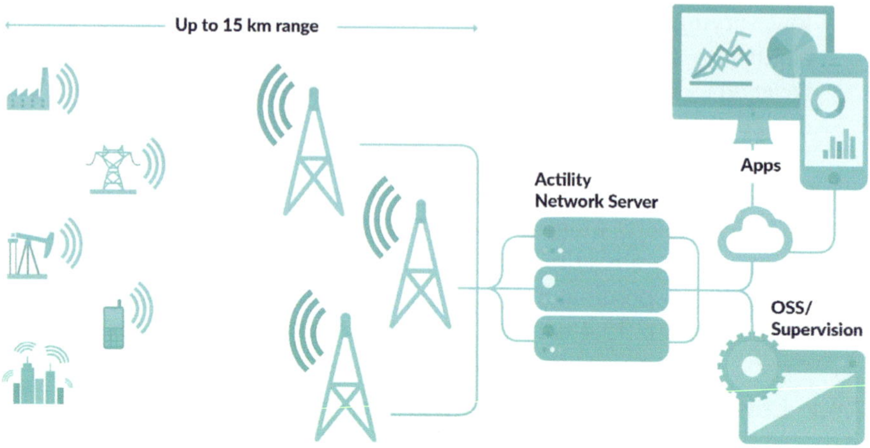

Figure 3.8 LoRaWAN technology.

- **NB-IoT**
  The narrowband Internet of Things (NB-IoT) is an IoT wireless protocol that employs low-power wide area network (LPWAN) technology. It was included in 3GPP Rel-13 for cellular wireless communication, with the goal of reducing deployment costs [39].
  NB-IoT technology communicates with existing GSM and LTE networks using low-bandwidth transmissions under licensed frequency bands. As shown in Figure 3.9, NB-IoT should support three modes of operation: stand-alone, guard-band, and in-band.
- **SigFox**
  SigFox is an emerging communication technology for IoT devices that employs an ultra-narrow band (UNB). SigFox offers LPWAN solutions in unlicensed sub-GHz bands, such as 868 MHz in Europe, 902 MHz in the US, and 920 MHz in Asia Pacific.

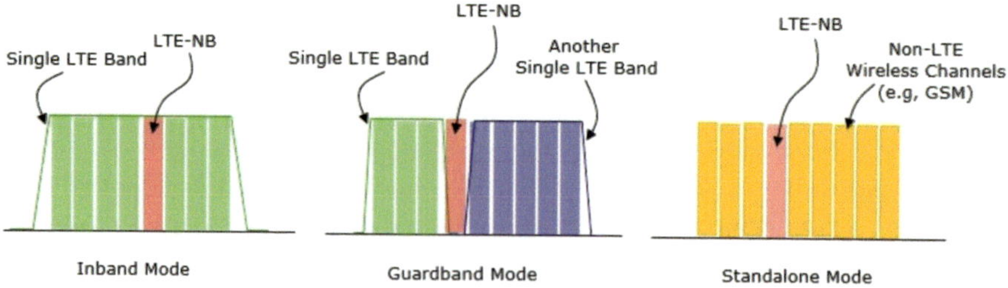

Figure 3.9 The three modes of NB-IoT deployment.

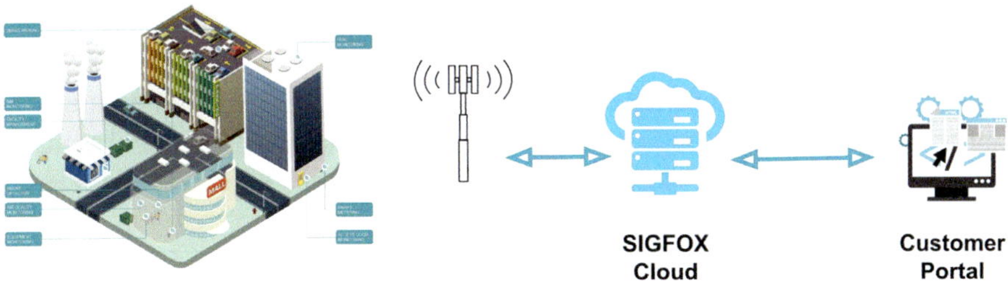

Figure 3.10 SigFox network architecture.

As depicted in Figure 3.10, the Sigfox network architecture connects various devices via antennas, processes data in a Sigfox cloud, and provides user access through the customer portal.
It is built on cellular networks and allows for the transmission of messages for IoT that require bandwidths of less than 1 kHz [40]. This network is based on one-hop star topology cell architecture and is fully independent of existing networks, offering benefits like long-range connectivity, ubiquity, low-energy consumption, and low cost [41, 42]. The SigFox network protocol uses patented base stations that have been integrated with software-defined radios (SDRs). BPSK modulation is used in the connection between end devices and the base station at a data rate of 100 bps and within a narrow band of a frequency of 100 Hz. Furthermore, a message sent by a SigFox device communicates with all accessible base stations and is stored in the SigFox cloud as one data point. The information stored in the Cloud SigFox could then be sent to platforms that enable the generation of data (statistics, curves, alarms, etc.) through API or callbacks.

3.5 Overview of Protocol Security within WBANs using Formal Verification

Wireless body area networks (WBANs) are being utilized more and more in a medical context. However, as a result of this increasing usage, there are issues over the security and privacy of sensitive medical data. To maintain the credibility and reliability of these networks, it is crucial to implement procedures that guarantee the confidentiality, integrity, and availability of information transmitted within WBANs. Formal verification approaches have emerged as an effective method to strengthen the security of the Internet of

Medical Things (IoMT). This section provides a comprehensive introduction to security protocols, focusing specifically on the use of formal verification methods in WBANs. Formal verification can be used to rigorously analyze and evaluate these protocols, allowing for the detection of potential vulnerabilities, verification of security features, and improvement in the overall trustworthiness of the system.

Al Hamadi et al. introduce a methodology [43] that employs a theorem to validate the functionality of a healthcare system based on a wireless body sensor network (WBSN). The researchers enhance a functional WBSN design suggested in a prior investigation [44] and construct an all-encompassing model to depict its behavior. Following that, the authors establish essential characteristics necessary for the successful functioning of the system and use theorem proving techniques to show that the suggested design efficiently meets these criteria. As an illustration, the authors verify a significant property of the WBSN system: the transmission of vital readings is triggered either when a critical value is detected, or once a periodic cycle is completed.

The primary motivation behind their work lies in ensuring the reliable functionality of the WBSN system, as its accuracy in sensing vital signs can have life-saving implications for patients. By accurately verifying the system's response to vital signs values and thresholds, as well as the sequential processes involved in reading and transmitting data, the authors aim to prevent critical incidents and optimize the efficiency of the healthcare system.

To achieve their goal, the authors adopt the Event-B method to model the WBSN system and utilize the Rodin platform for verification. As shown in Figure 3.11, system constraints that represent the static information are mapped into hypotheses, while the system's behavior is represented by events, executed only when their corresponding conditions are met. Moreover, design requirements that are under test are mapped into invariants, which are proven using the Rodin platform for the specific system model.

A detailed case study showcases the proposed methodology and illustrates its advantages over traditional simulation methods. The research highlights the effectiveness of the theorem proving in ensuring the correct implementation of WBSN functionalities and emphasizes the significance of formal methods in healthcare systems design and verification.

This chapter focuses on verifying the functional aspects of a WBSN system. However, it does not factor in the particular protocol used for data transmission between the network of sensors and their coordinator.

In [45], Chen et al. address the challenges of formal modeling and verification for both WSNs and WBANs using the expandable tool PAT

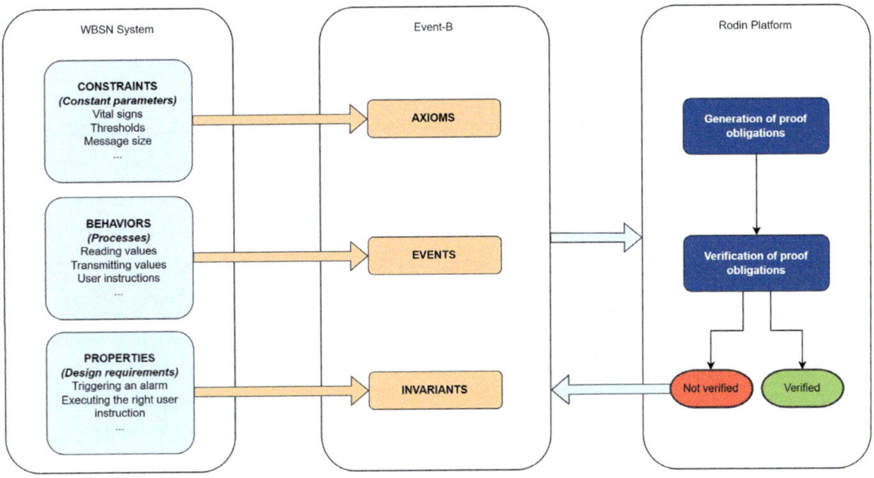

Figure 3.11 Verification methodology for the WBSN system.

(Process Analysis Toolkit) [46], a self-contained framework implementing various model checking techniques.

A location-based security approach in WSN is subjected to extensive formal verification by the authors. To facilitate mobility-free node behavior in WSN, they propose a CSP#-based abstract modeling language. They go beyond the standard Dolev-Yao attack model in PAT in both data structure and attack model design. Furthermore, they define the subsequent properties using LTL:

- **Security property:** It demands that messages be impenetrable to interception and decoding.
- **Internal authentication property:** The range of transmission of legitimate sensor nodes is not breached by adversaries.
- **External authentication property:** Adversaries, however, can connect with legal sensor nodes over a high bandwidth even when they are outside of those nodes' transmission range.

The verification results reveal that the security property is satisfied, while the internal and external authentication properties are not held.

Additionally, the authors conduct a verification of an authentication protocol that relies on dual antennas for WBANs. The attack model assumes an intruder can manipulate its transmission power and location. The results obtained from the verification process utilizing the Physical Authentication Token indicate that the authentication protocol, which relies on dual antennas for wireless body area networks (WBAN), is incapable of providing authentication assistance in situations when the intruder travels away from the network.

The verification model provided in this study does not take into account WBANs at the level of their functional communication MAC, focusing instead solely on node authentication. As a result, critical operations like data transmission based on critical thresholds still need to be addressed. To establish greater trust in the operation of WBANs, it is imperative to verify a range of functional properties associated with the communication protocol.

In [47], Ben Hamouda and Ben Hafaiedh address the significance of testing and verifying MAC protocols in WBANs due to their critical nature, where any flaws in these systems can potentially lead to life-threatening situations. S-TDMA MAC protocol, developed specifically for WBANs by other authors in [48] and [49], is the focus of their modeling and verification efforts. The S-TDMA protocol is based on time division multiple access (TDMA), a scheduled-based multiple access technique that organizes packet transmission into time frames and time slots.

To achieve their goal, the authors adopt the BIP framework, known for its formal semantics and support for rich interactions between components. They propose a formal model of the WBAN architecture that can scale with the number of sensor nodes. The authors model the coordinator and sensor nodes as atomic components within the BIP framework in a star topology. The coordinator node must be connected to every other node as it is in charge of their operation. Sensor nodes, on the other hand, are represented as atomic components facilitating the synchronization, transmission, and reception of various packets through ports using BIP connectors.

Having established the formal model, the authors proceed to formally verify several essential properties of the S-TDMA protocol, described using CTL. These properties include deadlock freedom, invariant verification, mutual exclusion, and fairness. By conducting these verification analyses, they ensure that the protocol operates correctly and meets the desired properties in terms of system behavior and performance.

In [50], Li et al. investigate a three-entity architecture for WBANs. They focus on a protocol proposed previously by Liu et al. [51] for user registration and authentication in the WBAN network. However, denial of service attacks, key-compromise impersonation attacks, and session key guessing attacks have been discovered, among other flaws in Liu et al.'s protocol. In order to tackle these concerns, the authors propose a new authentication protocol for WBANs with three distinct phases, namely initialization, registration, and authentication. Through informal analysis, the authors discuss the robustness of their proposed protocol against various threats, including replay attacks, DoS attacks, forgery attacks, and key-compromise impersonation attacks. It also provides anonymity, untraceability, mutual authentication, perfect forward secrecy for session keys, and immunity to the key escrow problem. For a more rigorous assessment, the authors employ BAN logic to perform a formal security analysis, confirming that their protocol successfully achieves the desired security features. Comparison results indicate that the proposed protocol enhances security, effectively addressing the weaknesses of the previous work while maintaining equivalent costs.

In [52], Almuhaideb and Alqudaihi address the limitations of existing authentication schemes in WBANs regarding node anonymity, key management, and size. To overcome these shortcomings, they propose a lightweight WBAN authentication protocol consisting of two protocols: authentication and re-authentication protocols. The proposed protocol presents a substantial advancement upon Kompara et al.'s scheme [53] by implementing crucial enhancements focused on reinforcing security. Primarily, the authors' improvements center on augmenting the hash function key size and implementing protective measures to conceal and secure the identities of all communication nodes. It also strategically employs an advanced key management system, emphasizing the generation of security parameters with a high degree of randomness. This approach achieves an equilibrium between enhancing security and optimizing operational efficiency within the system. The improved proposed protocol encompasses four phases: the initialization and registration phase, the authentication and key agreement phase, the re-authentication phase, and the secure key deletion phase. The authors conduct a comprehensive security analysis, utilizing both informal and formal methods, to validate the protocol's robustness against common security attacks such as brute force attacks, replay attacks, session hijacking attacks, eavesdropping attacks, and collision attacks. BAN logic is used to provide formal proof of key agreement and mutual authentication. The authors assume that their proposal introduces two crucial elements that still need to be present within the realm of existing literature, namely session key update and secure key deletion.

Rehman et al. [54] also focus on analyzing the authentication protocol proposed by Kompara et al. [53]. The detailed analysis of this scheme reveals the investigation of three types of attacks: in-compromise attack, sensor node impersonation attack, and base station compromise attack. To address its security flaws and enhance its efficiency, the authors propose a modified scheme that retains the three-level network model while ensuring anonymity and lightweight authentication.

To assess the security of the proposed scheme, the authors employ BAN logic for formal security verification and utilize the AVISPA tool to conduct informal verification. The scheme successfully withstands well-known attacks, as verified through these security analysis techniques.

In a related study, Rehman et al. [55] extend their previous research [54] and introduce an enhanced anonymous and hybrid authentication scheme. Their approach combines physiological signals, particularly ECG (electrocardiogram), with pre-deployed keys and efficient cryptography algorithms with low computational and memory requirements in order to implement strong and effective security against a wide range of commonly known attacks. There are four separate stages to the proposed scheme: bio-key extraction, registration, authentication, and key update. To ensure the protocol's authenticity, the authors employ BAN logic, a commonly used formal proof technique for authentication schemes, to verify sensing node and hub node mutual authentication. Through rigorous formal proof based on mathematical modeling, the authors achieve the four defined goals, thus demonstrating the scheme's security. Additionally, the authors conduct informal verification using the widely employed AVISPA tool, which further supports the safety and reliability of their proposed scheme for cryptographic protocol verification.

In [56], Ahmad et al. present a hybrid authentication system that uses a previously developed optimal cryptographic solution [54] in combination with physiological properties taken from data of pulsatile signals to construct a biometric key of unpredictable length. By taking 20 separate pulse samples, the authors confirm the randomness of the extracted bio-keys. The results indicate a higher level of entropy and a near-perfect unpredictability rate, suggesting the presence of strong security measures. The scheme's security goals are demonstrated, and its support for mutual authentication is demonstrated officially using the existing BAN logic. The simulations conducted by the AVISPA tool demonstrate that the scheme is both secure and resilient against prevalent flaws.

In their study [57], Sammoud et al. introduce a novel protocol for generating and distributing cryptographic keys in WBANs. The protocol leverages biometrics, specifically electrocardiogram (ECG) signals, to establish reliable and secure symmetric cryptographic keys. By employing this approach, the generated keys effectively safeguard communications within WBANs. The authors presume that WBAN nodes can carry out many sensing functions at once, which is consistent with the current trend toward devices like smart watches that incorporate multiple sensors (such as accelerometers, GPS, and ECG for heart rate monitoring) into a single wearable device. The proposed method can be broken down into two stages:

- Establishing the symmetric key between a node and its parent: Every WBAN node in a mesh/tree topology, aside from the root, connects to its parent node and shares a pre-installed symmetric key to protect transmitted data, including biometric key generation.
- The generation of the biometric key between child nodes facilitates private communication between two mesh-tree nodes that share an ascendant.

To demonstrate the protocol's resilience against prominent security threats, the authors first conduct an informal analysis. They assess the resilience of each stage of the key establishment protocol and present empirical evidence to demonstrate its efficacy in mitigating known threats. Additionally, to further validate the security of their proposal, the authors undertake formal verification utilizing two widely acknowledged tools, AVISPA and ProVerif.

As depicted in Figure 3.12, AVISPA incorporates four methods, namely OFMC, CL-AtSe, SATMC, and TA4SP, seamlessly integrated through the High-Level Protocol Specification Language (HLPSL).

The operations of the specified protocol are described using the HLPSL (High-Level Protocol Specification Language) to analyze the specified protocol. Initially, the protocol undergoes translation into an intermediate form (IF) using the HLPSL2IF translator. Subsequently, the resulting IF is employed as input for the four distinct back-ends.

The first stage efficiently repels active and passive attacks, as shown by the AVISPA simulations. In addition, the second stage demonstrates safety and meets all specified security objectives by preventing unauthorized access to the information required for biometrics-based key generation between two child nodes. The results derived by ProVerif are consistent with those acquired using AVISPA, hence validating the resilience and security of the suggested methodology.

Delgado-Vargas et al. introduce in [58] a new cryptographic protocol designed to ensure authentication, confidentiality, and integrity in WBANs. The protocol uses an authentication technique for keyless sensors and is formally analyzed with cryptographic protocol verification tools to confirm its right structure and adequate security. The architecture comprises four

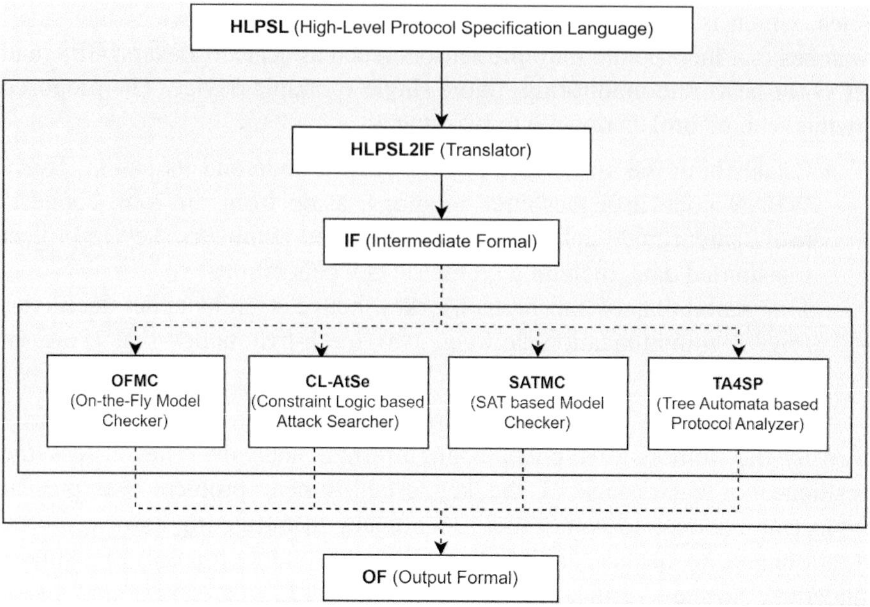

Figure 3.12 AVISPA tool architecture.

entities: a medical server, a coordinator node, sensors, and actuators. Communication between these entities is divided into phases, including setup and sensors' authentication, key generation, information sensing and encryption, information decryption, signing, and verification [59]. The protocol effectively ensures the security of data throughout the process of key generation, hence mitigating the risk of potential attackers gaining access to sensitive information that may be exploited for the purpose of carrying out spoofing attacks. Verification using Scyther and AVISPA demonstrates that the protocol successfully achieves authentication, confidentiality, and integrity.

3.6 Conclusion

Within eHealth systems, patients are provided with medical sensors that can detect, analyze, and calculate various physiological indicators, including temperature, heart rate, respiratory rate, and more. These medical sensors form a wireless body area network (WBAN), a type of wireless sensor network (WSN) specifically designed and employed for the human body.

Given the sensitivity of medical data, ensuring secure communications within the eHealth system is of paramount importance. Security and privacy considerations for the transfer of medical data from WBANs to gateways or remote servers are crucial for the acceptance and widespread adoption of eHealth systems. As a result, a multitude of security approaches have been suggested in the literature, indicating the substantial attention given to addressing communication security in WBANs.

The field of WBAN security techniques can be broadly classified into two primary categories: cryptographic and non-cryptographic authentication methods. Cryptographic authentication systems utilize modified versions of conventional cryptographic schemes in order to build secure channels of communication. In contrast, non-cryptographic authentication methods include systems relying on communication channels, biometric data, and proximity. These methods provide other authentication channels that rely less strongly on cryptographic procedures.

The objective of investigating these security measures is to tackle the difficulties linked to safeguarding WBAN communications and guaranteeing the privacy, accuracy, and accessibility of medical data. Researchers aim to create effective and dependable methods for securely transmitting medical information within WBANs. They achieve this by using both cryptographic and non-cryptographic authentication procedures. The ultimate goal is to promote the widespread acceptance and use of eHealth systems.

Based on the reviewed papers, BAN logic has become a dominant method for formalizing and proving security elements in WBANs. Although there are some limits to this logic, as stated in [60], the use of BAN logic has allowed researchers to examine authentication, secrecy, integrity, and other important security features of WBAN protocols. It has enabled the detection of weaknesses, the assessment of security measures, and the verification of protocol accuracy.

In addition, the AVISPA tool was found to be commonly used in the evaluated research as a resource for formal verification in WBANs. Researchers can use the tool to model protocols, specify security features, and test protocols' resistance to common threats. The widespread adoption of AVISPA attests to its usefulness and the improvement it has brought to the field of security analysis of WBANs.

References

[1] Vishnu, S., Ramson, S. J., & Jegan, R. (2020, March). Internet of Medical Things (IoMT)-An overview. In 2020, 5th International Conference on Devices, circuits, and Systems (ICDCS) (pp. 101-104). IEEE.

[2] Chatterjee, P., & Armentano, R. L. (2015, December). Internet of things for a smart and ubiquitous ehealth system. In 2015 international conference on computational intelligence and communication networks (CICN) (pp. 903-907). IEEE.
[3] FIORÈSE, Serge et MEINADIER, Jean-Pierre. Découvrir et comprendre l'ingénierie système. CEPADUES Editions, 2012.
[4] BJØRNER, Dines et HAVELUND, Klaus. 40 years of formal methods. In : International Symposium on Formal Methods. Springer, Cham, 2014. p. 42-61.
[5] ALUR, Rajeev et DILL, David. Automata for modeling real-time systems. In : International colloquium on automata, languages, and programming. Springer, Berlin, Heidelberg, 1990. p. 322-335.
[6] PETRI, Carl Adam. Communication with automata. 1966.
[7] REISIG, Wolfgang. Understanding Petri nets: modeling techniques, analysis methods, case studies. Heidelberg: Springer, 2013.
[8] SPIVEY, J. Michael et ABRIAL, J. R. The Z notation. Hemel Hempstead : Prentice Hall, 1992.
[9] ABRIAL, Jean-Raymond et HOARE, A. The B-book: assigning programs to meanings. Cambridge : Cambridge University Press, 1996.
[10] BERTOT, Yves et CASTÉRAN, Pierre. Interactive theorem proving and program development: Coq'Art: the calculus of inductive constructions. Springer Science & Business Media, 2013.
[11] MANNA, Zohar et PNUELI, Amir. The temporal logic of reactive and concurrent systems: Specification. Springer Science & Business Media, 2012.
[12] Clarke, E. M., & Emerson, E. A. (1981, May). Design and synthesis of synchronization skeletons using branching time temporal logic. In Workshop on logic of programs (pp. 52-71). Berlin, Heidelberg: Springer Berlin Heidelberg.
[13] Burrows, M., Abadi, M., & Needham, R. (1989). A Logic of Authentication: ACM Operating Systems Review. In Proceedings of the Twelfth ACM Symposium on Operating Systems Principles (Vol. 23, No. 5, pp. 34-37).
[14] ISO, NFEN : 9001 : Systèmes de management de la qualité-Exigences.
[15] BERARD, Béatrice, BIDOIT, Michel, LAROUSSINIE, François, et al. Vérification de logiciels. 1999.
[16] BAIER, Christel et KATOEN, Joost-Pieter. Principles of model checking. MIT press, 2008.

[17] XIN-FENG, Zhu, JIAN-DONG, Wang, BIN, Li, et al. Methods to tackle state explosion problem in model checking. In : 2009 Third International Symposium on Intelligent Information Technology Application. IEEE, 2009. p. 329-331.

[18] LARSEN, Kim G., PETTERSSON, Paul, et YI, Wang. UPPAAL in a nutshell. International journal on software tools for technology transfer, 1997, vol. 1, no 1,

[19] HOLZMANN, Gerard J. Parallelizing the spin model checker. In : International SPIN Workshop on Model Checking of Software. Springer, Berlin, Heidelberg, 2012. p. 155-171.

[20] GARDEY, Guillaume, LIME, Didier, MAGNIN, Morgan, et al. Romeo: A tool for analyzing time Petri nets. In : International Conference on Computer Aided Verification. Springer, Berlin, Heidelberg, 2005. p. 418-423.

[21] Sun, J., Liu, Y., Dong, J. S., & Pang, J. (2009). PAT: Towards flexible verification under fairness. In Computer Aided Verification: 21st International Conference, CAV 2009, Grenoble, France, June 26-July 2, 2009. Proceedings 21 (pp. 709-714). Springer Berlin Heidelberg.

[22] Alagar, V. S., Periyasamy, K., & Periyasamy, K. (2011). Specification of software systems. New York: Springer.

[23] Hoare, C. A. R. (1969). An axiomatic basis for computer programming. Communications of the ACM, 12(10), 576-580.

[24] ABRIAL, Jean-Raymond, BUTLER, Michael, HALLERSTEDE, Stefan, et al. Rodin: an open toolset for modelling and reasoning in Event-B. International journal on software tools for technology transfer, 2010, vol. 12, p. 447-466.

[25] Kaufmann, M., & Moore, J. S. (1996, June). ACL2: An industrial strength version of Nqthm. In Proceedings of 11th Annual Conference on Computer Assurance. COMPASS'96 (pp. 23-34). IEEE.

[26] Paulson, T. N. L. C., & Wenzel, M. (2013). A Proof Assistant for Higher-Order Logic. 2006-06-06]. http://isabelle.in.tum.de.

[27] O. Bello, S. Zeadally and M. Badra, "Network layer inter-operation of Device-toDevice communication technologies in Internet of Things (IoT)", Ad Hoc Networks, vol. 57, pp. 52-62, 2017.

[28] M. Andersson, Short-range Low Power Wireless Devices and Internet of Things (IoT), 1st ed. connectBlue, 2014, pp. 1-13.

[29] "11 Internet of Things (IoT) Protocols You Need to Know About", Rs-online.com, 2015.

[30] "IoT Technology | 2017 Overview Guide on Protocols, Software, Hardware and Network Trends", Postscapes.com, 2017.
[31] http://www.ieee802.org/15/pub/TG1.html
[32] Aguilar, S.; Vidal, R.; Gomez, C. Opportunistic Sensor Data Collection with Bluetooth Low Energy. Sensors 2017, 17, 159.
[33] Nieminen, J.; Savolainen, T.; Isomaki, M.; Patil, B.; Shelby, Z.; Gomez, C. IPv6 over BLUETOOTH(R) Low Energy; RFC 7668; IETF: Fremont, CA, USA, 2015.
[34] Wendy Warne. 2016. Bluetooth 5 Is Here. Retrieved December 14, 2016 from https://blog.bluetooth.com/bluetooth-5-is-here
[35] "IEEE Standard for Telecommunications and Information Exchange Between Systems - LAN/MAN Specific Requirements - Part 15: Wireless Medium Access Control (MAC) and Physical Layer (PHY) Specifications for Low Rate Wireless Personal Area Networks (WPAN)," in IEEE Std 802.15.4-2003 , vol., no., pp.1-680, 1 Oct. 2003, doi: 10.1109/IEEESTD.2003.94389.
[36] "IEEE Standard for Information technology– Local and metropolitan area networks– Specific requirements– Part 15.4: Wireless Medium Access Control (MAC) and Physical Layer (PHY) Specifications for Low Rate Wireless Personal Area Networks (WPANs)," in IEEE Std 802.15.4-2006 (Revision of IEEE Std 802.15.4-2003) , vol., no., pp.1-320, 7 Sept. 2006, doi: 10.1109/IEEESTD.2006.232110.
[37] A. Dongare, R. Narayanan, A. Gadre, A. Luong, A. Balanuta, S. Kumar, B. Iannucci, and A. Rowe, Charm: Exploiting geographical diversity through coherent combining in low-power wide-area networks, in Proceedings of the International Conference on Information Processing in Sensor Networks, 2018, pp. 6071.
[38] LoRa Alliance, LoRaWAN Specification (v1.0.3), Mar. 2018.
[39] A. Rico-Alvarino, M. Vajapeyam, H. Xu, X. Wang, Y. Blankenship, J. Bergman, T. Tirronen, and E. Yavuz, "An overview of 3GPP enhancements on machine to machine communications," IEEE Commun. Mag., vol. 54, no. 6, pp. 14–21, Jun. 2016.
[40] K. E. Nolan, W. Guibene and M. Y. Kelly, An Evaluation of Low Power Wide Area Network Technologies for the Internet of Things, in: Wireless Communications and Mobile Computing Conference (IWCMC), pp. 439444, 2016.
[41] A. Ali, G. A. Shah and J. Arshad, Energy Efficient Techniques for M2M Communication: A Survey, in: Journal of Network and Computer Applications, vol. 68, pp. 4255, 2016.

[42] G. Margelis, R. Piechocki, D. Kaleshi and P. Thomas, Low Throughput Networks for the IoT: Lessons Learned from Industrial Implementations, in: IEEE 2nd World Forum on Internet of Things (WF-IoT), pp. 181186, 2015.

[43] Al Hamadi, H., Gawanmeh, A., & Al-Qutayri, M. (2014, June). A verification methodology for a wireless body sensor network functionality. In IEEE-EMBS International Conference on Biomedical and Health Informatics (BHI) (pp. 635-639). IEEE.

[44] Chung, W. Y. (2009). Ubiquitous healthcare system based on a wireless sensor network.

[45] Chen, T., Yu, Z., Li, S., & Chen, B. (2016). From wireless sensor networks to wireless body area networks: formal modeling and verification on security using PAT. Journal of Sensors, 2016.

[46] https://pat.comp.nus.edu.sg/

[47] Hamouda, R. B., & Hafaiedh, I. B. (2017, October). Formal modeling and verification of a wireless body area network (WBAN) protocol: S-TDMA protocol. In 2017 International Conference on Internet of Things, Embedded Systems and Communications (IINTEC) (pp. 72-77). IEEE.

[48] Nie, Z., Li, Z., Huang, R., Liu, Y., Li, J., & Wang, L. (2015). A statistical frame-based TDMA protocol for human body communication. Biomedical engineering online, 14(1), 1-20.

[49] Chen, H., Nie, Z., Ivanov, K., Wang, L., & Liu, R. (2013, May). A statistical MAC protocol for heterogeneous-traffic human body communication. In 2013 IEEE International Symposium on Circuits and Systems (ISCAS) (pp. 2275-2278). IEEE.

[50] Li, X., Peng, J., Kumari, S., Wu, F., Karuppiah, M., & Choo, K. K. R. (2017). An enhanced 1-round authentication protocol for wireless body area networks with user anonymity. Computers & Electrical Engineering, 61, 238-249.

[51] Liu, J., Zhang, L., & Sun, R. (2016). 1-RAAP: An efficient 1-round anonymous authentication protocol for wireless body area networks. Sensors, 16(5), 728.

[52] Almuhaideb, A. M., & Alqudaihi, K. S. (2020). A lightweight and secure anonymity-preserving protocol for WBAN. IEEE Access, 8, 178183-178194.

[53] Kompara, M., Islam, S. H., & Hölbl, M. (2019). A robust and efficient mutual authentication and key agreement scheme with untraceability for WBANs. Computer networks, 148, 196-213.

[54] Rehman, Z. U., Altaf, S., & Iqbal, S. (2020). An efficient lightweight key agreement and authentication scheme for WBAN. IEEE Access, 8, 175385-175397.

[55] Rehman, Z. U., Altaf, S., Ahmad, S., Huda, S., Al-Shayea, A. M., & Iqbal, S. (2021). An efficient, hybrid authentication using ECG and lightweight cryptographic scheme for WBAN. IEEE Access, 9, 133809-133819.

[56] Ahmad, S., Rehman, Z. U., Altaf, S., Zaindin, M., Huda, S., Haroon, M., & Iqbal, S. (2022). Dynamic Key Extraction Technique Using Pulse Signal and Lightweight Cryptographic Authentication Scheme for WBAN. Sustainability, 14(21), 14625.

[57] Sammoud, A., Chalouf, M. A., Hamdi, O., Montavont, N., & Bouallegue, A. (2020). A new biometrics-based key establishment protocol in WBAN: Energy efficiency and security robustness analysis. Computers & Security, 96, 101838.

[58] Delgado-Vargas, K. A., Gallegos-Garcia, G., & Escamilla-Ambrosio, P. J. (2023). Cryptographic Protocol with Keyless Sensors Authentication for WBAN in Healthcare Applications. Applied Sciences, 13(3), 1675.

[59] Singh, A. K. (2014). A review of elliptic curve based signcryption schemes. International Journal of Computer Applications, 102(6).

[60] Nessett, D. M. (1990). A critique of the Burrows, Abadi and Needham logic. ACM SIGOPS Operating Systems Review, 24(2), 35-38.

4

IoMT Laws in Western Countries: An Overview of the Legal Landscape Governing the Use of IoMT Devices and Applications

Fatima Qasim Hasan[1], Shikha Goyal[1], and Fehmina Khalique[2]

[1]Plot No. 2, Yamuna Expressway, Sector 17A, India
[2]Plot Number 11, Knowledge Park II, India
E-mail: fatimaqasim.hasan@galgotiasuniversity.edu.in;
shikha.goyal@galgotiasuniversity.edu.in;
fehmina.khalique@lloydbusinessschool.edu.in

Abstract

Internet of Things (IoT) is a collection of tangible objects that are equipped with sensors, software, or have technological capabilities to share data with other internet-connected equipment or devices. With IoT gaining a rapid momentum across all industries, the healthcare industry has also gained from this development.

The combination of IoT with medical devices ensures a promising future for the healthcare industry. IoMT ensures connecting medical devices over the internet so that medical staff can monitor medical performance even remotely. However, with this advantage, there are serious legal and regulatory concerns that should be abided by. Thus, this chapter discusses IoMT laws in Western countries. It also discusses some of the recent health breaches, like the Life Labs data breach and the Virginia Commonwealth University personal data breach.

This chapter will focus on the Food and Drug Administration (FDA), National Institute of Standards and Technology (NIST), Health Insurance Portability and Accountability Act (HIPAA), and Federal Trade Commission (FTC) from the US, Medical Device Regulation (MDR) and General Data

DOI: 10.1201/9788770047395-4

Protection Regulation (GPDR) from EU, and Personal Information Protection and Electronic Documents Act from Canada. It will help in ensuring patient safety, regulatory compliance, market access, and the ethical and legal use of medical devices in the rapidly evolving field of healthcare technology. It will help foster innovation, protect patient data, and promote responsible and effective healthcare practices.

Keywords: IoMT, IoT, FDA, HIPAA, GDPR, cybersecurity, regulations, breach, USA, EU, Canada.

4.1 Introduction

IoT refers to a set of tangible objects that are furnished with sensors, processing power, software, and other technologies that can communicate and exchange data with other devices and systems by making use of the internet or other communications networks [1]. These devices enable them to collect and transmit data individually addressable and network-connected, but not necessarily internet-connected devices.

Because of the technological, financial, and social potential it possesses, the healthcare business is one of the numerous industries that has benefited from the rapid development of systems based on the Internet of Things (IoT). The integration of Internet of Things capabilities into medical systems enables these systems to offer better healthcare services such as remote patient monitoring, real-time diagnosis of medical disorders, and other similar activities, hence raising the level of care provided to human users and increasing their level of satisfaction [2]. It is expected that by 2027, the IoT market is projected to exceed $2.4 trillion annually [3].

IoMT encompasses both IoT and a variety of equipment used in healthcare services. IoMT represents the future of healthcare delivery systems, as it involves connecting all medical devices to the internet, allowing medical professionals to remotely monitor them. This evolution in healthcare enables faster and more cost-effective delivery of services. Figure 4.1 depicts IoMT in action, where sensors capture patient vital signs, transmit them to IoMT applications via the internet, and subsequently relay this information to healthcare experts and medical personnel, who can then provide a timely response to the patients.

According to Globe Wire, the benefits of the IoMT are predicted to drive the global market for IoMT to rise at a compound annual growth rate (CAGR) of 24.55% from US$55.324 billion in 2019 to US$257.162 billion in 2026 [4].

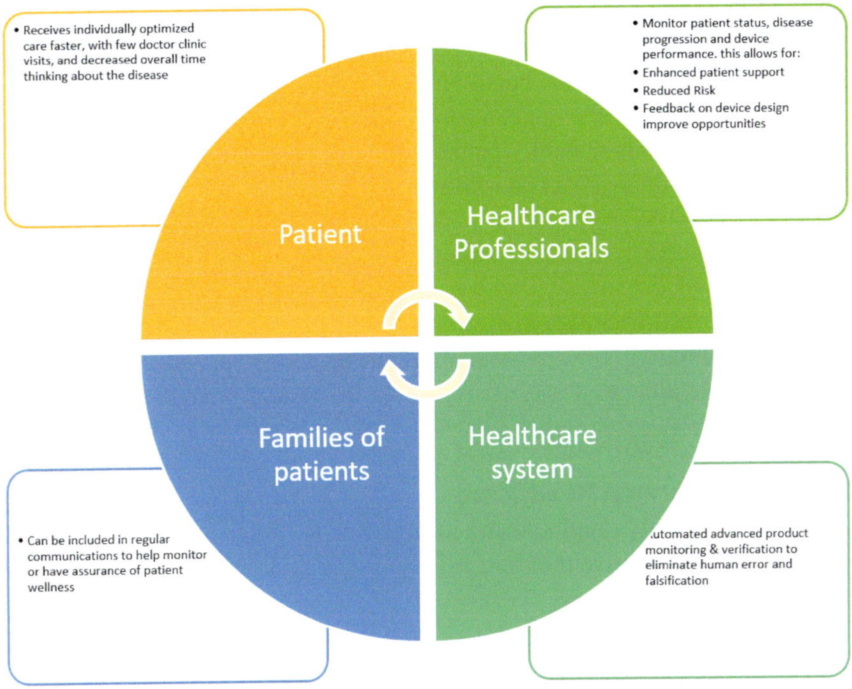

Figure 4.1 Stakeholders benefited from IoMT.

4.1.1 Relationship between IoT and IoMT

- IoMT is a subset of IoT: IoMT can be regarded as a specialized field within the IoT framework. It emphasizes specifically the application of IoT technologies in the healthcare industry [5].
- IoMT encompasses the incorporation of medical devices with IoT infrastructure to facilitate connectivity, data collection, and remote monitoring of healthcare-related parameters. It seeks to enhance healthcare delivery, promote patient care, and facilitate proactive health management [6].
- IoT + medical devices = IoMT: It can lead to optimized results for patients, healthcare professionals, patients' families, and the healthcare system at large.

4.1.2 Significance of IoMT

The significance of IoMT is evident in the present technological and healthcare domain. It is elaborated through the following points.

4.1.2.1 Improved and efficient patient care

IoMT is beneficial for collecting data in an efficient manner that is convenient for the patient as well as the health provider.

IoMT devices offer enhanced data accuracy, reduced risk factors, improved time management, remote monitoring capabilities, and superior predictive capabilities [7]. Their relevance in healthcare solutions is increasingly apparent, making them an ideal choice for screening, predicting, and monitoring emerging infectious diseases like COVID-19 [8].

4.1.2.2 Remote monitoring

The implementation of a remote monitoring facility is advantageous for the health provider as it makes it easy to do routine activities along with continuous health surveillance_[9].

4.1.2.3 Data-driven healthcare

IoMT monitors and provides health information to caregivers as well as health providers as a preventive measure to identify early identification of a medical issue or reduce critical cases [10].

4.1.2.4 Smart hospital

IoMT provides health intelligence in smart hospitals to aid the best medical facilities with early diagnosis and patient care. Smart hospitals revolutionize the healthcare industry by digitalizing healthcare, which, in the long run, will be scalable and efficient for a smart city project [11]. IoT plays an integral component in the advancement of medical care by making it smart and intelligent.

The first phase of the smart hospital initiative involves the implementation of smartphone-based appointment registration, which allows patients to schedule appointments based on the availability of doctors. Additionally, a mobile application is being developed to facilitate inquiries and provide test result reports. These advancements aim to enhance the efficiency and convenience of hospital services [9].

4.1.2.5 Mobile health

Applications for m-health are the way of the future, and they will become an important tool for delivering healthcare. For instance, people with type 1 diabetes can receive assistance with self-management through text messaging on their cell phones. Treatment adherence and diabetic self-efficacy can improve as a result of this approach [10].

4.1.2.6 Reduce cost and expenses

Remote patient monitoring is used to transmit data back to physicians along with automatic renewal requests, allowing doctors to prescribe appropriate medication depending on the patient's condition. This will reduce the expenditures and budget that are now paid while caring for patients who are not taking their medicines on time [12]. For example, a portable ECG device measures and records ECG readings at any time and in any location through an ECG monitoring system based on IoT technology [10].

4.1.2.7 Data-driven decision-making and error reduction

Beyond aiding in decision-making, data generated by IoT devices plays a pivotal role in optimizing healthcare operations by minimizing errors, waste, and overall system costs. Many individuals grapple with chronic conditions like heart disease and diabetes, among others. Thanks to the analytical power of IoT, patients can now receive more individualized care and treatment. Networked, smart gadgets can be utilized to track the health of the elderly and patients with chronic conditions. With this understanding, medical professionals will be more qualified to heal patients [11].

4.1.2.8 Faster disease diagnosis

Real-time infection detection aids in the provision of appropriate medical treatment and, importantly, helps control the epidemic [13]. For example, a portable PCR system based on a chip allows for real-time differential detection of malarial parasites [14]. Moreover, it has been found that patients who are unable to attend hospitals for their regular check-ups physically reveal a preference for utilizing internet (IoMT) devices. Accurate real-time statistics by Internet of Medical Things (IoMT) machines make the healthcare facility dependable and efficient. These machines enable healthcare professionals to promptly identify problems and determine appropriate solutions within a short timeframe [15].

4.1.2.9 Personalized medicine

The concept of "personalized" medicine has garnered significant attention and generated considerable anticipation in recent years. The foundation of personalized medicine rests upon the recognition that individuals display unique and intricate characteristics across molecular, physiological, environmental exposure, and behavioral dimensions. Consequently, it is suggested that interventions targeting diseases should be customized to align with these peculiar characteristics [16].

4.1.2.10 Improved treatment

To enhance the efficacy of treatment methods, it is imperative to explore avenues for improvement. The utilization of this technology empowers medical practitioners to make well-informed decisions based on empirical evidence, thereby promoting a high level of transparency in their decision-making processes [17].

In addition to its widespread application in the healthcare sector, IoMT and Software as a Medical Device (SaMD) are now being embraced and put into practice within hospital settings and residences, thereby making it susceptible to cyberattack and invasions against vulnerable open medical network device. These attacks and invasions also result in data breaches and higher expenditures for healthcare delivery and can have an ill effect on patient health outcomes [18]. The exponential proliferation of the IoMT devices has elicited apprehensions about the realm of cybersecurity vulnerabilities and the safeguarding of sensitive patient information. The inherent interconnectivity of these devices gives rise to vulnerabilities that have the potential to result in data breaches and compromise the safety of patients. There is a growing emphasis among regulatory bodies and industry stakeholders on the imperative of ensuring the security of IoMT devices. This entails

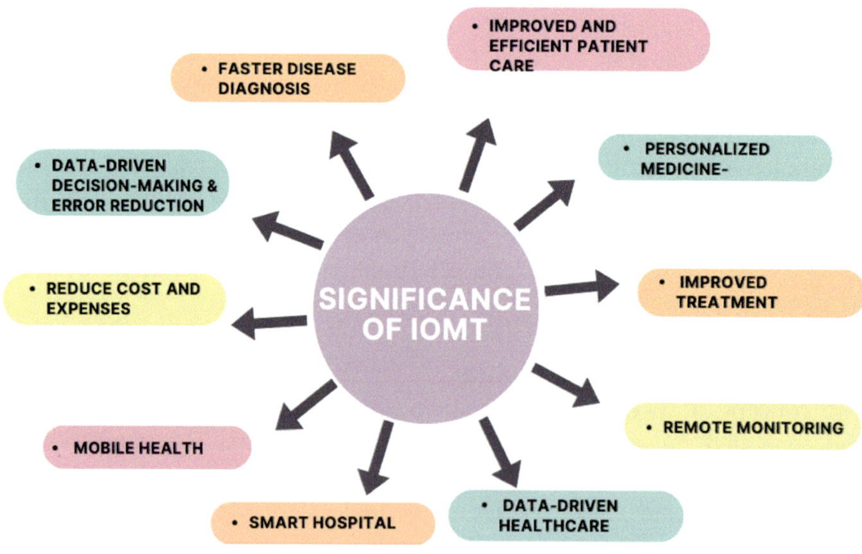

Figure 4.2 Stakeholders benefited from IoMT. Source: Authors creation.

incorporating robust security measures into the very fabric of connected medical devices, thereby addressing potential vulnerabilities and mitigating risks [19]. The results of these attacks, as well as their financial and security implications, have prompted various government organizations and agencies, such as trade associations, technical associations, standards organizations, research centers, political parties, and non-governmental organizations, to proactively protect the assets, the interests, and welfare of the people [20].

4.2 Laws in Western Countries

The advent of the Internet of Medical Things (IoMT) has led to strict legal regulations in Western nations to protect patient confidentiality and guarantee the safe implementation of networked medical devices. Adherence to data protection regulations, including the Health Insurance Portability and Accountability Act (HIPAA) in the US and the General Data Protection Regulation (GDPR) in the EU, is emphasized by law. These rules require IoMT applications to have strong security protocols, clear permission procedures, and open data standards. As Western countries adopt digital health technologies, ongoing legal advancements seek to achieve a balance between innovation promotion and personal health information protection.

4.2.1 Laws in USA

The implementation of effective regulations is necessary to govern the sector and protect consumers from potential risks associated with the use of this technology. Dealing with cyber threats in the IoMT is crucial, and this may necessitate the use of technological security solutions. Equally important is the establishment of appropriate rules and regulations [18]. Various aspects of this business may be subject to regulations by several existing US organizations; however, the current framework needs to be revised. The US legislation on IoMT is discussed briefly in this section.

1. The US Department of Health and Human Services Federal Drug Administration (FDA)
2. The Federal Trade Commission, another autonomous agency under US government jurisdiction
3. The Department of Health and Human Services' Office for Civil Rights (OCR) enforces the Health Insurance Portability and Accountability Act (HIPAA).

4.2.1.1 The US federal drug administration (FDA)

Protecting patient health information on the IoMT is critical to ensuring privacy and maintaining the security of sensitive medical data. Recently, there has been a significant increase in proactive measures taken by the Food and Drug Administration (FDA) to enhance the security of IoMT devices. The Food and Drug Administration of the United States (FDA or US FDA) is a federal department of the Department of Health and Human Services. The FDA is in charge of protecting and promoting public health by regulating and supervising food safety, tobacco products, caffeine products, dietary supplements, prescription and over-the-counter pharmaceutical drugs (medications), vaccines, biopharmaceuticals, blood transfusions, medical devices, electromagnetic radiation emitting devices (ERED), cosmetics, animal foods and feeds [3], and veterinary products [21]. In response to growing concerns about cyberattacks on internet-connected devices used in healthcare settings, the FDA has issued new cybersecurity recommendations for internet-connected devices – medical condition. The recommendations are part of President Joe Biden's comprehensive $1.7 trillion federal budget plan that he signed in December [22].

In accordance with the new regulations, all new medical device applicants are now required to present a strategy outlining how they will track, recognize, and deal with cybersecurity risks as well as give "reasonable assurance" that their devices are secure. Additionally, they must frequently release security updates and fixes, especially for emergency circumstances. A "software bill of materials" listing every piece of software utilized in the applicants' devices, including open-source software, is also required [23].

The organization has issued comprehensive guidelines and regulatory frameworks about the seamless integration of medical devices and the IoMT. The FDA categorizes IoMT devices according to their possible dangers and assigns them to several regulatory paths. IoMT devices can be categorized as Class I (low risk), Class II (moderate risk), or Class III (high risk) by the FDA. The classification defines the level of regulatory scrutiny and pre-market clearance or approval required. Before IoMT devices can be legally announced in the United States, they may need pre-market clearance or approval from the FDA. The device's classification determines the regulatory pathway used. Class I devices normally go through a pre-market notification (510(k)) process; however, Class II devices may need a 510(k) clearance or a pre-market approval (PMA) application. A PMA application is typically required for Class III devices [24].

4.2.1.1.1 Regulatory control and compliance

Regulatory control and compliance IoMT devices are subject to several regulatory controls to assure their safety and efficacy. The Food and Drug Administration examines design controls, software validation, and clinical data, labeling, and manufacturing processes to determine compliance with regulatory requirements. Monitoring device efficacy and safety also requires post-market surveillance and adverse event reporting [25].

The FDA provides guidance documents and standards to IoMT device manufacturers and developers. These documents provide recommendations and best practices to aid in the creation, testing, and regulatory compliance of these technologies. Compliance with these guidelines serves to guarantee that IoMT devices meet all applicable regulatory requirements [26].

4.2.1.1.2 Considerations regarding cybersecurity

The FDA recognizes the importance of addressing cybersecurity threats associated with IoMT devices. The agency issued guidance on medical device cybersecurity, emphasizing the need for manufacturers to implement adequate safeguards to protect patient data and device functionality from potential cyber threats. The FBI reported in 2022 that 53 percent of internet-connected medical equipment and other digital items used in hospitals have known significant vulnerabilities. Insulin pumps, intra cardiac defibrillators, mobile cardiac telemetry, and pacemakers were among the medical equipment identified in the research as being vulnerable to cyberattacks resulting in inaccurate data and administering drug overdose, which would result in endangering the patient's health [27].

To accomplish its public health goals, FDA is open to working with interested parties, by pooling resources and knowledge through appropriate channels. Thus, the Food and Drug Administration (FDA) may effectively collaborate to meet urgent public health requirements and close knowledge gaps, thereby fostering creative development of the products within its purview. Cooperation Research and Development Agreements (CRADAs), memorandums of understanding (MOUs), contracts, cooperation agreements, and other public–private partnership frameworks are only some of the ways businesses and the FDA formalize their collaboration [28].

A memorandum was signed between the FDA and the National Institute of Standards and Technology (NIST) of the United States. The collaboration with NIST was to encourage and support the latest manufacturing technologies in the 21st century [29].

4.2.1.2 The national institute of standards and technology (NIST)

NIST provides cybersecurity guidelines for the IoT. It offers policies and guidelines for connected devices for security reasons but does not make compliance mandatory on every connected device. For example, if an individual buys a Fitbit gadget from Walmart for himself, the data obtained and disseminated does not get protection by the HIPAA law. However, if a similar device is purchased from a healthcare practitioner, it would be subject to HIPAA guidelines [30].

Here are some ways in which the NIST framework falls short:

(1) The NIST framework is not adequate for managing risks since its adoption is entirely discretionary. As a result, it is not a suitable alternative to centralized systems for managing sensitive data [31].

Because organizations are complex and threats are unique, the NIST framework cannot be used universally to address security breaches and threats.

4.2.1.3 Health insurance portability and accountability act (HIPAA)

USA has implemented a legislative law named HIPAA. Its major goal is to protect patient health information by creating data privacy and security safeguards. Its major goal is to protect patient health information by creating data privacy and security safeguards. These provisions are designed to ensure the confidentiality and integrity of sensitive medical data. By adopting HIPAA, the United States hopes to preserve people's privacy rights while also ensuring the security of their personal health information [32].

By linking medical devices and technologies, the legislative law HIPAA on IoMT seeks to protect the confidentiality and safety of individual's health data. The HIPAA Privacy Rule creates comprehensive national laws to safeguard health information that has the potential to reveal an individual's identity. This applies to entities such as health service providers, healthcare plans, and healthcare clearing centers that disseminate or save health data via internet platforms. The Privacy Rule defines limitations for the use and exposure of protected health information (PHI). Furthermore, individuals have unique rights regarding their protected health information (PHI) [32].

The HIPAA Security Rule complements the Privacy Rule by establishing a framework for the protection of electronic protected health information (e-PHI). The aforementioned regulation applies to organizations designated as protected, mandating the execution of organizational, physical, and digital safeguards to make it confidential and available to electronically protected health information (e-PHI). An incident of data exposure was revealed after 16 years. More than 4,000 patients' protected health information was exposed by the Virginia Commonwealth University (VCU) Health System, specifically its transplant center. VCU Health detected the compromise in February 2022, the sensitive data of 441 individuals, including their social security numbers, dates of birth, and medical record numbers, were subjected to unauthorized exposure [33]. The Security Rule incorporates a comprehensive set of regulations about a variety of information security aspects. These regulations include risk analysis, access controls, encryption, audit controls, and contingency planning for emergencies, among other essential components [32].

This law gives consumers an alternative to safeguard the confidentiality and safety of their healthcare information; it is only relevant if the healthcare information collector is an HIPAA-addressed firm. In particular, the aforementioned requirements do not apply if the collector does not fit under the scope of HIPAA. For instance, healthcare practitioners who are involved in the collection and utilization of this information to deliver services to the customer do not fall under the ambit of HIPAA [34]. HIPAA protection applies only to specific entities instead of different entities.

HHS' Office for Civil Rights (OCR) released a notice of potential rulemaking outlining various possible amendments to the HIPAA Privacy Rule. A Final Rule is now due, with the HIPAA modifications anticipated to go into effect in 2023 [35].

4.2.1.3.1 The proposed recommendations to the HIPAA privacy rule

The latest HIPAA guidelines now allow patients to personally review their PHI and to make notes or take photographs of their personal health information details. Earlier, the period of access was 30 days, but it has been reduced to 15 days. The new recommendations also restrict the transference of their e-PHI to a third party other than e-PHI, which is maintained in an EHR. However, covered entities must respond to requests from other covered entities providers and health plans for access to certain records. The recommendation also confers a right to the individual to instruct a covered entity to get his e-PHI transferred on a personal health application. It also further states that an individual must receive an e-PHI free of cost. When the covered entity receives the summary of PHI, it is his responsibility to inform the individual of their right to either obtain or direct the PHI copies to a third party. The recommendations also grant permission to the armed forces to use or disclose the PHI to all uniformed forces. The definition of the covered entity was broadened and included its ability to disclose the PHI to prevent a threat to health and safety in case the damage is seriously and reasonably foreseeable. The covered entities must post the estimated fee schedules for the access and disclosures on the websites. Furthermore, the mandatory rule for an individual to send the acknowledgment after obtaining notice of Privacy Practices is excluded [36].

4.2.1.4 National institute of standards and technology interagency reports (NISTIR)

NISTIR publishes the work of NIST in the form of interim or final reports. NISTIRs are also responsible for reporting the results of NIST projects in a more comprehensive form.

A few reports on IoT have been summarized below:

- **8259 NISTIR**: This study provides guidelines to IoT device makers to assist them in implementing the recommendations in SP 800-213. It acts as a basic activity to help manufacturers in satisfying the cybersecurity demands of their consumers [37].
- **NISTIR 8259A**: This publication is another fundamental activity that offers IoT device makers extra assistance in addressing cybersecurity standards [37].
- **NISTIR 8259B, 8259C, and 8259D**: Together with SP 800-213, these three NISTIRs create a unit that helps assure alignment between the government and IoT device designers addressing IoT device cybersecurity for federal agencies. NISTIR 8259B, 8259C, and 8259D provide a starting point for manufacturers developing IoT devices for the federal government market [37].
- **NIST IR 8425**, an interagency report, is 3. The Profile of the IoT Core Baseline for Consumer IoT Products is now available in its final form in this document. It combines the consumer Internet of Things (IoT) cybersecurity requirements from NIST's white paper on Recommended Criteria for cybersecurity labeling for consumer Internet of Things (IoT) products [38].

The Federal Trade Commission is in charge of implementing consumer protection legislation. For IoMT devices that lie outside of the FDA's regulatory jurisdiction, the FTC may come to the rescue, assuring consumer data protection, which includes IoMT devices that produce, gather, or distribute end-user health data. The FTC, however, does not explicitly address the cybersecurity danger presented by such gadgets [30].

This regulation specifically applies to the data collected by Internet of Medical Things (IoMT) devices, with a focus on safeguarding patients' information within the European Union [39].

4.2.2 European laws

The European Union (EU) boasts a vibrant and innovative medical device sector, where small- and medium-sized enterprises actively participate. This thriving industry is underpinned by a robust commitment to patient and user safety, forming the basis of the legislative framework that facilitates the seamless functioning of the internal market [40].

The medical device and *in vitro* diagnostics legislation replaced the old laws which were applicable for the preceding 20 years. The goal was to develop robust, clear standards that are both sustainable and safe for supporting innovation. These laws included key innovations to modernize the existing structure, including a new pre-market examination procedure involving a panel of experts at the EU level. It also enhanced the standards for designation and processes [41].

This legislation increased openness by implementing the complete EU databank and providing a unique device identifier tracking mechanism for medical equipment. Patients were also given implant cards with information about medical implants [41].

Post-market surveillance requirements were mandatory to monitor the manufacturer's actions [41].

Digital health technologies (DHTs), which include IoMT devices such as wearable and virtual assistants, have gained traction in the EU because of their ability to empower people to control their health and well-being. These devices monitor a variety of health-associated data, including level of activity, heart rate, and sleep duration, as well as calorie consumption. These devices in the long run help to reduce the medical cost and help the patients toward self-care or self-health management [42].

Effectively regulating DHTs, including IoMT devices, is essential to guarantee consumer safety and to address potential risks that may arise from their usage beyond the originally intended purpose set by the manufacturer [42]. The European Medical Devices Regulation (MDR) plays a significant role in regulating medical devices, and its classification rules and post-market surveillance system provisions apply to DHTs. The MDR aims to anticipate and address the actual use of DHTs, ensuring that manufacturers acquire knowledge about how their products are used in real-world scenarios. This information helps to make informed regulatory decisions based on the impact of DHTs and holds manufacturers responsible for known or encouraged misuse of their products [42].

In addition to the MDR, the European Commission has been involved in funding research and innovation projects related to digital health and IoT platforms in healthcare. For instance, the Horizon 2020 program has allocated significant funding for efforts in research and innovation, including the deployment of digital technologies in European healthcare [43].

4.2.2.1 General data protection regulation (GDPR)

Various policies and standards about the security and privacy of patient data exist within the IoMT ecosystem. These regulatory guidance and frameworks play a crucial role in ensuring the appropriate protection of sensitive information within this interconnected network. The EU General Data Protection Regulation (GDPR), a legal framework that monitors the protection of personal data as well as the upkeep of privacy and security requirements, is one famous example [44]. General Data Protection Regulation (GDPR): the general data protection policy sets guidelines for companies to collect and process the information of the individual. GDPR recognizes the right to privacy. This law empowers the consumer to exercise their control over the information processed by the controller. The organization collecting and processing data, including health data, must comply with Articles 10 and 33 of the GDPR, which provide that data security of the process must be assured after the adoption of appropriate safeguards when utilizing health data [45].

The General Data Protection Regulation of Europe transfers data ownership and control to consumers. Shockingly, the healthcare sector and the health research community have remained silent even though they collect precisely the type of data that the GDPR seeks to protect [46]. This law makes the company liable for any data published without the consent of the consumer [47]. It gives patients enhanced rights and more power in the management and ownership of their health data, and it makes an effort to define the rights of individuals and the protection of their personal health information in digital healthcare exchanges [48].

The GDPR enhances the protection of the right to access personal health data and sets a 30-day response deadline, down from the previous 40 days, for patient access requests by healthcare organizations. Additionally, the GDPR introduces the requirement of a data protection impact assessment (DPIA) to enhance transparency between patients and healthcare service providers. Data controllers must perform a DPIA before processing sensitive health information to identify potential data processing risks and devise solutions for them [48]. This law takes appropriate steps to establish relationships with third countries and international organization.

4.2.2.2 Medical device regulation

MDR stands for Medical Device Regulation. It was introduced in April 2017, and it brings about significant changes to the European regulatory framework for medical devices. This includes the introduction of new primary and secondary responsibilities for the EMA and national competent authorities regarding the assessment of particular product categories. The Regulation officially came into force in May 2017, with a phased transition period [49].

Under the Medical Devices Directive, previously, medical devices were mandated to serve a medical purpose. However, this approach resulted in some products, like non-corrective contact lenses, which resembled medical devices but lacked a medical purpose, being categorized as general products rather than medical devices. To improve regulatory oversight of such products, Annex XVI of the MDR includes a list of six items, including devices used for liposuction, brain stimulators, and lasers for tattoo removal, among others. These products now necessitate the publication of common specifications before they can be marketed, and the European Commission is currently in the process of preparing these specifications [50].

4.2.3 Canadian laws

The Personal Information Protection and Electronic Documents Act (PIPEDA), a federal law enacted in the year 2000, is applicable to all commercial organizations, irrespective of their geographical location or the nature of their clientele [45].

The PIPEDA applies universally to all Canadian enterprises, regardless of their location, that handle personal information in the course of commercial operations that transcend either provincial or national boundaries (this includes provinces that have essentially equivalent laws).

The PIPEDA governs commercial organizations that collect, use, or disclose personal information, including personal health information, within a province. PIPEDA would also apply to healthcare professionals who receive payment from the public health insurance system [52].

The definition of personal information under PIPEDA and provincial law has to be updated to incorporate inferences about persons' personal information utilizing technologies such as AI, big data, and robots. This change is a vital step toward safeguarding personal data since most inferences about people are derived without their knowledge or agreement, and the use of the inference harms their interests unless the use of the data is justified [45].

The PIPEDA requires data collectors to acquire data for certain reasons. As a result, if the data was not disclosed at the time of collection, it will be difficult and hazardous to utilize it for secondary purposes such as study [53].

While PIPEDA does not apply to public hospitals since their essential operations are not commercial, non-core activities, such as a pharmacy operating a commercial organization on hospital premises, may be subject to the Act. Because Quebec, British Columbia, and Alberta have provincial privacy rules that are essentially identical to PIPEDA, PIPEDA will not be applied in those jurisdictions to private-sector commercial operations that occur inside the province's territorial limits [45].

Before collecting, using, or disclosing a person's personal information, an organization must get that person's permission. Additionally, people have the right to see and question the veracity of the personal information a company holds on them. In terms of the gathering, using, and disclosing of personal health information, legislation has also been passed in Ontario, New Brunswick, Nova Scotia, and Newfoundland and Labrador [51].

According to PIPEDA, the right to privacy of individuals must be balanced against organizations' legitimate interests in acquiring, using, or disclosing personal information [54]. When evaluating the best interests of the individual and the organization, a reasonable person's viewpoint must be used. This balancing of interests is required for PIPEDA compliance [54].

Under PIPEDA, "no-go zones" are defined as goals for which it is not appropriate to collect, use, or disclose an individual's personal information [54]. These goals are based on previous research, discussions with pertinent stakeholders, and nationwide polls of Canadians. Collecting, using, or disclosing personal information illegally are all examples of no-go zones. Individuals profiled or classified in a manner that is unjust, unethical, or discriminatory, thereby breaching the principles and protections outlined in human rights legislation.

PIPEDA applies to all federally regulated organizations that do business in Canada. The Act also applies to the personal information of their workers [54].

Among these organizations are the following:

Airports, planes, and airlines; banks and authorized foreign banks; interprovincial or international transportation firms; telecommunications companies; offshore drilling activities; and radio and television broadcasters are all examples of authorized foreign banks [54].

The breach of e-health security and privacy caused by the attack on LifeLabs, a laboratory testing company in Canada, is only one of many recent examples. The event brought to light the concerns of privacy and safety that are associated with the increasing reliance of the medical industry on e-health platforms. The data breach that occurred in 2019 exposed confidential information about millions of LifeLabs customers, including their names, addresses, passwords, birth dates, health card numbers, and lab test results [55–57].

The event highlighted the vulnerability of healthcare companies to cyber-attacks and the need to implement adequate security measures in the e-health sector. Experts claim that the medical sector has often lagged behind other types of enterprises in terms of the cybersecurity practices that they have implemented [55]. Inadequate security precautions and procedures were identified as a contributing factor to the event at LifeLabs. It served as a signal to healthcare companies that the protection of patient data should be their priority and that they should enhance their security architecture in order to withstand any attacks [57].

As a reaction to the breach, LifeLabs enlisted the assistance of cybersecurity experts, negotiated with the perpetrators of the attack, and ultimately paid a ransom to regain access to the data that had been compromised [56]. Even though the company made steps to fix the system vulnerabilities that led to the breach and offered identity theft protection services to people whose information was compromised [57], the occurrence raised concerns about the probable utilization of the stolen data for fraudulent activities and identity theft [57]. The company made attempts to fix the system problems that led to the breach.

This had an impact on the purchasing decisions of millions of customers, particularly in the provinces of British Columbia and Ontario, as well as in Newfoundland, Labrador, and Saskatchewan [56]. Dedicated phone lines were set up to convey more information to people affected by the hack, and actions were taken to minimize the potential risks associated with the breach [58].

In general, the attack on LifeLabs serves as a reminder of the need for robust security and privacy measures in the e-health business. This highlights the need for proactive cybersecurity practices in preserving sensitive patient information and fighting against the possibility of cyber assaults.

In response to the incident, LifeLabs worked with cybersecurity professionals and cybercriminals to recover the stolen data [56]. To restore access to the material, the corporation paid the attackers a ransom [59]. However, there were concerns voiced about the delay in telling the public about the breach since there were fears of further assaults [56].

The event brought to light the significance of e-health security and privacy. It acted as a wake-up call for the healthcare business, emphasizing the vulnerabilities and insufficient security mechanisms in place [55]. The LifeLabs data leak highlighted the need for healthcare organizations to implement strong security controls and procedures to secure patient information [58]. It also emphasized the hazards associated with the growing dependence on electronic health records as well as the significance of improving the resilience of healthcare systems to cyberattacks [57].

4.2.4 Comparative analysis of USA, European, and Canadian laws on internet of medical things (IoMT) and data privacy

Table 4.1 Comparative analysis of USA, European Union, and Canadian laws on Internet of Medical Things (IoMT) and data privacy. Source: Authors creation.

USA	European Union	Canada
The USA has a fragmented regulatory landscape with different agencies overseeing various aspects of IoMT. The FDA focuses on medical device safety and cybersecurity, while HIPAA primarily deals with the privacy of health information.	The EU has a comprehensive and unified regulatory framework, including MDR and GDPR, which covers both medical device safety and data privacy.	Canada has PIPEDA, which primarily focuses on data privacy and applies to commercial organizations, including those handling health data.
The FDA classifies IoMT devices based on risk levels and requires pre-market clearance or approval. It emphasizes cybersecurity guidelines and post-market surveillance.	The EU MDR classifies medical devices and also covers IoMT devices. It places a strong emphasis on post-market surveillance and real-world usage, making manufacturers responsible for known or encouraged misuse.	PIPEDA does not directly regulate medical devices but covers the privacy of personal health information. Canada relies more on the FDA's regulatory standards for medical devices.

Table 4.2 *Continued.*

USA	European Union	Canada
While the FDA addresses cybersecurity, HIPAA ensures data privacy. The USA places a strong emphasis on safeguarding patient health information.	The GDPR comprehensively covers data privacy and security, including health data. It gives individuals more control over their data and requires organizations to conduct data protection impact assessments.	PIPEDA focuses on data privacy, requiring consent for data collection and setting limits on data use. It balances privacy rights with legitimate organizational interests.
Enforcement varies between agencies, with the FDA and OCR responsible for different aspects. Violations can result in fines and legal actions.	The EU has robust enforcement mechanisms for both MDR and GDPR, with significant fines for non-compliance.	PIPEDA enforcement includes fines and legal actions, but penalties may not be as severe as those under the GDPR.
The USA's regulations primarily affect products and services within its borders, with some international influence through collaborations and standards.	The EU's regulations have extraterritorial applicability, affecting any organization handling EU citizens' data or selling medical devices in the EU.	PIPEDA's impact is primarily domestic, but it affects international organizations handling Canadian data.
The FDA places a significant emphasis on cybersecurity for IoMT devices, issuing guidelines, and recommendations.	The EU MDR also addresses cybersecurity but focuses more on the broader safety and effectiveness of devices in real-world scenarios.	PIPEDA does not specifically address cybersecurity but requires organizations to protect personal information.

4.3 Conclusion

Internet of Medical Things industry has advanced healthcare by allowing collection, analysis, and exchange of patient data through networked medical devices and systems. However, in order to preserve patient privacy, data security, and legal compliance, the use of IoMT technology must be controlled by strong legislative frameworks.

In EU, IoMT systems, and healthcare providers must adhere to GDPR rules that include gaining informed permission, adopting adequate security measures, and guaranteeing transparent data practices.

Controlling IoMT devices in the EU is also facilitated by the Medical Device Regulation (MDR). The medical devices must adhere to safety and performance criteria laid out by the MDR, which include data protection and cybersecurity. It emphasizes the need for manufacturers to design products with privacy and security in mind, as well as continuously updating and patching vulnerabilities to reduce possible hazards.

The FDA provides guidance documents and standards to IoMT device manufacturers and developers. The FDA ensures that these devices are safe, trustworthy, and efficient. It also inquires their data privacy and security practices. Manufacturers implement patient privacy procedures against any risk related to unauthorized access to medical data.

In the United States, the Health Insurance Portability and Accountability Act (HIPAA) establishes privacy and security requirements to protect individual health information. HIPAA emphasizes IoMT systems and healthcare providers handling protected health information (PHI) to apply measures to secure PHI, take consent from the patient, and give patients with access to their own health data. The collection, usage, and sharing of sensitive data in Canada is governed by the Personal Information Protection and Electronic Documents Act (PIPEDA). Organizations deploying IoMT systems must adhere to PIPEDA's privacy principles, which include obtaining individual consent, protecting data, and granting individuals access to their own information. These laws and regulations collectively aim to strike a balance between the potential advantages of IoMT technology and the safeguarding of patient rights and data. Healthcare providers, manufacturers, and other entities must adhere to these legal frameworks to ensure the privacy, security, and reliability of the collected data by IoMT devices.

It will take time and work to ensure the privacy of the patients and adjust these regulations with the fast-changing technology and promote innovation in healthcare.

Acknowledgments

I express sincere gratitude to the Almighty and everyone in my publication team for making this chapter possible.

References

[1] Internet of things: Available at: https://en.wikipedia.org/wiki/Internet_of_things. [accessed September 23, 2023]

[2] Kotronis et al. (2019). Evaluating Internet of Medical Things (IoMT)-based systems from a human-centric perspective. *Internet of Things. 8*, 100125. DOI:10.1016/j.iot.2019.100125.

[3] THE INTERNET OF THINGS 2020: Here's what over 400 IoT decision-makers say about the future of enterprise connectivity and how IoT companies can use it to grow revenue: Available at: https://www.businessinsider.com/internet-of-things-report?IR=T [accessed September 23, 2023]

[4] $55 Billion Global Internet of Medical Things Market Expected to Grow at a CAGR of 24.55% Between 2021 and 2026: Available at: https://www.globenewswire.com/news-release/2022/1/28/2374901/28124/en/55-Billion-Global-Internet-of-Medical-Things-Market-Expected-to-Grow-at-a-CAGR-of-24-55-Between-2021-and-2026.html [accessed September 23, 2023]

[5] Razdan, S. and Sharma, S. (2022) Internet of medical things (IoMT): overview, emerging technologies, and case studies. *IETE technical review. 39*(4), 775-788. DOI: 10.1080/02564602.2021.1927863

[6] Kelly et al. (2020). The Internet of Things: Impact and implications for health care delivery. *Journal of medical Internet research*, *22*(11), 20135. DOI: 10.2196/20135

[7] Siddiqui et al. (2021). IoMT cloud-based intelligent prediction of breast cancer stages empowered with deep learning. *IEEE Access*, *9*, 146478-146491. DOI: 10.1109/ACCESS.2021.3123472.

[8] Panja et al. (2023). Fuzzy-logic-based IoMT framework for COVID-19 patient monitoring. *Computers & Industrial Engineering*, *176*, 108941. DOI: 10.1016/j.cie.2022.108941.

[9] Vishnu et al. R. (2020)."Internet of Medical Things (IoMT) - An overview," in the proceeding of the 2020 5th International Conference on Devices, Circuits, and Systems (ICDCS): Coimbatore, India, 2020, 101-104.

[10] Baig et al. (2015). Mobile healthcare applications: system design review, critical issues and challenges. *Australasian physical & engineering sciences in medicine*, *38*, 23-38. DOI: 10.1007/s13246-014-0315-4.

[11] Saba, T. "Intrusion Detection in Smart City Hospitals using Ensemble Classifiers," 2020 13th International Conference on Developments in eSystems Engineering (DeSE), Liverpool, United Kingdom, 2020, 418-422, DOI: 10.1109/DeSE51703.2020.9450247.

[12] Arora, S. (2020) IoMT (Internet of Medical Things): Reducing cost while improving patient care. *IEEE Pulse*, *11*(5), 24-27. DOI: 10.1109/MPULS.2020.3022143

[13] Gupta et al. (2023). *Blockchain for Secure Healthcare Using Internet of Medical Things (IoMT).* Springer International Publishing AG, 13-25, DOI: 10.1007/978-3-031-18896-1
[14] Nair et al. (2016.) Differential diagnosis of malaria on Truelab Uno®, a portable, real-time, micro PCR device for point-of-care applications. *PLoS One*, *11*(1), 0146961. DOI: 10.1371/journal.pone.0146961
[15] Wagan et al. (2022). Internet of medical things and trending converged technologies: A comprehensive review on real-time applications. *Journal of King Saud University-Computer and Information Sciences*, 9228-9251. DOI: 10.1016/j.jksuci.2022.09.005
[16] Goetz, L.H. and Schork, N.J., 2018. Personalized medicine: motivation, challenges, and progress. *Fertility and sterility*, *109*(6), pp.952-963.
[17] Gupta et al. (2023). *Blockchain for Secure Healthcare Using Internet of Medical Things (IoMT).* Springer International Publishing AG, 79-91, DOI: 10.1007/978-3-031-18896-1
[18] Sadhu et al. (2022). Prospect of internet of medical things: A review on security requirements and solutions. *Sensors*, *22*(15), 5517. DOI: 10.3390/s22155517
[19] The Internet of Medical Things - Anticipating the Risk: Available at: https://www.isaca.org/resources/isaca-journal/issues/2019/volume-4/the-internet-of-medical-things-anticipating-the-risk [accessed September 23.2023]
[20] Internet of Medical Things (IoMT) advances and brings new challenges: Available at: https://network-king.net/internet-of-medical-things-iomt-advances-and-brings-new-challenges/ [accessed September 23, 2023]
[21] Food and Drug Administration: Available at: https://en.wikipedia.org/wiki/Food_and_Drug_Administration [accessed September 23, 2023]
[22] Hireche et al. (2022). Security and privacy management in the Internet of Medical Things (IoMT): A synthesis. *Journal of Cybersecurity and Privacy*, *2*(3), 640-661. DOI: 10.3390/jcp2030033
[23] FDA Bans Sale of IoMT Devices That Fail Cybersecurity Requirements: Available at: https://www.portnox.com/blog/fda-bans-sale-of-iomt-devices-that-fail-cybersecurity-requirements/ [accessed September 23, 2023]
[24] Premarket Approval (PMA): Available at: https://www.fda.gov/medical-devices/premarket-submissions-selecting-and-preparing-correct-submission/premarket-notification-510k [accessed September 23, 2023]
[25] Premarket Approval (PMA): Available at: https://www.fda.gov/medical-devices/premarket-submissions-selecting-and-preparing-correct-submission/premarket-approval-pma [accessed September 23, 2023]

[26] FDA Releases Guidance On Cybersecurity In Medical Devices: Available at: https://www.meddeviceonline.com/doc/fda-releases-guidance-on-cybersecurity-in-medical-devices-0001 [accessed September 23, 2023]
[27] FDA requires medical devices be secured against cyberattacks: Available at: https://edition.cnn.com/2023/03/29/tech/fda-medical-devices-secured-cyberattacks/index.html [accessed September 23, 2023]
[28] Partnerships: Enhancing Science Through Collaborations With FDA: Available at: https://www.fda.gov/about-fda/partnerships-enhancing-science-through-collaborations-fda [accessed September 23, 2023]
[29] MOU 225-21-006: Available at: https://www.fda.gov/about-fda/domestic-mous/mou-225-21-006 [accessed September 23, 2023]
[30] Stein et al. (2018). The current ethical and regulatory status of the Internet of Medical thing (IoMT) and the need for a new IoMT law. *Journal of Healthcare Ethics & Administration*, *4*(2), 32-38. DOI: 10.22461/jhea.6.7162
[31] Shanmugam, B. and Azam, S. (2023) Risk Assessment of Heterogeneous IoMT Devices: A Review. *Technologies*, *11*(1), .31. DOI: 10.3390/technologies11010031
[32] Summary of the HIPAA Privacy Rule: Available at: https://www.hhs.gov/hipaa/for-professionals/privacy/laws-regulations/index.html [accessed September 23, 2023]
[33] VCU Health Notifies Patients of Transplant Donor, Recipient PHI Data Breach: Available at: https://healthitsecurity.com/news/vcu-health-notifies-patients-of-transplant-donor-recipient-phi-data-breach [accessed September 23, 2023]
[34] HIPAA and Protecting Health Information in the 21st Century: Available at: https://jamanetwork.com/journals/jama/article-abstract/2682916 [accessed September 23, 2023]
[35] HIPAA Updates and HIPAA Changes in 2023: Available at: https://www.hipaajournal.com/hipaa-updates-hipaa-changes/ [accessed September 23, 2023]
[36] NIST Releases Draft Guidance on Internet of Things Device Cybersecurity: Available at: https://www.hipaajournal.com/hipaa-updates-hipaa-changes/ [accessed September 23, 2023]
[37] NIST Releases Draft Guidance on Internet of Things Device Cybersecurity: Available at: https://www.nist.gov/news-events/news/2020/12/nist-releases-draft-guidance-internet-things-device-cybersecurity [accessed September 23, 2023]

[38] NIST IoT Cybersecurity Program Releases Two New Documents: Available at: https://csrc.nist.gov/News/2022/nist-iot-cybersecurity-program-nist-irs-8425-8431 [accessed September 23, 2023]
[39] The Internet of Medical Things—Anticipating the Risk: Available at: https://www.isaca.org/resources/isaca-journal/issues/2019/volume-4/the-internet-of-medical-things-anticipating-the-risk [accessed September 23, 2023]
[40] Overview: Available at: https://health.ec.europa.eu/medical-devices-sector/overview_en [accessed September 23, 2023]
[41] New Regulations: Available at: https://health.ec.europa.eu/medical-devices-sector/new-regulations_en [accessed September 23, 2023]
[42] Yu, H. (2022). Regulation of Digital Health Technologies in the European Union: Intended versus Actual Use*. In I. Cohen, T. Minssen, W. Price II, C. Robertson, & C. Shachar (Eds.), *The Future of Medical Device Regulation: Innovation and Protection* (pp. 103-114). Cambridge: Cambridge University Press. doi:10.1017/9781108975452.009
[43] The Internet of Things in European healthcare: Available at: https://digital-strategy.ec.europa.eu/en/policies/internet-things-european-healthcare [accessed September 23, 2023]
[44] Hireche et al. (2022). Security and privacy management in the Internet of Medical Things (IoMT): A synthesis. *Journal of Cybersecurity and Privacy*, *2*(3), 640-661. DOI: 10.3390/jcp2030033
[45] Sarabdeen et al. (2022). Creating standards for Canadian health data protection during health emergency–An analysis of privacy regulations and laws. *Heliyon*, *8*(5). DOI: 10.1016/j.heliyon.2022.e09458
[46] Turning the Tables — The New European General Data Protection Regulation: Available at: https://www.nejm.org/doi/full/10.1056/NEJMp1806637[accessed September 23, 2023]
[47] Art. 1 GDPR Subject-matter and objectives: Available at: https://gdpr-info.eu/art-1-gdpr/ [accessed September 23, 2023]
[48] Yuan, B. and Li, J. (2019). The policy effect of the general data protection regulation (GDPR) on the digital public health sector in the european union: an empirical investigation. *International journal of environmental research and public health*, *16*(6), 1070. DOI: 10.3390/ijerph16061070
[49] Medical Device Regulation comes into application: Available at: https://www.ema.europa.eu/en/news/medical-device-regulation-comes-application [accessed September 23, 2023]

[50] Melvin, T. (2022) The European Medical Device Regulation–What Biomedical Engineers Need to Know. *IEEE Journal of Translational Engineering in Health and Medicine*, *10*, 1-5. DOI: 10.1109/JTEHM.2022.3194415

[51] PIPEDA in brief: Available at: https://www.priv.gc.ca/en/privacy-topics/privacy-laws-in-canada/the-personal-information-protection-and-electronic-documents-act-pipeda/pipeda_brief/[accessed September 23, 2023]

[52] Bernier, A. Knoppers, B.M.(2020) Pandemics, privacy, and public health research. *Canadian Journal of Public Health*, *111*, 454-457. DOI: 10.17269/s41997-020-00368-5

[53] Laurie et al. (2015). Accessing health and health-related data in Canada: The expert panel on timely access to health and social data for health research and health system innovation. *Council of Canadian Academies.*

[54] Guidance on inappropriate data practices: Interpretation and application of subsection 5: Available at: https://www.priv.gc.ca/en/privacy-topics/collecting-personal-information/consent/gd_53_201805 [accessed September 23, 2023]

[55] Life Labs cyberattack one of 'several wake-up calls' for e-health security and privacy: Available at: https://www.cbc.ca/news/science/lifelabs-data-breech-security-ehealth-1.5400817 [accessed September 23, 2023]

[56] Life Labs pays ransom after cyberattack exposes information of 15 million customers in B.C. and Ontario: Available at: https://www.cbc.ca/news/canada/british-columbia/lifelabs-cyberattack-15-million-1.5399577 [accessed September 23, 2023]

[57] Life Labs users wise to worry about fraud, ID theft after mass data breach say experts: Available at: https://www.cbc.ca/news/canada/british-columbia/lifelabs-hack-very-serious-says-expert-1.5400196 [accessed September 23, 2023]

[58] Here's how the cyberattack at Life Labs impacted Sask. residents Michaela Solomon: Available at: https://regina.ctvnews.ca/here-s-how-the-cyberattack-at-lifelabs-impacted-sask-residents-1.4734338 [accessed September 23, 2023]

[59] Data of 15M Patients Stolen, Retrieved in Life Labs Cyberattack: Available at: https://www.healthitsecurity.com/news/data-of-15m-patients-impacted-retrieved-in-lifelabs-cyberattack [accessed September 23, 2023]

5

A Cybersecurity Framework for IoBNT: Inception and a Comprehensive Review

Vaishali Meena and Gaurav Indra

Department of IT, Indira Gandhi Delhi Technical University for Women, India
E-mail: vaishali019phd22@igdtuw.ac.in; gauravindra@igdtuw.ac.in

Abstract

The Internet of Bio-Nano Things (IoBNT) is an emerging research domain with immense potential in healthcare applications. The physical protection of patients is of paramount importance to prevent malicious attacks on their bodies. Potential physical attacks include administering medicine with malicious nanomachines or injecting harmful nanomachines into patients. Additionally, the usage of terahertz waves on human skin can result in tissue damage, emphasizing the need for robust communication and sensing standards. Wearable bio-electronic devices encounter obstacles concerning their widespread acceptance and adoption. While there have been limited examples of fully functional and approved bioelectronic devices, collaboration between research teams, clinical organizations, and technology companies is crucial for progress. Challenges in bio-cyber interfaces (BCI), such as ligand-receptor selection and realistic modeling of artificial structures, need to be addressed. Biocompatibility, biodegradability, and biofouling are crucial considerations for designing devices that directly interact with the biological environment. The interconnection of millions of IoBNT devices leads to the generation of big data, requiring efficient data management and analytics. Data quality, noisy data, and missing values pose challenges that need to be addressed through data validation and advanced analytics algorithms. New data collection policies should be developed to prevent data from being linked, shared, and analyzed.

DOI: 10.1201/9788770047395-5

The security of IoBNT is a critical challenge, considering the potential misuse of sensitive patient data and the risk of bio-cyber terrorism. Existing security mechanisms for traditional wireless networking need to be improved to meet the diverse system requirements of IoBNT. Lightweight security mechanisms and access controls that are material-constrained and compatible with nanonetworks are required. Authentication schemes and encryption techniques must be carefully selected, considering the resource limitations of IoBNT devices. Biochemical cryptography and bio-inspired algorithms offer promising solutions for secure communication and data protection. The chapter will emphasize the interdisciplinary nature of the challenges faced in IoBNT, requiring collaboration among fields such as physics, mechanical engineering, chemical engineering, biology, and information technology. Standardization initiatives can play a pivotal role in unifying information security in IoBNT, while user training and awareness are crucial for widespread adoption. Future research should focus on developing real-time security systems to detect and mitigate attacks, particularly in the context of theragnostic processes. By addressing these security challenges and capitalizing on the research opportunities, IoBNT can realize its full potential in revolutionizing healthcare by enabling early detection, remote diagnosis, targeted drug delivery, and other innovative applications.

Keywords: Bio-cyber interface (BCI), Internet of Bio-Nano Things (IoBNT), bio-electronics device security, bio-inspired security approaches.

5.1 Introduction

Over the last decade, the Internet of Things has attracted considerable attention in research and development. It involves connecting machines and different objects embedded with computation capabilities to extend the internet into various domains. While there are efforts to develop general IoT devices, specific applications require small, concealable, and non-intrusive devices. Recent research on nanomaterials such as carbon nanotubes or graphene has led to the concept of the Internet of Nano Things (IoNT), which aims to interact with nanoscale devices. From healthcare to security to the military, the IoT contains great potential. Nanoobjects are readily concealable, locatable, and deployable for sensing, processing, networking, and processing on account of their diminutive size.

However, it is imperative to contemplate the potential disadvantages associated with IoNT devices thoroughly. Artificial devices that depend on electromagnetic (EM) communications and synthesized materials may result in detrimental consequences for human health or environmental degradation in specific settings. An innovative avenue of research emerges with the integration of synthetic biology tools and nanotechnology in the development of nanoscale systems and devices. By manipulating, repurposing, modifying, and reengineering biological cells, this strategy is implemented. Bio-nano things can be developed through the analogy between biological cells and conventional embedded computing devices in the Internet of Things. It is well-known that bio-nanomaterials utilize the energy of cells for functions including processing, communication, and perception. Biological systems, as opposed to conventional electronic devices, are powered by biomolecules and biochemical reactions. This distinction lends support to the concept of the IoBNT, which, across all of its fields, promises to influence networking and communication. In response to these issues, the notion of the IoBNT has surfaced. By combining tools from synthetic biology and nanotechnology, IoBNT engineers embedded biological computing devices. Bio-nanomaterials facilitate applications such as environmental control of contaminants and pollutants and *in vivo* sensing and actuation networks by utilizing the functions and biochemical domains of biological cells.

IoBNT signifies a fundamental change in the fields of network engineering and communication. This study presents new obstacles in the development of environmentally friendly and secure approaches to information exchange, interaction, and networking in the biochemical domain. Additionally, it establishes a connection to the electrical domain of the internet. The development of IoBNT has received significant investments from government agencies and industries worldwide. It presents new opportunities for research and development in fields like healthcare, security, and environmental monitoring. However, careful consideration must be given to ensure the safe and responsible deployment of IoBNT devices to minimize potential risks and maximize their benefits. IoBNT leverages DNA-based instructions, biochemical data processing, chemical energy transformation, and molecular communication (MC), which involves the transmission and reception of molecules. These fundamental aspects enable a wide range of applications within the IoBNT framework, including:

(i) ***In vivo* sensing and actuation:** Bio-nano things implanted in the human body can collaborate to gather health-related information. By sending this information to doctors outside the internet, they can follow orders such as links and prescriptions from doctors.

(ii) Controlling internal communication: Bio-nano things can be used to repair or block communication between our internal organs. This is especially important for the nervous and endocrine systems, which play a significant role in many diseases.

(iii) Environmental control and cleanup: Bio-nanoobjects deployed in natural ecosystems will monitor and identify toxins and pollutants.

They can collaborate to modify and reduce the effects of these chemicals through processes such as bioremediation. For example, bacteria can be used to clean up oil spills. This chapter follows a specific structure: initially, it defines bio-nano things within the context of tools accessible through synthetic biology and nanotechnology. It proceeds to examine the application of communication engineering in crafting the telecommunications of bio-nano things, delving into the complexities associated with engineering networks of these entities and establishing connections to the internet. Following this, it outlines additional challenges in research for achieving the IoBNT. The chapter wraps up with a conclusion, summarizing the main points covered.

In the context of IoBNT, BNT can be defined as distinct structural and functional entities operating and interacting within the biological environment. These bio-nano things have their origins in biological cells, and their existence is made feasible through the integration of synthetic biology and nanotechnology. They exhibit functionalities comparable to those found in embedded computing devices within the Internet of Things (IoT), including sensing, processing, actuation, and communication with other bio-nano things. The fundamental building blocks for bio-nano things are biological cells. Cells, which serve as the essential units of life, comprise a membrane enclosing a mixture of specialized molecules with specific functions and compositions. These molecules can also be organized into functional structures. Drawing parallels between the components of a typical IoT-embedded computing device and the element of a cell reveals striking similarities.

For instance, the densely packed genetic instructions within a cell's DNA molecules, encoding protein structures and regulatory sequences, acting as the cell's "data units," can be compared to the control unit that contains the embedded software of a device. Likewise, the chemical content of the cell's cytoplasm, composed of molecules synthesized by the cell following DNA instructions, can be compared to the memory unit storing embedded system data values. Other molecules and structures exchanged with the external environment, such as vesicles, can also be considered part of the cell's memory unit. The molecular machinery involved in transcription and translation, which converts DNA instructions into protein molecules, can be associated with the processing unit of an embedded system. The reservoir of adenosine-triphosphate (ATP) molecules within the cell, synthesized using energy from the external environment, can be seen as the power unit that supplies energy for the cell's biochemical reactions. Signaling pathways within cells, consisting of specific chains of chemical reactions, can be likened to transceivers in embedded systems. These pathways facilitate the exchange of information-bearing molecules among cells. In addition, the ability of cells to recognize other molecules or respond to physical stimuli such as light or any stress, as well as changing the chemical nature of the environment or being mechanically affected by the cell such as flagella, pili, or cilia, can affect hearing and functioning of the system. The recent pandemic and ongoing lockdown measures have fueled an increased interest in the search for electronic and telecommunications services.

The IoBNT system involves the use of bio-nanonetworks (networks of nanoscale computing devices) to understand chemical and biological changes in the environment, particularly in the human body. Data collected from these nanonetworks is sent to data centers over the internet for later processing. Additionally, these nano-nets can perform medical functions based on remote orders from doctors. Applications of bio-nano nets or bio-nano things in medicine are numerous. They can assist in tasks such as targeted drug delivery (TDD), continuing healthcare, tissue engineering, and cancer screening. However, due to the restrictions in transceiver size, computing power, and propagation of bio-nanoobjects, wireless communication devices are not suitable for supporting communication in nanonetworks. Therefore, new communication systems specifically designed for these nanonetworks are required.

One example of such communication technology is molecular communication (MC), which involves the transmission and reception of molecules to exchange information within the nanonetwork. Nano-electromagnetic (EM) communication, acoustic communication, and nano-mechanical communication in the terahertz band are other communication technologies investigated in bio-nanoobjects. In order to guarantee the optimal functioning of IoBNT devices and systems, seamless connectivity between *in vivo* nanonetworks and other networks, such as the internet, is essential to support complex clinical applications. Hybrid interface devices are required to provide *in vivo* access to other nanonetworks. The device must understand two elements of the communication protocol: biochemical signals produced by nanonetworks in the body and electromagnetic signals received from the internet. The biological network interface is the connection between the biological domain and the cyber domain. Biological network interfaces can transmit biochemical signals from *in vivo* nanonetworks to the internet, etc. The design and modeling of biological communication networks is an important but challenging aspect of IoBNT use. Interdisciplinary research has focused on developing bio-electronic materials that lead to processes such as second skin, biological connections, and biological materials. This model provides the basis for the design and use of bio-electronic interfaces. Bioelectronic interfaces can be formed from materials with electronic properties that can be affected by biomolecular complexes. The change in voltage affects the current flowing in the circuit. Examples of popular bioelectronic interface technologies include wireless drug sensors, RFID devices, and electronic tattoos. Establishing a seamless connection between *in vivo* nanonetworks and external networks requires the creation of interconnected devices that can understand and interpret the communication process of biochemical and electromagnetic signals. The research collaboration has led to the development of bioelectronic interface systems and technologies that enable the integration of IoBNT systems into real-world healthcare applications. Wireless chemical sensors are crucial for spotting changes in the chemical substrates of products. These sensors can wirelessly send the data gathered over the internet to programs that will analyze and further process it. Nanomaterial-based inks are used in inkjet printing of circuits to produce implantable RFID technology. These devices may detect different physical parameters using radio frequency identification (RFID) technology and broadcast them to adjacent devices like mobile devices. Additionally, electronic skin-attachable sensors based on tattoos can be used to collect data on sweat glands and lymph nodes. For clinical application, ongoing physiological monitoring is essential.

However, designing effective bio-cyber interfaces presents several challenges. The biggest challenge is to accurately model the molecular data collected by *in vivo* sensors as equivalent electromagnetic signals. This conversion process is essential for seamless communication between the biological and cyber domains. Additionally, there are concerns related to data security and user safety. The access provided by IoBNT applications to the human body can be exploited for malicious purposes, leading to potential bio-cyber terrorism. Attackers may target vulnerabilities in IoBNT applications and infrastructure to manipulate bodily functions, extract user information without detection, or disrupt normal body functions. To ensure the widespread adoption of IoBNT systems, it is crucial to address these security concerns. Robust security measures need to be implemented to protect the devices and the privacy of individuals. Trust in the security and privacy of these resource-constrained devices is paramount for their acceptance and integration into healthcare systems. Establishing conventional and novel security measures that are suitable for these devices is essential. This work aims to provide a roadmap, highlighting the progress made in IoBNT security and identifying the future steps required to enhance security, reduce the impact of cyberattacks, and safeguard individuals by means of illicit profiling and surveillance. The wireless chemical sensors, inkjet printable electronics, and electronic tattoo-based sensors offer innovative ways to collect and transmit data in IoBNT systems.

Nevertheless, it is imperative to prioritize the resolution of security concerns and guarantee the safety of users in order to achieve extensive implementation of these technologies. It is critical to establish confidence in the privacy and security of IoBNT systems through the implementation of robust security measures that prevent unauthorized access and cyberattacks. The increasing number of internet users and the widespread adoption of internet-based applications have led to a surge in connected devices. Projections indicate that by the end of 2025, the internet will have over 75 billion connected devices. Consequently, the research and development of the Internet of Things (IoT) concept has garnered significant attention over the past 15 years. The Internet of Things comprises numerous physical devices, including sensors, actuators, and personal electronic devices that connect and communicate over the internet. Presently, IoT applications find extensive use in diverse areas such as smart transportation, real-time monitoring, smart cities, smart grids, environmental monitoring, health, and smart buildings. With the progress in information science and nanotechnology, the application scope of the Internet of Things has broadened, giving rise to new concepts like the Internet of Nano Things (IoNT), Internet of Bio Things (IoBNT), and Internet Biodegradable Factors (IoBDT). Although these concepts are in their early stages, the roots of nanotechnology trace back to the 1950s. Richard Feynman initially discussed the potential for manipulating materials from the atomic scale and achieving miniaturization in his influential talk titled "There's Plenty of Room at the Bottom" in 1959. The year 1974 saw the introduction of the term "Nanotechnology" by Norio Taniguchi to refer to accuracy at the atomic and molecular levels. The investigation and application of materials and devices at the atomic scale constitute nanotechnology, which unites numerous disciplines such as medicine, chemistry, engineering, and biology. Nanoentities are devices that possess the ability to perform operations such as data collection, computation, processing, and transmission at the nanoscale. Their dimensions span from 1 to 100 nanometers (nm). Promising

IoBNT application environments. Further analysis is provided on energy storage technologies and wireless power transfer (WPT) methods, which provide insight into the energy-related obstacles and possible resolutions in IoBNT.

An exhaustive examination is also conducted on the security, privacy, biocompatibility, and coexistence of IoBNT systems. Due to the intimate interaction between IoBNT and complex biological systems, it is critical to ensure the security and privacy of these systems. In addition to discussing mitigation strategies, this chapter examines the difficulties and potential dangers associated with unauthorized access, data breaches, and cyber–physical assaults in IoBNT. Furthermore, this chapter examines the biocompatibility of BNTs and their ability to coexist with biological systems, emphasizing the criticality of biocompatibility in the design and implementation of IoBNTs. Finally, consideration is given to the coexistence challenges of IoBNT, which include interference with other devices and ongoing biological processes. This chapter offers valuable insights into the multidimensional aspects of the emerging field of IoBNT by conducting an exhaustive and novel review of electrical and optical bio-cyber interfacing technologies, addressing the challenges associated with big data, energy harvesting, and storage, and discussing security, privacy, biocompatibility, and coexistence issues. The chapter provides an overview of the existing research, highlights significant obstacles, and delineates possible future avenues for progress in the domain of IoBNT.

The objective of this chapter is to present a thorough synopsis of the latest developments pertaining to the IoBNT, encompassing its theoretical underpinnings as well as its practical applications. The chapter commences by providing a comprehensive overview of the IoBNT framework, which includes natural IoBNT systems that function as sources of inspiration for the development of artificial IoBNT systems. Nervous nanonetworks, bacterial nanonetworks, and plant communication networks are examples of these natural systems. It is anticipated that the integration of natural and artificial IoBNT systems will create new opportunities for IoBNT applications.

5.2 Network Architecture and Communication of IoBNT

In the context of IoNT and IoBNT, network architecture designs, including various communication paradigms, are discussed to ensure good integration and good communication between nanodevices and macroscopic components. This model extends electromagnetic, molecular, acoustic, and mechanical communication, allowing nanoobjects to interact by exchanging various information, for example, synchronization signals, sensing parameters, results of logic operations, instructions, and commands [15].

Molecular communication and nano-electromagnetic communication are currently the primary research focuses for IoNT and IoBNT networks [16]. These interconnected models can utilize similar communication technologies. Nano-electromagnetic communication contains the transmission and reception of radio frequency waves within the terahertz band, while molecular communication operates by transferring and receiving information through the release and response of specific molecules [21]. Nevertheless, several challenges persist, such as ensuring sufficient coverage, compatibility, energy efficiency, and data transfer rates when employing various communication methods. Although theoretical knowledge and practical models exist in the literature, achieving communication at the nanoscale remains a challenging endeavor. This complexity is attributed to the need for biocompatibility in nanodevices and the unique signal propagation characteristics within biological tissues [22].

The network structures of both IoNT and IoBNT are intended to establish connections between the electrical and biochemical realms, integrating devices at the nanoscale. Specifically, in IoNT, the primary components consist of nano nodes, nano routers, bio-nano-interface devices, and gateways [15]. In contrast, the IoBNT architecture incorporates bio-cyber interfaces, gateways, and application-specific server elements.

The IoBNT network enables the detection of chemical and biological changes in the environment and transmits the collected data to a central data center for further processing and analysis [44]. The IoBNT concept must be realized to bridge the gap between the network's electrical and biological domains by establishing seamless integration and communication between nanoscale and macro-scale components. Figure 5.1 describes the architecture of IoMT; let us delve into each component of the IoBNT architecture:

5.2.1 Bio-nano things

These are nanodevices that not only possess computational capabilities at the nanoscale but also exhibit the ability to detect and measure various phenomena within that scale. For instance, nanodevices can detect chemical compounds with extraordinary sensitivity, even at levels as minuscule as billionths. They can also detect the existence of infectious agents, such as viruses or detrimental bacteria. Nanodevices consist of different hardware elements, and all the necessary software and programming are integrated

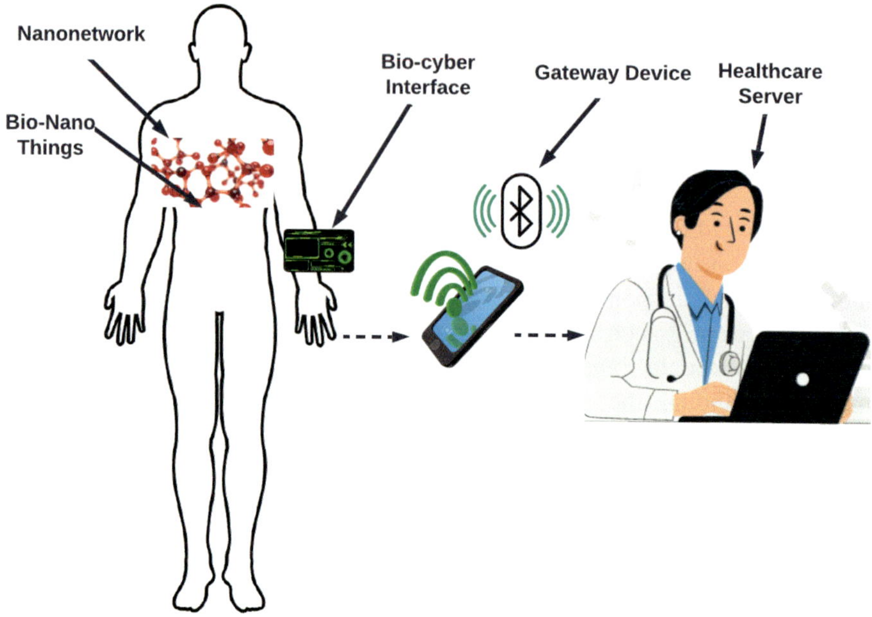

Figure 5.1 IoMT architecture [46].

into their information processing units. There exist two primary categories of nanodevices: electronic nanodevices and biological nanodevices. Cutting-edge materials in the realm of advanced nanotechnology, such as carbon nano tubes (CNT) and graphene nano ribbons (GNR) [17], play a crucial role in the development of electronic nanodevices.

Conversely, biological nanodevices are crafted by employing nanotechnology methodologies alongside biological materials, involving the reprogramming of biological substances such as cells, viruses, bacteria, bacteriophages, red and white blood cells, and stem cells. Additionally, biomolecules like liposomes, nanospheres, nanocapsules, micelles, dendrimers, fullerenes, and DNA capsules can be artificially synthesized to develop nanodevices. Hybrid nanodevices that combine both approaches are also possible. The size of nanodevices can vary from macro molecules to typical biological cells.

The composition of nanodevices can be pure biological [21], including proteins, DNA sequences, lipids, and biological cells. Alternatively, it can combine biological and non-biological materials such as magnetic particles and gold nanorods. Naturally occurring nanodevices include many nanodevices found in nature, such as protein motors that bind specific molecules and facilitate their transport by filaments, liposomes that can store and release specific molecules, and biological cells coated with negative materials to perform negative functions such as mercury uptake.

5.2.1.1 Nanonetworks

The nanonetwork encompasses a range of nanoscale devices, including nano transmitters, nano receivers, nano routers, and specialized nanodevices designed for specific functions such as sensing, actuation, monitoring, and control. In the context of intra-body nanonetworks deployed within the human body, either through oral ingestion or injection, these networks facilitate biomedical applications *in vivo*. Composed of nanoscale devices such as nanomachines, nano routers, and nano micro interfaces, the nanonetwork operates collectively to carry out sensing and actuation tasks [17]. Through interconnectedness, nanomachines collaborate in a distributed manner to execute various tasks. Their compact size allows for placement in hard-to-access areas within tissues, enabling minimally invasive therapeutic operations.

5.2.1.2 Bio cyber interface

The illustration in Figure 5.2 highlights the striking similarity between the elements of a biological cell and the components of a typical IoT computing device, drawing parallels such as the nucleus as the CPU unit and ribosomes as sensors. The nano–micro interface acts as a crucial intermediary for communication between nano and micro scales, commonly known as the BCI or bioelectronics device in this chapter for inclusivity. Its primary function is to facilitate the conversion of electrical signals, received as commands from healthcare providers' medical servers, into biochemical signals that intra-body nanonetworks, and vice versa, can understand. The BCI represents an advanced and hybrid device with the capability to enable seamless communication between nanoscale and microscale devices. The device receives data collected from nanonetworks, processes the nanoscale data in its processing unit, converts it into a format suitable for normal use (such as the internet), and connects to micro-devices.

The components and operations of the bio-cyber interface will be discussed in detail below.

5.2.2 Transduction unit

The bio-cyber interface is equipped with a transduction unit that plays a crucial role in converting electrical signals from external devices into biochemical signals that can be effectively interpreted by bio-nano things

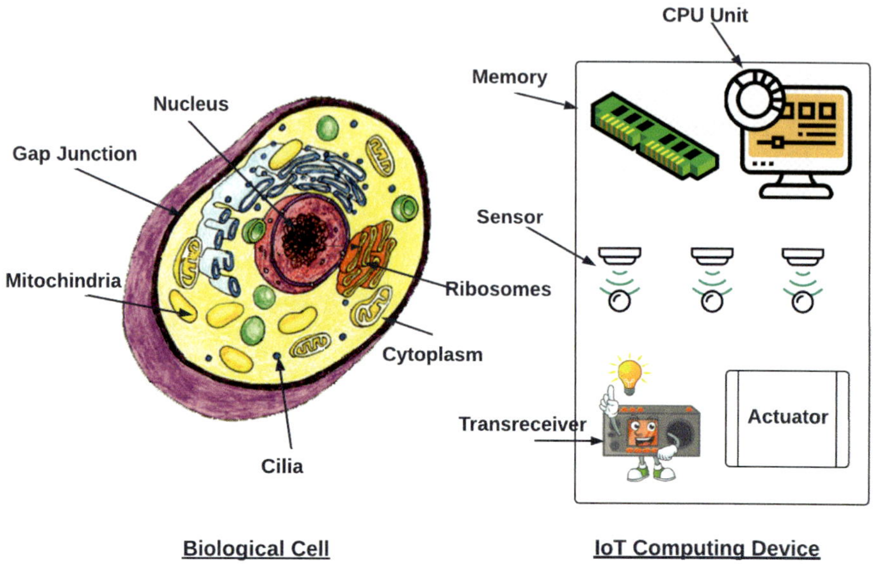

Figure 5.2 Elements of a biological cell and components of a typical IoT device [18].

[22]. To accomplish this conversion, the transduction unit relies on the utilization of various materials, such as biomaterials, artificially synthesized biomaterials, non-biological materials, or a combination of these approaches, resulting in hybrid designs [23]. The transduction unit itself can be further categorized into two distinct components, namely the electro-bio transduction unit and the bio-electro transduction unit.

5.2.2.1 Electromagnetic to bio-chemical signal conversion unit

The electro-bio transduction unit is of paramount importance as it facilitates the conversion of biochemical signals from external devices into electromagnetic signals, thereby allowing their transmission to *in vivo* nanonetworks for additional processing. The essential components of this apparatus comprise a decoder, a drug storage unit, an external physical effect source, and an injection chamber. The decoder, which functions as the recipient of signals originating from external devices, converts them into logic gates. The logic gates, which symbolize binary directives, elicit particular physical consequences in the surroundings, including magnetic, optical, or thermal radiofrequency (RF) signals. An external physical effect source, such as a thermal, optical, or magnetic field, is strategically positioned around the drug storage device in order to induce these physical effects. This source activates the nanomachines within the unit, leading to the release of their contents in response to changes in the external environment. Another critical element, the injection chamber, administers the released molecules into the network of blood vessels, ensuring their efficient distribution throughout the body to facilitate their intended therapeutic or diagnostic functions.

5.2.2.2 Bio-chemical to electromagnetic signal conversion unit

The bio-electron transduction unit plays a crucial role in converting molecular signals into electrical signals by detecting the concentration of received molecules. According to the study mentioned in [33], this unit utilizes a cell structure as a bioluminescence bio-reporter. The bio-reporter operates based on the principle of a bio-luminescence reaction, wherein the presence of an analyte triggers the generation of a reporter protein.

5.2.3 Communication unit

The IoBNT paradigm aims to connect the human body with the internet, and the bio-cyber interface serves as a crucial component in achieving this connection. Its role is to wirelessly transmit aggregated data from the body to healthcare providers. The bio-cyber interface is designed to enable communication with both intra-body nanonetworks and the internet, requiring two distinct communication units for external communication and intra-body communication.

5.2.3.1 Intra-body nanonetwork communication

Conventional wireless communication technologies need to be improved for intra-body communication due to the small size of nano-transceivers within the human body. To address this challenge, novel communication technologies have been explored, including molecular communication (MC) and nano-electromagnetic communication in the terahertz band.

a) **Molecular communication:** It involves the exchange of information between biological nanomachines via information encoding molecules. From a communications engineering perspective, MCs are built around key components, including donor bio-nanomachines, receiver bio-nanomachines, and the environment. Transmitter bio-nanomachines encode information molecules by varying the molecule concentration or using other appropriate methods according to the application. The bio-nanomachine transmitter then releases the encoded information into the environment.

The diffusion medium utilized in *in vivo* applications is typically an aqueous solution, which facilitates the movement of molecules toward the intended site. The efficacy of the disclosure procedure is still being determined. Active diffusion involves the vesicle-bound transportation of molecules to their intended locations via molecular motors. Passive or diffusion-based communication involves the replacement of information molecules with those that diffuse into the environment. Receptor bio-nanomachines capture information molecules from the exposure environment and identify them by the reaction. These reactions can generate signals for other molecules, perform certain functions, or form new molecules.

b) **Nano-electromagnetic communication:** Intra-body communication through nano-electromagnetic (EM) waves at the THz band has been proposed as a viable option [17]. This approach utilizes EM waves to transmit information between a source and a destination within the body. Recent advancements in the utilization of nanomaterials, including carbon nanotubes and graphene derivatives such as graphene nanoribbons, have facilitated the achievement of nanoscale electromagnetic communication [21]. The THz band offers advantages for intra-body communication, including reduced susceptibility to scattering effects and its non-ionizing nature, ensuring safety for biological tissues [19].

5.2.3.2 Communication with the internet

Wireless connectivity between bio-cyber interfaces and smartphones is crucial for enabling internet access for patients with bio-cyber implants. Smartphones have become an integral part of various IoT applications due to their widespread availability, advanced computational capability, and open-source nature. They can be utilized as gateway devices to facilitate communication between bio-cyber interfaces and the internet.

Wireless chemical sensors (WCS) and wireless body area networks (WBANs) are two wireless technologies compatible with bio-cyber interfaces and smartphone devices. WBANs employ implanted sensors to transmit data about physical abnormalities to internet-based medical applications wirelessly. Extensive research in WBANs has contributed to its maturity compared to IoBNT. On the other hand, WCS has been actively explored in chemical engineering for over a decade. These wearable patches can detect bodily chemical values and transmit them to connected smartphones for analysis and processing by healthcare applications. To identify suitable wireless technologies for bio-cyber interface design, a thorough review of the literature was conducted, focusing on domains like WBANs and WCSs. Various aspects, such as data rates, sizes, power requirements, transmission range, real-time versus on-demand data transfer, and warning capability, were carefully considered during the design process. The choice of wireless technology depends on specific system requirements and the intended mode of operation for the bio-cyber interface.

Several wireless technologies are available to establish human-to-internet connectivity. Active wireless technologies, including IEEE 802.15.6, Zigbee, and Bluetooth, utilize transponders to transfer and receive radio frequency waves over long distances with high data rates. These different technologies require a continuous power supply for proper operation. However, passive wireless technologies such as RFID and near-field communication (NFC) enable communication without needing a continuous power source.

5.2.4 Power supply

A reliable power supply is an essential prerequisite for bio-cyber interfaces to function seamlessly, facilitating the acquisition, manipulation, and transmission of data. Nevertheless, despite notable advancements, the existing condition of lithium rechargeable batteries fails to satisfy the ever-changing requirements of emerging technologies and the limitations imposed by their size. In order to confront this obstacle, scholars, including those affiliated with MIT, have been diligently investigating alternative methodologies. The initiatives above encompass the reduction in the size of battery sources, the formulation of energy-harvesting methods that rely on bodily movements, and the exploration of wireless battery recharge methods. These initiatives are focused on addressing the drawbacks related to the dimensions and functionality of batteries, specifically as they pertain to implants utilized in wireless body area networks (WBANs) and analogous implementations.

The objective is to advance battery technology by increasing the duration and efficacy of power supplies for bio-cyber interfaces. By progressing these energy solutions, scholars aim to spur the creation of more sophisticated and environmentally sustainable bio-cyber interfaces, thereby catering to the discipline's ever-changing demands.

5.2.5 Adhesion system

Regarding bio-cyber interfaces, which are conceptualized as bio-electronic devices that can be worn or adhered to, the selection of patch material is a topic that is continuously investigated across disciplines. The distinctive attributes of human skin contribute to this, comprising remarkable stretchability (surpassing 100% strain), a coarse texture (maximum height of 40 μm), and the existence of sweat and hair. Achieving sufficient adhesion between skin patches and the human epidermis presents a formidable obstacle.

Care must be taken when selecting adhesive materials for these patches in order to prevent complications such as cytotoxicity, skin contamination, injury, infection risks, and loss of wet adhesion, all of which have the potential to reduce their efficacy. Scholars are currently engaged in active efforts to identify appropriate adhesion materials for bio-cyber interfaces that can effectively mitigate these concerns and ensure dependable and secure attachment to human skin. The objective is to create adhesive solutions capable of surmounting these obstacles and preserving a strong and long-lasting bond with the human epidermis.

5.2.6 Gateway

Gateway devices play a critical role within the Internet of Things (IoT) ecosystem by acting as intermediaries connecting sensors to the internet. These electronic devices, encompassing smartphones, tablets, notebooks, and minicomputers, facilitate uninterrupted connectivity by transmitting data between sensors and the internet. Gateway devices offer a significant benefit in that they facilitate patient mobility while ensuring optimal signal reception from sensors that have restricted transmission ranges, including Bluetooth LE, NFC, and RFID technologies. The purpose of wearable bioelectronic devices is to accommodate mobile devices. An example of this is the integration of an RFID reader into a smartphone, which prevents the necessity for an external RFID reader. Likewise, smartphones have emerged as the most suitable platforms for bioelectronic devices employing Bluetooth LE for communication.

Access points, such as Wi-Fi access points and cellular base stations, are critical components of the network infrastructure. By facilitating the routing of body sensor data to the medical server, these access points guarantee dependable communication between peripheral devices and the server, which is essential for the analysis and processing of the data. The uninterrupted connectivity facilitates effective monitoring and management of healthcare.

5.2.7 Healthcare server

The healthcare server functions as a centralized storage system where sensory data gathered from the human body is stored, analyzed, and processed.

It serves as a vital component for real-time health monitoring, allowing prompt responses to emergencies by sending alert messages. To ensure the confidentiality and integrity of sensitive biomedical data, access to the server is restricted to authorized entities. These measures safeguard patient privacy and security, enabling authorized users to transmit commands and retrieve collected data for analysis and informed decision-making.

5.3 Security Challenges

In addition to enabling a wide range of innovative biomedical uses, the introduction of skin-implanted bioelectronics and the IoBNT mechanism will also make it possible for the adversary to use it for malicious purposes due to its wireless connectivity. Using bio-electronic gadgets, the attackers will have the apparent potential to create brand-new terrorist techniques to hurt the patient remotely. Bio-cyber terrorism is the term used to describe the malicious use of intra-body nanonetworks and bio-electronic devices to get malicious access to the human body via the internet in order to steal personal information or spread new illnesses. To carry out lethal and life-threatening acts from a distance, bio-cyber-terrorism can benefit from wirelessly accessing the human body. Therefore, security protections must be included in the bio-electronic device itself or in a separate component, which may increase the size of the device or make it impossible to use situations. Another option is to assign security tasks to nearby, external devices that have more advanced resources than bioelectronics-based devices. For instance, some researchers on the subject of IMD (implantable medical device) suggest giving security capabilities to external devices like Med-Mon and Cloaker. However, to create a secure connection with external devices, the bioelectronic device must perform a simple authentication method at least once. Bio-electronic devices will also be connected to a gateway device (like a smartphone) to send and receive information from the healthcare professional.

As a result of the technical distinctions between nanonetworks and bio-cyber interfaces, this section addresses their respective security requirements. No matter the underlying technical changes, the security objectives are constant. Security risks to IoBNT may be modeled using the STRIDE method of hazard. STRIDE is an acronym that stands for Information Disclosure, Denial of Service, Elevation of Privilege, Spoofing, Tampering, Repudiation, and Information Tapping. These six classifications offer a thorough breakdown of dangers and may be further broken down into related threats. Each danger category has a corresponding security objective:

Tampering-Integrity, Spoofing-Authentication, Repudiation, Confidentiality, Non-Repudiation, Information Disclosure, Denial of Service Availability, and Elevation of Privileges-Authorization.

- **Authentication:** Authentication ensures that the identity of each communication party is verified and that the data originates from a reputable source, preventing unauthorized users from accessing or modifying the information. Messages and users alike require authentication [29].
- **Integrity:** Integrity ensures that messages sent between authorized parties are not tampered with or altered by unauthorized parties.
- **Non-repudiation:** Each communication transaction is recorded under the traditional networking paradigm in order to detect network anomalies and identify the assailant should they attempt to exploit their privileges. Non-repudiation may be compromised if an adversary obtains access to the logs and deletes the data to nullify any existing traces.
- **Confidentiality:** Confidentiality assures that the attacker won't find out what the sender and recipient were communicating about. Only authorized personnel must access the data after being verified in advance by some procedure.
- **Availability:** With this objective, the device's services and communication will always be accessible upon request.
- **Authorization:** The authorization property ensures that only entities with the authority to order a certain operation can do it. To be authorized, an entity must first have completed the standard login (ID, password) process to prove its identity.

5.3.1 Challenges of nanonetworks

Changes in the surrounding environment, including pH levels, temperature, and other conditions, can have a significant impact on how well nanomachines perform. A malevolent attacker might change the surrounding conditions to hinder communication. Additionally, there are a few hypothetical attacks that an attacker may launch if they manage to obtain physical access to a person's body to disrupt the operation of nanomachines. For instance, attackers might introduce nanomachines that have been reprogrammed to damage the earlier therapeutic nanonetwork. The physical medium in which nanonetworks are installed is vulnerable to distinct fluidic medium physical assaults that are unique to the area in which they are deployed. For instance,

- Viruses in the human body might interfere with the communication of deployed nanomachines.

- The patient's body's natural immune system, which may mistake the nanomachines for invaders, would attempt to eliminate them.
- Due to the signal transmission and changes in the propagation medium, data may become unreliable.

The following are other unique nanonetworking challenges:

a) **Challenges to Safety:** Patients must be physically protected to prevent an assailant from accessing their bodies and harming them. Physical assaults can be launched by inserting malicious nanomachines into the patient's body or by giving them medication that has been tainted with harmful code. Communication and detecting standards ought to be kept up since using THz waves on human skin might result in heat and affect skin tissue.

b) **Nanonetwork addressing:** Another noteworthy issue related to nanonetworks is the naming and tending of nanomachines. A nano arrangement encompasses many nanomachines, and it is not conceivable to address each nanomachine with a special character. Nevertheless, imaginative tending to frameworks such as FCNN (Work Centric Nano Organizing) offers an arrangement for tending to issues. Rather than tending to each hub, the FCNN-based method designates addresses to body capacities and areas.

c) **Energizing nanomachines:** The issue of control supply is basic in nanomachines since they are not associated with an outside control source. Moreover, the battery unit is the biggest unit in terms of mass, which may increase the estimate of nanomachines, which is undesirable. As a result, vitality rummaging procedures for pulling vitality from inside the body must be inquired about.

d) **Design of the transmitter/sender and receiver:** The improvement of nano handsets is the primary step toward the acknowledgment of completely utilitarian nanonetworks, and two hypothetical strategies will be utilized to construct the imagined nano handsets: organic structures empowered by manufactured science and nanomaterials-based structures. The molecular communication hypothesis still depends on presumptions since there is no counterfeit. Thus far, nanotechnology has been applied to microsystems; however, the hypothesis is replete with numerous design options for nanotransmitters and receivers, some of which may need more practicality. A clear distinction exists between the terms "hypothesis" and "hone"; extra thinking ought to, in hypothesis, go with test affirmation. *In vitro* damp labs, specifically, ought to be imagined for healthcare applications that will be uncovered to extra clinical ponders.

5.3.2 Common challenges with bio-cyber interfaces

The collection of procedures required to transfer data from the biochemical domain of bio-nano things networks to the internet cyber domain, which is based on electrical circuits and electromagnetic communications, and vice versa, is referred to as a bio-cyber interface in this chapter. The designing of chemical and physical forms able to absolutely examine the atomic properties where data is contained and change over them into the control of electromagnetic parameters is one of the essential impediments to the acknowledgment of these interfacing. The improvement of inventive chemical and organic sensors made attainable by nanotechnology, which guarantees unheard-of detecting capabilities, can be a step within the right heading.

These sensors are regularly made of materials with electromagnetic properties that can be changed by atoms or particle complexes, like natural receptors bound to particles, and as a result, tweak the current in an electrical circuit. The essential issues with this detecting strategy for IoBNT applications are its tall idleness, constrained selectivity, need for standardized reaction, and, more urgently, its unidentified biocompatibility, which is taken into thought following. Another challenge to the arrangement of bio-cyber interfacing is biocompatibility, which is characterized here as the property of a designed framework to constrain its activity on the natural environment only to its aiming work, without any undesirable modification of organic parameters.

We imagine the plausibility of making bio-cyber interfacing by encasing organic nanosensors and electromagnetic (EM) nano-communication units inside the previously mentioned counterfeit cells. Typically, since the previously mentioned nanosensors are moderately small, current promising inquiries about nano-communications have been found to utilize EM waves. EM nano-communication unit would have a wireless interface with the electrical gear exterior of the organic environment, the counterfeit cell would guarantee biocompatibility, and the natural nanosensor would oversee bridging the chemical and electrical spaces in this plan. For intra-body IoBNT applications, another choice is to thrust the EM space toward the physical boundary between the organic environment and the exterior world, such as the skin. In this course, electronic tattoos may consolidate a bio-cyber interface that may sense biochemical data from cells on the epidermis, sweat organs, or apprehensive terminations and wirelessly communicate it to adjacent outside electronic gadgets, much like those based on RFID innovation, which permits clients to verify gadgets inside near extend.

5.3.3 Open issues, other challenges, and future research directions

These networks' real-world applications need help. These difficulties also raise open research questions and potential future study directions.

- **Nanotechnology and standards:** Nanonetworks have short-range (1 nm to 1 m) *in vivo* communication modalities. Additionally, there is a lot of biological noise around us. Data loss, delays, and network congestion can all result from these communication problems in nano-communication.
- **Data management and analysis:** The quantity of novel devices connected to the internet and nanonetworks is expected to increase significantly. Presently, the methodology and examination of data pose a substantial challenge. Regarding nanonetworks, considerable attention will be devoted to this issue. Furthermore, further investigation is warranted regarding the development of advanced algorithm models for data analysis that are capable of functioning on nanoscale devices.
- **Smart biomaterials:** Although there are numerous distinctive sorts of biocompatible in-capsular sensors (camera, pH, temperature, gas, etc.), the advancement of ingestible sensors and shrewd biomaterials is still in its earliest stages.
- **Security and privacy:** The recent nanonetwork schemes mostly contain their applications in the medical, biological, chemical, and personal domains that do not yet have defined standards and frameworks. Since there is currently an excessively big threat surface and multiple attack channels, these networks are exposed [48]. Currently, more important than other application areas is assuring the security, availability, and integrity of the stored data and moving it around the network. By creating the conditions for harmful events like data tampering, theft, espionage, and potentially bioterrorism, this deficiency could endanger people and civilizations [29]. Because of this, trust management systems, user access control systems, and efficient data compression models are required. There are numerous unexplored research areas, such as substance administration, portability administration, benefit conglomeration and disclosure, vitality preservation, vitality collecting, control exchange, nano gadget tending to, and integration with next-generation advances (SDN, NFV, Blockchain, Metaverse, etc.), in addition to the challenges already mentioned.

In addition to opening new IoBNT possibilities, the ability to link to and control the human body over the internet also creates opportunities for hackers to utilize it for nefarious purposes. The patients will be seriously at risk from this incident, which is referred to as "bio cyber terrorism." Therefore, the greatest and most crucial obstacle to the development and use of bioelectronic devices is security. Since these devices provide data that contains the patient's most confidential information, it is extremely confidential. By exploiting this data, hackers and enemies can launch a variety of attacks with potentially deadly results with the patient's condition and the healthcare provider's improper prescription practices. It is necessary to prevent security breaches along the communication path from the device to the healthcare provider. It is impossible to find solutions to the security problems of IoBNT in the current mechanisms of conventional wireless networking. Because IoBNT's networking technology is new and has a variety of system requirements, Get-to-control and security approaches for IoBNT should be straightforward to utilize and harmonious with the resource-constrained and lightweight IoBNT devices and nanonetwork.

a) **Cryptographic fundamentals:** Robust cryptographic measures are essential for ensuring user privacy in IoBNT, especially as they deal with patients' sensitive physiological data. However, the resource-constrained nature of IoBNT poses challenges for implementing computationally expensive symmetric and asymmetric cryptography systems. To address this issue, researchers have explored lightweight cryptographic techniques suitable for the IoBNT environment. These lightweight cryptographic methods aim to strike a balance between security and computational efficiency while operating in resource-limited settings. Implementing lightweight cryptography can help safeguard patients' private data without overburdening the nanonetwork's constrained resources.

   The choice of an IoBNT-compatible cryptographic system depends on the cryptosystem's energy, memory, and execution time requirements. Dressler and Kargl have presented the latest area of bio-chemical cryptography, which appears promising for nanonetworks. Techniques for biochemical cryptography that have been proposed thus far encrypt data using DNA molecules. There are several ideas for encryption schemes that use DNA cryptography.

b) **Authentication:** Intra-body nanonetworks face challenges in implementing traditional authentication and access control techniques. Verification of the data source and messages sent to gateway devices becomes essential before transmission to intra-body nanonetworks. Authentication techniques need to account for several types of nano-communication, including molecular communication (MC), nano-electromagnetic communication, and nano-acoustic communication. A recent proposal suggests using path loss dependence on distance utilized as a device identifier for nano-electromagnetic communication, enabling the distinction between data transmitted by authorized and unauthorized transmitters. However, this authentication approach might not be feasible for MC due to the unique communication characteristics involved.

To address the issue of molecular communication authentication at the nanoscale, researchers may explore using biological molecules, such as DNA and RNA, as sources of encryption. This approach presents novel challenges and may require collaboration between biologists, computer scientists, and biochemists to explore innovative solutions.

c) **Encryption:** Key management in nanonetworks poses significant challenges, whether it involves proactive distribution prior to data transmission or pre-distribution prior to network implementation. At the nanoscale, both approaches have limitations. Pre-distribution becomes impractical due to the limited storage capabilities of nanodevices, making it infeasible to store many paired keys. *In vivo* nanonetwork applications with constrained online access to nanonetworks also render proactive or on-demand key distribution impractical, as it necessitates continuous online connectivity to the devices. Some researchers have also proposed using ECC for devices with constrained resources. However, real-time implementation of ECC-based primitives remains computationally expensive. Quantum-based encryption algorithms have shown promise in resource-limited devices. Given the severe resource constraints in nano-communication networks, there may be more viable options than public-key cryptography. Instead, cryptographic mechanisms based on biochemical or DNA cryptography may be more suitable at the nanoscale.

Bio-inspired algorithms, which draw inspiration from nature, are currently being employed to tackle computer and networking challenges. Bio-inspired computing aims to translate problem-solving principles observed in nature into algorithms for computing applications. Bio-inspired security algorithms constitute a subset of this field, leveraging tactics used by nature to fend off attackers. The human immune system serves as a natural defense mechanism, protecting the body from invaders and foreign viruses. In the realm of wireless sensor network cybersecurity, researchers have proposed biologically inspired algorithms like Genetic Mutation, the Artificial Immune System, and Ant Colony Optimization to counter cyberattacks effectively. These bios-inspired algorithms offer promising approaches to defend against several types of attacks in the context of IoBNT. As numerous algorithms can be employed to mitigate security risks in IoBNT, utilizing bio-inspired algorithms emerges as a potential and scalable security solution. Developing robust security solutions for IoBNT through the utilization of bio-inspired algorithms is an essential objective for future research and development.

5.4 Conclusion

As IoBNT advances, it is important to address the security aspects of these technologies. Currently, the security landscape for IoBNT has yet to mature fully, leaving room for potential attackers to exploit vulnerabilities. Even non-sophisticated attacks can have significant consequences for the safety and integrity of IoBNT technologies. This presents an opportunity for standardization initiatives to establish unified information security practices within the IoBNT domain. Lessons learned from well-established fields like IoT, wireless body area networks (WBANs), and implantable medical devices (IMDs) can contribute to identifying potential attack vectors in IoBNT systems. In addition to software and hardware security mechanisms, user training and awareness are crucial for the widespread adoption and secure usage of IoBNT technologies. Educating users about potential risks, best practices for secure operation, and the importance of data privacy can significantly enhance the overall security posture. Furthermore, continuous research and development efforts should focus on the real-time detection and mitigation of security attacks that may impact the theragnostic process in IoBNT.

By addressing these security challenges, the IoBNT community can establish robust security measures, promote standardization, and build user confidence in the reliability and safety of IoBNT technologies. As the field progresses, it is essential to foster collaboration among researchers, industry experts, and policymakers to develop comprehensive security frameworks that protect the integrity, privacy, and functionality of IoBNT systems.

References

[1] Y. A. Qadri, A. Nauman, Y. B. Zikria, A. V. Vasilakos, and S. W. Kim, "The Future of Healthcare Internet of Things: A Survey of Emerging Technologies," in IEEE Communications Surveys & Tutorials, vol. 22, no. 2, pp. 1121-1167, Second quarter 2020, doi: 10.1109/COMST.2020.2973314.

[2] The Internet of Things: How to Capture the Value of IoT. Hershey, PA, USA: McKinsey & Company, May 2018.

[3] R. Minerva, A. Biru, and D. Rotondi, Towards a Definition of the Internet of Things (IoT), Telecom Italia, Rome, Italy, May 2015.

[4] N. Yang, Z. Wang, R. Gravina, and G. Fortino, "A survey of open body sensor networks: Applications and challenges," in Proc. 14th IEEE Annu. Consum. Commun. Netw. Conf. (CCNC), Las Vegas, NV, USA,2017, pp. 65–70.

[5] H. Qiu, X. Wang, and F. Xie, "A survey on smart wearables in the application of fitness," in Proc. IEEE 15th Int.Conf. Depend. Auton. Secure Comput. 15th Int. Conf. Pervasive Intell. Comput. 3rd Int. Conf. Big Data Intell. Comput. Cyber Sci. Technol. Congr. DASC Pi Com/DataCom/Cyber Sci., Orlando, FL, USA, 2018, pp. 303–307.

[6] Global Wearables Market Grows 7.7% in 4Q17 and 10.3% in 2017 as Apple Seizes the Leader Position, Says IDC, Int. Data Corporat. Framingham, MA, USA, 2018.

[7] L. Filipe, F. Fdez-Riverola, N. Costa, and A. Pereira, "Wireless body area networks for healthcare applications: Protocol stack review," Int.J. Distrib. Sensor Netw., vol. 11, no. 10, pp. 1–23, 2015.

[8] Q. Mao, F. Hu, and Q. Hao, "Deep learning for intelligent wireless networks: A comprehensive survey," IEEE Commun. Surveys Tuts.,vol. 20, no. 4, pp. 2595–2621, 4th Quart., 2018.

[9] J. Pan and J. Mc Elhannon, "Future edge cloud and edge computing for Internet of Things applications," IEEE Internet Things J., vol. 5, no. 1,pp. 439–449, Feb. 2018.

[10] G. Manogaran, R. Varatharajan, D. Lopez, P. M. Kumar,R. Sundarasekar, and C. Thota, "A new architecture of Internet of Things and big data ecosystem for secured smart healthcare monitoring and alerting system," Future Gener. Comput. Syst., vol. 82, pp. 375– 387, May 2018.

[11] Y. N. Malek et al., "On the use of IoT and big data technologies for real-time monitoring and data processing," Procedia Comput. Sci.,vol. 113, pp. 429–434, Sep. 2017.

[12] M. M. Alam, H. Malik, M. I. Khan, T. Pardy, A. Kuusik, andY. L. Moullec, "A survey on the roles of communication technologies in IoT-based personalized healthcare applications," IEEE Access,vol. 6, pp. 36611–36631, 2018.
[13] M. M. Mutlag, M. K. A. Ghani, N. Arunkumar, M. A. Mohammed, and O. Mohd, "Enabling technologies for fog computing in healthcare IoT systems," Future Gener. Comput. Syst., vol. 90, pp. 62–78, Jan. 2019.
[14] H. Baali, H. Djelouat, A. Amira, and F. Bensaali, "Empowering technology enabled care using IoT and smart devices: A review," IEEE Sensors J., vol. 18, no. 5, pp. 1790–1809, Mar. 2018.
[15] Kuscu, Murat, and Bige D. Unluturk. "Internet of bio-nano things: A review of applications, enabling technologies and key challenges." arXiv preprint arXiv:2112.09249 (2021).
[16] Senturk, Seyda, Ibrahim Kok, and Fatmana Senturk. "Internet of Nano, Bio-Nano, Biodegradable and Ingestible Things: A Survey." arXiv preprint arXiv:2202.12409 (2022).
[17] M. H. Miraz, M. Ali, P. S. Excell, and R. Picking, "Internet of nano things, things and everything: future growth trends," Future Internet,vol. 10, no. 8, p. 68, 2018.
[18] R. Nawaratne, D. Alahakoon, D. De Silva, P. Chhetri, and N. Chilamkurti, "Self-evolving intelligent algorithms for facilitating data interoperability in iot environments," Future Generation Computer Systems,vol. 86, pp. 421–432, 2018.
[19] H. Fouad, A. S. Hassanein, A. M. Soliman, and H. Al-Feel, "Analyzing patient health information based on iot sensor with ai for improving patient assistance in the future direction," Measurement, vol. 159, p.107757, 2020.
[20] Manojkumar, Sreelakshmi. "Security and possible applications towards internet of nano things in near future." (2022).
[21] I. F. Akyildiz, M. Pierobon, S. Balasubramaniam, and Y. Koucheryavy, "The internet of bio nano things," IEEE Communications Magazine,vol. 53, no. 3, pp. 32–40, 2015.
[22] Zafar S, Nazir M, Sabah A, Jurcut AD. Securing Bio-Cyber Interface for the Internet of Bio Nano Things using Particle Swarm Optimization and Artificial Neural Networks based parameter profiling. Comput Biol Med. 2021 Sep;136:104707. doi: 10.1016/j.compbiomed.2021.104707. Epub 2021 Jul 31. PMID: 34375900.

[23] Garcia-Sanchez, Antonio-Javier, et al. "Dynamic Multi-Hop Routing in Terahertz Flow guided Nanosensor Networks: A Reinforcement Learning Approach." IEEE Sensors Journal (2023).
[24] Lemic, Filip & Abadal, Sergi & Tavernier, Wouter & Stroobant, Pieter & Colle, Didier & Alarcón, Eduard & Marquez-Barja, Johann & Famaey, Jeroen. (2019). "Survey on Terahertz Nanocommunication and Networking: A Top-Down Perspective".
[25] I. K¨ok and S. ¨Ozdemir, "Deepmdp: A novel deep-learning-based missingdata prediction protocol for iot," IEEE Internet of Things Journal, vol. 8,no. 1, pp. 232–243, 2020.
[26] P. K. D. Pramanik, A. Solanki, A. Debnath, A. Nayyar, S. El-Sappagh,and K.-S. Kwak, "Advancing modern healthcare with nanotechnology,nanobiosensors, and internet of nano things: Taxonomies, applications,architecture, and challenges," IEEE Access, vol. 8, pp. 65 230–65 266, 2020.
[27] M. A. Cruz Alvarado and P. Bazàn, "Understanding the internet of nanothings: overview, trends, and challenges," E-Ciencias de la Información,vol. 9, no. 1, pp. 152–182, 2019.
[28] N. A. Ali, W. Aleyadeh, and M. AbuElkhair, "Internet of nano things network models and medical applications," in 2016 International Wireless Communications and Mobile Computing Conference (IWCMC), IEEE, 2016, pp. 211–215.
[29] G. Velvizhi, S. Shantha kumar, B. Das, A. Pugazhendhi, T. S. Priya,B. Ashok, K. Nanthagopal, R. Vignesh, and C. Karthick, "Biodegradable and non-biodegradable fraction of municipal solid waste for multifaceted applications through a closed loop integrated refinery platform: Paving a path towards circular economy," Science of the Total Environment, vol.731, p. 138049, 2020.
[30] C. Steiger, A. Abramson, P. Nadeau, A. P. Chandrakasan, R. Langer, and G. Traverso, "Ingestible electronics for diagnostics and therapy," Nature Reviews Materials, vol. 4, no. 2, pp. 83–98, 2019.
[31] B. Chen et al., "A Security Awareness and Protection System for 5G Smart Healthcare Based on Zero-Trust Architecture," in IEEE Internet of Things Journal, vol. 8, no. 13, pp. 10248-10263, 1 July1, 2021, doi: 10.1109/JIOT.2020.3041042.
[32] M. Agiwal, A. Roy, and N. Saxena, "Next generation 5G wireless networks: A comprehensive survey," IEEE Commun. Surveys Tuts.,vol. 18, no. 3, pp. 1617–1655, 3rd Quart., 2016.

[33] I. Ahmad, S. Shahabuddin, T. Kumar, J. Okwuibe, A. Gurtov, and M. Ylianttila, "Security for 5G and beyond," IEEE Commun. Surveys Tuts., vol. 21, no. 4, pp. 3682–3722, 4th Quart., 2019.

[34] A. Akhunzada, S. U. Islam, and S. Zeadally, "Securing cyberspace of future smart cities with 5G technologies," IEEE Netw., vol. 34, no. 4pp. 336–342, Jul./Aug. 2020.

[35] R. Arnold and D. Longley, "Zero-knowledge proofs do not solve the privacy-trust problem of attribute-based credentials: What if alice isevil?" IEEE Commun. Stand. Mag., vol. 3, no. 4, pp. 26–31, Dec. 2019.

[36] N. A. Azeez and C. V. der Vyver, "Security and privacy issues in ehealth cloud-based system: A comprehensive content analysis," Egypt.Informat. J., vol. 20, no. 2, pp. 97–108, 2019.

[37] A. Banchs, D. M. Gutierrez-Estevez, M. Fuentes, M. Boldi, and S. Provvedi, "A 5G mobile network architecture to support vertical industries," IEEE Commun. Mag., vol. 57, no. 12, pp. 38–44, Dec. 2019.

[38] S. Buzzi, I. Chih-Lin, T. E. Klein, H. V. Poor, C. Yang, and A. Zappone, "A survey of energy-efficient techniques for 5G networks and challenges ahead," IEEE J. Sel. Areas Commun., vol. 34, no. 4, pp. 697–709, Apr.2016.

[39] J. Cao et al., "A survey on security aspects for 3GPP 5G networks,"IEEE Commun. Surveys Tuts., vol. 22, no. 1, pp. 170–195, 1st Quart.,2020.

[40] Chen, J. Yang, J. Zhou, Y. Hao, J. Zhang, and C.-H. Youn, "5Gsmartdiabetes: Toward personalized diabetes diagnosis with healthcare big data clouds," IEEE Commun. Mag., vol. 56, no. 4, pp. 16–23, Apr.2018.

[41] L. Chettri and R. Bera, "A comprehensive survey on internet of things (IoT) toward 5G wireless systems," IEEE Internet Things J., vol. 7,no. 1, pp. 16–32, Jan. 2020.

[42] S. Zafar et al., "A Systematic Review of Bio-Cyber Interface Technologies and Security Issues for Internet of Bio-Nano Things," in IEEE Access, vol. 9, pp. 93529-93566, 2021, doi:10.1109/ACCESS.2021.3093442.

[43] E. B. Steager, M. S. Sakar, C. Magee, M. Kennedy, A. Cowley, and V. Kumar, "Automated biomanipulation of single cells using magnetic microrobots," Int. J. Robot. Res., vol. 32, no. 3, pp. 346_359, Mar. 2013.

[44] D.-H. Kim, P. K. Wong, J. Park, A. Levchenko, and Y. Sun, "Microengineered platforms for cell mechanobiology," Annu. Rev. Biomed. Eng.vol. 11, no. 1, pp. 203_233, Aug. 2009.O. Ergeneman, G. Dogangil,

M. P. Kummer, J. J. Abbott, M. K. Nazeeruddin, and B. J. Nelson, "A magnetically controlled wireless optical oxygen sensor for intraocular measurements," IEEE Sensors J., vol. 8, no. 1, pp. 29_37, Jan. 2008.

[45] T. Nakamura and A. Terano, "Capsule endoscopy: Past, present, and future," J. Gastroenterol., vol. 43, no. 2, pp. 93_99, Feb. 2008.

[46] J. M. Dubach, D. I. Harjes, and H. A. Clark, "Fluorescent ion-selective nano sensors for intracellular analysis with improved lifetime and size,"Nano Lett., vol. 7, no. 6, pp. 1827_1831, Jun. 2007.

[47] C.-J. Chen, Y. Haik, and J. Chatterjee, "Development of nano technol-ogyfor biomedical applications," in Proc. Conf., Emerg. Inf. Technol. Taipei,Taiwan: IEEE, 2005, pp. 1_4.

[48] R.W. Carlsen and M. Sitti, "Bio-hybrid cell-based actuators for microsystems,"Small, vol. 10, no. 19, pp. 3831_3851, Oct. 2014.

[49] J. W. Aylott, "Optical nanosensors_ An enabling technology for intra-cellular measurements," Analyst, vol. 128, no. 4, pp. 309_312, 2003.

[50] B. P. Timko, T. Dvir, and D. S. Kohane, "Remotely triggerable drug delivery systems," Adv. Mater., vol. 22, no. 44, pp. 4925_4943, Nov. 2010.

[51] G. Pan and L. Wang, "Swallowable wireless capsule endoscopy: Progress and technical challenges," Gastroenterol. Res. Pract., vol.2012, Oct.2011, Art. no. 841691.

[52] Mandal, S., Khan, D.A. & Jain, S. Cloud-Based Zero Trust Access Control Policy: An Approach to Support Work-From-Home Driven by COVID-19 Pandemic. New Gener. Comput. 39, 599–622 (2021).

[53] S. Rostampour, N. Bagheri, Y. Bendavid, M. Safkhani, S. Kumari and J. J. P. C. Rodrigues, "An Authentication Protocol for Next Generation of Constrained IoT Systems," in IEEE Internet of Things Journal, vol. 9, no. 21, pp. 21493-21504, 1 Nov.1, 2022, doi:10.1109/JIOT.2022.3184 293.

[54] Chang, Yuxia, Chen Fang, and Wenzhuo Sun. "A blockchain-based federated learning method for smart healthcare." Computational Intel-ligence and Neuroscience 2021 (2021).

[55] Singh, Saurabh, et al. "A framework for privacy-preservation of IoT healthcare data using Federated Learning and blockchain technology." Future Generation Computer Systems 129 (2022): 380-388.

[56] Li, D., Luo, Z. & Cao, B. Blockchain-based federated learning method-ologies in smart environments. Cluster Comput 25, 2585–2599 (2022).

[57] H. Jin, X. Dai, J. Xiao, B. Li, H. Li and Y. Zhang, "Cross-Cluster Federated Learning and Blockchain for Internet of Medical Things,"

in IEEE Internet of Things Journal, vol. 8, no. 21, pp. 15776-15784, 1 Nov.1, 2021, doi: 10.1109/JIOT.2021.3081578.

[58] Dutta, M, A. K. Singh, and A. Kumar. "An efficient signcryption scheme based on ECC with forward secrecy and encrypted message authentication." 2013 3rd IEEE International Advance Computing Conference (IACC). IEEE, 2013.

[59] Kandasamy, Kamalanathan, et al. "Digital Healthcare-Cyberattacks in Asian Organizations: An Analysis of Vulnerabilities, Risks, NIST Perspectives, and Recommendations." IEEE Access 10 (2022): 12345-12364.

[60] Adekunle, A. A., and S. R. Woodhead. "An aead cryptographic framework and tinyaead construct for secure wsn communication." 2012 Wireless Advanced (WiAd). IEEE, 2012.

[61] Nguyen, Dinh C., et al. "Federated learning for internet of things: A comprehensive survey." IEEE Communications Surveys & Tutorials 23.3 (2021): 1622-1658.

6

Risk Monitoring Strategy for Confidentiality and Integrity of Healthcare Data

Pragynasmita Sahoo, Sirsha Basak, and Sushruta Mishra

Kalinga Institute of Industrial Technology, Deemed to be University, India
E-mail: 2105048@kiit.ac.in; 2106159@kiit.ac.in;
sushruta.mishrafcs@kiit.ac.in

Abstract

Existing protection endeavors make an effort to provide CIA (confidentiality, integrity, and availability) security safeguards. The streams of traffic in the field of subtle health care requisition are essential. When discussing the accessibility of confidential healthcare, the first thing that springs to mind when considering care data or the confidentiality of highly valued data is that the user should securely access it. Sensitive healthcare information must be safeguarded to limit unauthorized access, disclosure, and modification. The most favored way is to execute tiered modeling of safety measures because there is no such protection that allows us to make our systems completely secure. In this study, the modular encryption standard (MES) and the augmentation of conditions are mathematically described. A centrism-tiered paradigm for protecting the confidentiality of healthcare data is provided by probability tracking of sensitive information. A machine learning technique based on a fuzzy inference system combined with neural networks is used to improve decision-making regarding the risk monitoring plan of MES. Data collection, data cleaning, data analysis, and interpretation of results are the methods/tools that can be used to analyze the accuracy and error rate of MES. Data collection has been implemented through techniques such as sampling, data acquisition, and data preparation. Data cleaning is used for data validation, data imputation, and data transformation. Data analysis has

DOI: 10.1201/9788770047395-6

always been carried out through descriptive statistics, inferential statistics, and interpretation of results.

Keywords: Health equity, modular encryption standard (MES), adaptive neuro-fuzzy inference system, data confidentiality, risk monitoring, reliability viewpoint, medical domain.

6.1 Introduction

A crucial component of the healthcare sector is the confidentiality of patient data. It is crucial to prevent unauthorized access to the sensitive patient information that healthcare organizations gather since it might be used to identify specific patients. Given the growing dependence on computerized case studies and the increase in cyber threats, there is a considerable danger that this information may be compromised.

The security program of every healthcare organization must include a risk monitoring plan. The method aids organizations in identifying possible threats to the confidentiality of patient information, evaluating the likelihood and severity of those threats, putting measures in place to lessen those threats, and tracking the efficacy timing of that supremacy. This process is continual, necessitating constant attention to make sure the risks are properly controlled [1].

Finding the hazards that may jeopardize patient information is the first step in the risk monitoring plan for healthcare information confidentiality. Various factors, such as technology flaws, human mistakes, and hostile assaults, might result in risks. Each risk is first identified, and then its likelihood and effect are evaluated to decide which alleviation strategies should be prioritized. The right controls are then put in place to lessen the chance or impact of the threats, and their efficiency is reviewed over time to carry on to offer sufficient security.

In conclusion, a strong risk monitoring approach is essential to maintaining the privacy of medical data. It aids healthcare organizations in maintaining patient privacy, regulatory compliance, and reputation safety.

6.1.1 Brief of risk monitoring in healthcare

Using information gathered through risk monitoring activities, the protection tracking plan is put into action by survey or manual means, reporting on information relevant to intended purposes for risk monitoring and providing inputs to ongoing risk assessment and response processes. The protection tracking plan documentation differs from the collection of risk-monitoring techniques on the basis of risk hypotheses, restrictions, precedence, and tolerance levels, which are implemented once. The main goal of the protection tracking plan is to discuss how different entities' risks will be tracked. Activities for risk monitoring should be correlated and shared throughout the organization's levels (or with other organizational units). With the help of this, the dissemination of risk assessment findings might influence the planning or execution of risk responses throughout the whole organization. Risk detection, monitoring, assessment, mitigation, and prevention of remote and directorial paradigms, procedures, and reports are being compromised by the protection monitoring in medical domain strategies. By employing risk monitoring, healthcare organizations' benefits, sales, mandates, reimbursement amounts, brand values, and patient safety are all routinely and aggressively protected. Categorization of healthcare protection monitoring has always placed a strong emphasis on the significance of victim security and the prevention of medical mistakes that jeopardize an organization's capacity to fulfill its goal. Give patients safeguards and protection against monetary culpability. However, the increasing move of healthcare protection plans has gotten increasingly difficult over time due to advancements in technologies, rising cybersecurity concerns, the rapid advancement of medical knowledge, and the industry's constantly shifting administrative, legitimate, parliamentary, and reciprocate environments [2]. Figure 6.1 highlights the overall process of risk monitoring in the healthcare domain.

6.1.2 Comparison of health monitoring research review

In a specific type of investigation called monitoring, a question is repeatedly examined over time while continuing to gather data and giving a proper aspect to reach the thing. The main goal of monitoring is to ensure that all programs on length adhere to a clear or implied coordinate of standards that may be enforced by monitoring. In contrast to other types of exploration, which may aim to produce information with lower immediate policy applicability, monitoring is specifically deliberate to have experimental significance for policy-making in the shorter term. Monitoring may or may not yield useful information for long-term planning. The distinctive aspect of monitoring is that sensitive information is often provided in a descriptive rather than an illuminating manner. Typically, one needed help to use a protection plan to compute and analyze as-yet-unknown paths, or methodologies, which would

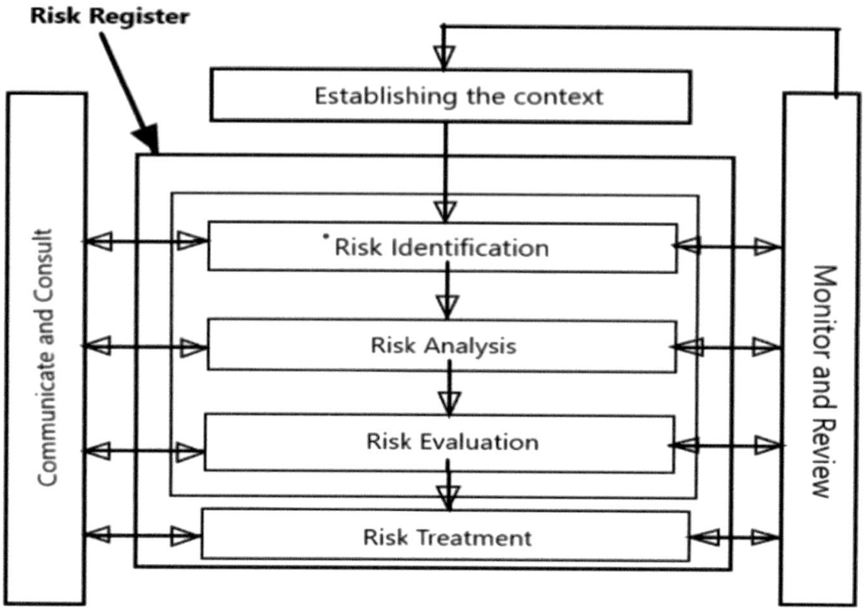

Figure 6.1 Processes implemented for risk monitoring.

prompt for further abstract and careful explicatory research. A monitoring system's data can be utilized for observing substitutes in the parameters of variation in a certain health measure over time between various socioeconomic groupings over a certain period; the frequency and circumstances of significant elements that are known to affect health, such as poverty, severance, housing circumstances, academic achievement, or utilization of appropriate health services, can also be learned by monitoring. These factors would naturally be expected to have an impact on health concerns. The monitoring data mostly demonstrates particular ineffective outcomes concerning how similar components often could not be predicted to be produced; however, occasionally, they can be appropriate to make. A reported loss in health status without proportional decreases in the usage or quality of relevant health services, for instance, would point to the need to explore substitutes in medical considerations other than the medical domain and probable ineffective factors. Similar outcomes must easily take into account results from additional research in summation to abidance inferred through monitoring. A collection of exploratory questions, the capacity to analyze those questions on a regular, continuous basis, and a formal procedure of regularly linking outcomes or discoveries with the targeted objective of instructional policy are the basic components of any monitoring system. Any protection plan must have a few fundamental qualities that always remain the same, regardless of the points or topics covered. The information gathered must first, like with any survey, be trustworthy and accurately shielded, clearly demonstrating what it represents. Still, in the monitoring profession, objectivity will frequently matter more than perfection. In many resource-poor countries, for instance, births and deaths are disproportionately under-reported among the poor, pastoral, and other irregular population groups, making the actual information too biased to use to assess the valuation directly. If the under-described were aimlessly distributed across social groups, however, similar records could be helpful for acquiring a valuation in spite of their inexactitude and biased donations. In summation, in accordance with the general technical qualities of the survey, other more specific necessities are required for protection planning such as transparent rules pertinence, clarity to allow the original labor force to use the methods for statistics group and for examination and investigation on an ongoing, routine basis, affordability to take into account the coffers needed for all stages of the monitoring process, not just data collection, and sustainability to allow the data collection. It can be challenging to meet these requirements, especially when they are combined. For example, it may be difficult to make the rules for data collection and analysis transparent and clear while also making them affordable and sustainable. However, it is important to meet these requirements as much as possible in order to ensure the accuracy and reliability of the data collected [3].

The chapter is structured as follows. Section 6.1 highlights the general introductory part regarding security aspects in healthcare data integrity. Section 6.2 discusses the significant background studies carried out in this analysis. Section 6.3 outlines the constituents of healthcare risk monitoring. Section 6.4 highlights the strategic risk monitoring method. The section discusses the generic standards and practices of healthcare risk monitoring. Section 6.6 denotes the implementation aspects of the study in the medical domain. Finally, Sections 6.7 and 6.8 present the future scope and conclusion of the chapter.

6.2 Literature Survey and Background Works

Ariba et al. conducted a survey on hazard identification, risk assessment, and risk control in a woodworking company [4]. Chen et al. surveyed a commonly used semiquantitative technique for peril protection strategy, known as the risk matrix approach (RMA), as well as its usual modifications, and explained the fundamental principles of risk as the research foundation [5]. Gul and Ganeri surveyed the inadequacies of a precise risk score computation and reduced decision-making inconsistency; a fuzzy methodology is provided in this research that allows experts to utilize linguistic variables for assessing two aspects that are the parameters of the matrix method [6]. Popov et al. surveyed the coverage of Google Scholar, Scopus, and the Web of Science's three main bibliometric databases, which will be systematically and thoroughly compared. We thus offer a longitudinal and eclectic collation of the three databases based on a sample of 146 prominent academics from five major subject fields [7]. Schwarz et al. surveyed the assessment of situations that had previously been discovered with process hazard analysis (PHA) tools like HAZOP, and semiquantitative risk analysis (SQRA) methods like LOPA were created. With obstacles stopping the chain of occurrences from spreading to the end of the accident, these SQRA tools describe a scenario as a series of events. Frequencies, failure rates, and effects are expressed in orders of magnitude [8]. Korombel et al.'s survey is based on the distinguishing characteristics of several qualitative and quantitative methodologies for evaluating the risks of actual investment projects. In order to make it easier to choose the most practical method for a certain project, the article analyzes a few of the current risk assessment techniques in terms of their application's benefits and drawbacks [9]. The Swedish Geotechnical Society surveyed that in order to cut the expenses associated with unfavorable outcomes of geotechnical risks, the society has established a standard framework for risk management in geotechnical engineering projects [10]. An effective tool for analyzing, ranking, and defining priorities in risk management is the risk assessment matrix. According to the ISO 31000 risk management framework, this article provides an overview of the important factors, benefits, drawbacks, strengths, and limitations of this instrument [11].

They looked at a real-world public health case because it gave us risk data from our own experiences that we could use to judge the real-world ramifications of the published worry that risk matrices would provide forecasts that were worse than random. By creating a risk assessment matrix with a public health risk scenario – the risk of contaminated blood transfusion infection – that presents a negative connection between damage frequency and severity, they investigated this projected concern [12]. Kaya et al. surveyed the usage of risk matrices in a profound medical domain in England, and the instructions for using them are examined in this study. The document analysis of the warning assessment procedures, methods, and techniques employed in English hospitals examines the relevance of critiques of risk matrices from outside of healthcare. The results show that there are many different risk matrices in use, some of which may be more likely to prioritize risks incorrectly due to their design [13]. They surveyed that the fast growth of information technologies has led to an increase in risk and security problems, which now affect all organizations regardless of size. Managers must adopt techniques for assessing and managing risk as part of a carefully thought-out process in order to get the desired results [14]. This case emphasizes risk factors associated with unfavorable incidents where cutting-edge technical solutions do not perform as intended [15]. Will Maimaris et al. examine how capital and topographical medical domain system structures affect hypertension awareness, treatment, and control in this systematic review (a study that employs established criteria to find all the literature on a specific issue). The introduction of financial incentives to healthcare professionals for the diagnosis and treatment of hypertension and the expansion of insurance coverage in nations like the US, where mankind is reimbursed for healthcare through security policies and other measures, could all have an impact on hypertension care at this level of medical domain paradigms [16]. Chiozza et al.'s surveys on productive impersonal peril supervision should be encouraged and constantly enhanced within the framework of clinical governance. It should be included in all medical domains and workers' daily routines rather than being seen as a distinct task. To create a patient-centered and guarded structure, effective interdisciplinary collaboration is necessary, as is a willingness to consider mistakes and learn from them [17]. Oliver Kessler et al. described a theoretical model that was used to describe the level at which CRM elements have been implemented within the organization [18].

6.3 Constituents of Risk Monitoring in Healthcare

In summation to the circumstances of any structure for tracking, a monitoring system concentrates on medical valuation as well as healthcare, which have several prerequisites, which include appropriate exploration questions, closely related social groups to compare, appropriate health indicators and their determinants, appropriate estimates of the differences in those indicators between the various social groups, and a systematic procedure for illuminating and implementing the appropriate results.

Figure 6.2 schematically depicts several strategies in a continuous process to draw attention to numerous critical challenges unique to covering medical valuation.

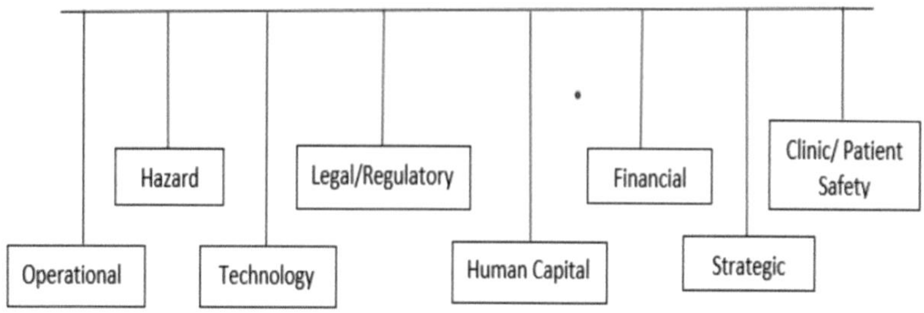

Figure 6.2 Eight risk domains of risk monitoring.

Finding the knowledge in the first place is a crucial challenge that will only produce lesser equity. It is technically proven that in order to achieve fairness, one must swim against the current of dominant intensities, which may be detected as driven by sweat, to distribute society's rewards further indifferently. Therefore, to bring social change among different social groups, information must be placed within an environment that is conscious of the forces and crucial performers. Lawmakers should guard to be told, and this frequently requires not only trying to move leaders but also cranking the proletariat community to produce and preserve a constant force on ministers to pursue their target. In this regard, participatory exploration techniques may be very beneficial since they not only produce previously unattainable information, such as community perceptions of unmet health or healthcare, by not just meeting their needs but also giving them a stake in solving the issues, and proletariat organizations may be more inclined to continue applying pressure to leaders for as long as is required. The picture also clearly shows how addressing equality is an ongoing, circular process that connects information collecting and analysis with espousal and gesture for change.

6.3.1 Identify risk

Since threat monitoring involves supervising queries and new threats that constantly arise, it is challenging to face all the pitfalls a healthcare reality has to face. Still, through the use of institutional and diligent knowledge and by engaging everyone – cases, workers, directors, and payers – healthcare danger directors can spot traps and potentially disastrous situations that would be difficult to foresee otherwise.

6.3.2 Estimated and rank risk

Once connected, it is simple to rate, rank, and prioritize hazards based on their prospect of occurring and the effect that will have on the situation. On the basis of these metrics, more funds are distributed, and duties are assigned. Colorful maps and threat matrices, which may be used to negotiate this and detect potential dangers as well as to develop communication and cooperative decision-making, are also recommended to investigate and report sentinel information.

6.3.3 Events

According to the Joint Commission, sentinel events are "any unexpected event in a health care setting resulting in death or serious physical or cerebral injury to a case or cases, not related to the natural course of the case's illness." Case safety issues are addressed incontinently through quick response and thorough disquisition admits guard events to reduce the unborn threat. Staff response and clarity can be measured by establishing a plan to enable the estimation and enforcement of remedial behavior. Lookout incidents do not necessarily arise from sins and vices. Healthcare associations may still create an environment of esteem, faith, and collaboration between employees and leadership by establishing transparency and rigorous evaluation.

6.3.4 Submit conformance reports

As stipulated in the Joint Commission agreement, guard occurrences, drug offenses, and faults with medical equipment must all be reported to confederate, situations, and other tracking organizations. In order to protect sensitive information, incidents like wrong-point or ambulatory enucleation, factory bruises, antidote offenses, etc., must be proven, enciphered, and reported.

6.3.5 Apprehend close-by overlook, catchings and learn from them

"Close-by Overlooks" and "good catches" often occur when mistakes or guard occurrences are prevented by luck or divine intervention. These are generally the fashionable techniques to detect and assist with impending hazard elements. In order to implement prevention measures and fashionable practices, professionals should create a culture that promotes reporting and admitting. Consider going beyond the outrageous to find ineffective failures. Active failures are flagrant and closely related, such as when a nanny administers the incorrect medication to treat a case. Conversely, idle faults are typically concealed and can only be found via analysis and close inspection. The colorful source of negative events and situations is examined and documented while taking into account the first and less immediately evident causes.

6.3.6 Implement tried and true incident analysis models investigation

To comprehend revealed failures and reasons, as well as linkages among difficult elements, models created for analyzing accidents are applied. For instance, inadequate personnel, discomfort, and exhaustion can result in serious medical crimes. The application of well-designed models improves the functioning and efficacy of threats. The Sharp and Blunt End Evaluation of Clinical Crimes models are two misfortune survey replicas used in medical domain warning operations. In order to aid in identifying the causes and products of medical errors, failure mode and goods analysis are stationed in entail detailed textiles.

6.3.7 Infuse in an acknowledged ultimatum potency

RMIS requirements for information systems are also encouraging vibrant channels for reporting and mitigating problems. With the help of these technologies, you may establish guard situations, track threats, submit a film, benchmark data points, and enhance assiduity in comparison. Reports can be produced for a variety of reasons, including losses, events, open claims, and missed time from work due to injuries, to mention a few. RMIS can significantly improve threat operating systems by optimizing their performance through readily available and reliable systems and providing overall cost savings through the automation of repetitive chores.

6.3.8 To capture the appropriate ratio of threat backing and transfer retention

Risk management refers to a company's methods for swiftly and successfully tracking the backing loss brought on by dangers. Threat retention and insurance programs, such as tone insurance and internal insurance, are the pathways via which threats are transferred.

6.3.9 Recognition factors

These factors include monitoring the dangerous elements that affect the ways in which organizations operate and their resources, as well as any individuals or other affiliations that they may have. To guarantee that the data required to create credible, threat-based judgments remains available throughout time, organizations continuously assess threat elements of relevance. Monitoring the numerous threat factors (such as problematic origin and problematic happenings, erratic and preparing circumstances, antagonist potential and intent, and targeting of organizational operations, means, or individualities) can provide crucial information on changing conditions that may have an impact on an association's ability to carry out its core operations and business functions. Threat assessments can be updated on a regular basis according to the suitable incidence that is intended to be applicable using information omitted from the continuing monitoring of threat variables. The absolute goal is to maintain constant evidential awareness of the legislative leadership paradigm, organizational conditioning, charge/business procedures, statistics paradigm, and operating environments, and, thus, to be aware of all threat factors that might influence the threat that associations are experiencing. As a result, associations take into account the role threat factors play in the execution of the threat response plan while petitioning the warning analysis habitats or warning factors (i.e., range, motive, theoretic, limitations, threat forbearance, precedents, and trade-offs). For instance, it is anticipated that the reliability viewpoint of the statistics paradigm (i.e., the peril elements uniform within that paradigm) will typically only reflect the relevant portion of the organizational risk response, with actions taken at the organizational level or in relation to the mission/business process providing the majority of that response.

In some cases, more than monitoring alone is needed to offer enough information about the reliability viewpoint of the statistics paradigm to assess the entire risk that organizations are taking. One may anticipate that highly competent, fully furnished, and inspired peril origin will compete with the widely used defense strategies (e.g., circumventing or manipulating such structure).

6.3.10 Simplified menace analysis

This entails expediting the peril computation process utilizing the findings from continual threat factor monitoring. Threat assessments are simplified in the right situations at the right frequency. Similar judgments usually take into consideration, for instance, the present level of threat to and the importance of fundamental organizational and operational business functions. Associations must reevaluate the goal, compass, hypotheticals, and restrictions of the assessment in order to decide whether or not all tasks in the danger assessment process are relevant.

6.3.11 Specialized enterprises

The intricacy of a specialized role requires gathering, analyzing, presenting, and interpreting the data that must be taken into consideration when creating any protection planning, with the training and skills of the original labor force executing all these duties. A theoretically perfect strategy will not be useful for covering if people who must use it cannot maintain it over time. This problem affects everyone, but it is especially severe in nations with few resources since there are not nearly enough qualified specialists. Resource-poor countries also face constraints in terms of the structure for the collection of information, including the total costs of both the original purchase and the ongoing conservation of needful outfits and technology. Despite these constraints, it is likely far and wide, indeed in the poorest country with the least coffers, to do much further with data and coffers than is presently being done. They are geared particularly to the requirements of experimenters in resource-poor countries. To gear up the requirements of experimenters in resource-poor countries, a 1998 publication by the WHO describes online vacuity and provides practical suggestions regarding data for sources and pointers for covering health equity. The publication suggests a real, grounded illustration of using the data sources, similar to the demographic and health checks and living norms measure study, which is conducted in numerous lesser developed nations. These numerous checks can be used to assess trends over time in a range of pointers of equity in maternal and child health as well as healthcare. Injuries in healthcare delivery and some equity needles can also be proved by simple ways, similar to exit interviews at health installations that have been in place only a time or so. The equity hand experience should soon give a rich and creative illustration of an approach for covering necessary health equity in resource-poor settings, including strategies to modify the checks and structure.

6.4 Strategic Risk Monitoring Plan

Healthcare organizations must have a risk management plan that is both set and ongoing. The association's strategy for identifying, managing, and mitigating danger is outlined in the threat monitoring plan. Pharmaceutical inferiority and all division heads should be afraid of and involved in the creation and continuing assessment of the plan. Plans for medical domain warning protection express the confederation threat operation methodology's goals, compass, and purpose. They also describe the duties and positions held by the employees involved in threat reduction and peril administration. The structure of a risk monitoring plan varies by association and is determined by the study of real data, real being systems, and the specifics of each medical domain materiality. However, all medical domain hazard monitoring strategies should have the following abecedarian components.

6.4.1 Instruction and tutelage

Risk monitoring plans should specify the circumstances for hand training, which should include first exposure to hands, continuous and in-service training, periodic reviews and department testimony, and episode-determined training.

6.4.2 Occurrence and descent complaints

The peril tracking goal should outline procedures for developing and reacting to occurrence and descent complaints to increase patient satisfaction and lower liability of action. Response times, employee responsibilities, and expected behavior must be clearly stated and conveyed.

6.4.3 Goals, aspirations, and criterion

The aim and dominance of the medical domain peril observation should be clearly defined in risk monitoring plans. It is important to clearly state your goals for lowering responsibility state, protecting incidents and close calls, and the total cost of the department testimony. Also, the strategy should be explicit and mandate, announcing on perceptible and practical facts.

6.4.4 A transmission strategy

While the medical domain peril must observe aims to encourage honest and open communication, details on how and with whom to do so should be included in the healthcare peril observation aim. It is important to demonstrate the coming method and follow-up conditioning. The strategy must explicitly state how the compartment and the C-suite workforce should report. The strategy should also encourage a blame-free environment and support anonymous reporting.

6.4.5 Contingency proposal

Peril observes that the strategy must include backup plans for unfavorable systematic malfunctions and devastating events like crashing longitudinal health records, safety violations, and malware. The strategy must also contain emergency readiness for repercussions such as symptom breakouts, prolonged potential outages, violent storms, or large-scale explosions.

6.4.6 Chronicling guidelines

Every medical domain interconnection needs a rapid and user-friendly method for identifying, categorizing, and monitoring potential hazards and negative events. These structures must also have mandatory communication processes.

6.4.7 Reaction and alleviation

Aims for peril to the medical domain structure must also include collaborative mechanisms for reacting to reported hiccups and incidents, such as acute reaction, research, communication, and recurrent negligence prevention.

The medical domain ultimatum observing scheme must be a live document that is continually improved and simplified based on current statistics, emerging pitfalls, assignments learned, and substitutes in the medical domain and drug use. When these updates and modifications are made, the plan should incorporate provisions for connections and preparation [19].

6.5 Standardization to Risk Management in Healthcare

By integrating and organizing draft, warning, and wither working techniques, our methodology makes it feasible for them to contribute to a systemic study of threat, which is not achievable when they are used in silos. It is crucial to emphasize that while a design is transient and one-of-a-kind and a process is typically continuing and repetitive, both have underlying structures. The preparation will be focused on the proper case-by-case delivery of care in the context of healthcare processes. Because a design and a process are structurally similar, we may use design operation techniques to discuss danger in medical domain procedures. In addition, many cross-functional systems, like those involved in innovation, are present in the processes of providing healthcare. Additionally, the methodology's fourth phase uses failure modes and goods analysis (FMEA), an HRA approach that has, by far, been most widely embraced in the healthcare industry in recent years. It has been used in a variety of industries, including lowering the risk associated with blood transmission, hypodermic pharmaceutical transmissions, streamlining medication delivery systems, and hospital medicine customs. Additionally, the Joint Commission on Accreditation of Health Care Organizations and the Healthcare Assiduity has recently promoted FMEA as a technique for lowering the risk of instances [20]. A full explanation of each phase of the established approach is provided in the accompanying Figure 6.3.

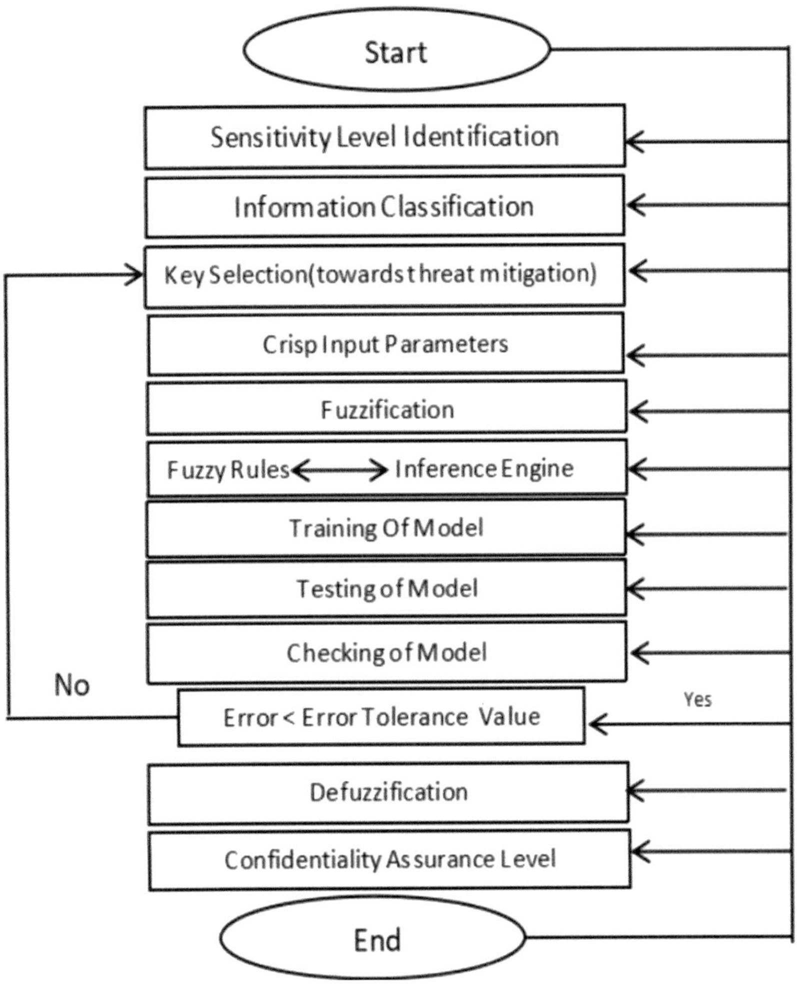

Figure 6.3 Schematic flowchart of methodology in risk management.

6.5.1 Environmental survey

The environmental survey is intended to help people choose and get familiar with important healthcare procedures. Additionally, this is the time when the colorful characters in charge of the procedure in question join the team working on the analysis. The working platoon gains its first understanding of process conditioning and related overflows of quantitative data, clinical information, and organizational information. This serves as the foundation for the recognition of desperation, which is explored further via rosters and interviews, two of the classic procedures used in threat identification. Rosters may be intentionally used in tone-evaluation procedures and reviews as a technique to keep track of the assignments learned from previous events. Conversely, when it is not feasible to gather the working platoon together for danger identification sessions, interviews are routinely employed in their place. They are often held in a private setting where the participant is encouraged to share his views honestly and fearless criticism or retaliation [20].

6.5.2 Charting an operation

In this alternative stage of the technique, common tools for designing threat operations are used to acquire a more detailed explanation of the state of the solo procedure, including the recognition of the players responsible for them. The procedure is broken down into steps, which are further dissected and transformed into constraints until an acceptable level of detail is attained. The effort failure construction may be utilized to negotiate this assignment efficiently. The labor failure construction is the source of the tree structure that makes up the effort failure construction. However, it is more concerned with processes than products. Abecedarian process conditioning is present in the effort failure construction's smallest location. The labor failure construction and the effort failure construction do, however, justify the time dimension because they were created in a design planning setting. Consequently, this has been included in the suggested technique by using process inflow maps. By using precedence linkages, flow maps enable the detection of conditioning in the smallest ABS position in accordance with a logical time sequence. Additionally, conditioning may be physically positioned inside a matrix structure in an inflow map, where vertical lanes correspond to various process stages and square paths to the performer that executes control. The term "cross-functional inflow map" refers to this structure [20].

6.5.3 Threat recognition and evaluation

The final stage of the suggested method involves comprehending the analyzed procedures and then spotting related dangers once more with the aid of a diagram-perfect functioning instrument. The peril failure form, which is a source-aware grouping of diagram flaws that organizes and specifies the overall danger exposure of the design, is used to link threat sources in the first place. Each pitching location offers a discussion of potential threats to the design in a less detailed manner. The current technique bases the determination of the peril failure form circumstances on the mastery of the operation under consideration acquired during the initial two-way communication, environment survey, and charting of a map, as well as on the experience of the working platoon members. The number of scenarios should be chosen to ensure that the peril failure form is both comprehensive – including all potential danger sources – and simple to comprehend and apply to avoid mistakes. Threat sources are split into interior and exterior remains by a first generic bracket. The danger origin in the earliest class can be effectively avoided and controlled, but those in the second class are beyond the control of the process actors and can only be avoided, for example, by changing conditioning where they can. Interior danger sources are very important since they can be managed [21].

6.6 Implementation in Medicare Pharmacy

The application of the created methodology to medication functioning procedure at a sanatorium pharmacy department is explained to show how it should be applied to assess health processes.

Figure 6.4 illustrates the system factors contributing to the adverse events that took place in a hospital system.

This case was named since medicine and other medium operations are some of the most interdisciplinary procedures taking place in a sanatorium. In fact, it involves numerous conditionings carried out by many divisions, including central drugstores and functioning apartments, starting from when accounts are purchased from vendors before being used to treat patients. As a result, the way similar processes are exhaustively managed tells us a lot about efficacy and productiveness. Some authors proved that a significant amount of a sanitarium's overall expenditures go toward planning and documenting [22]. Also, adverse events due to invalid medicine authority (adverse medicine events) are frequent sources of harm in patients receiving

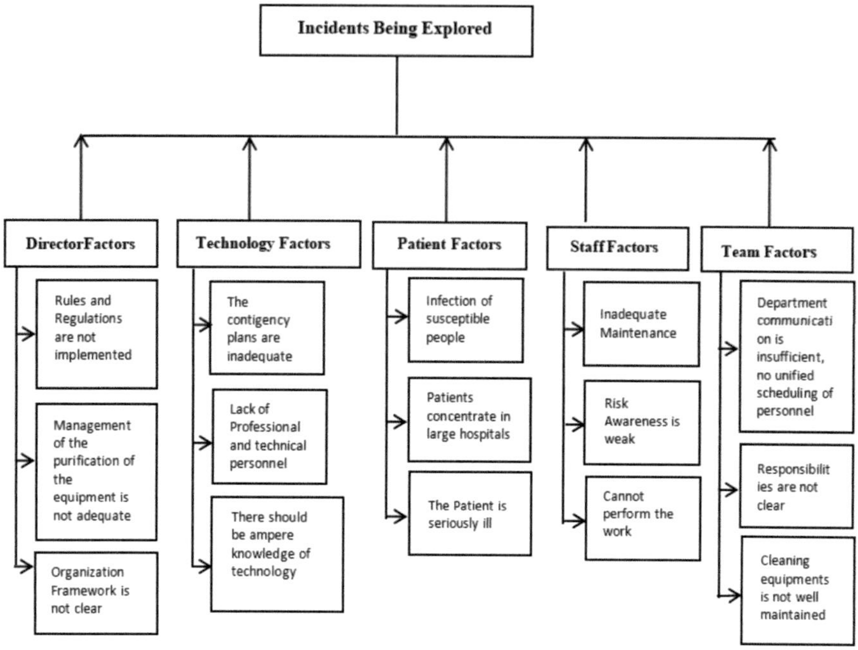

Figure 6.4 Risk management in a hospital operating system.

rehabilitation, and they can start at any point throughout a medical procedure. Since adverse occurrences that occur later in the medication functionality procedure may have their origins in this hub of hospital equipment, we decided to examine the planning procedure of a pharmacy department. In this case study, a 1372-bed teaching hospital in Torino is the subject (Italy). With a total area of 14 dispensaries and 5822 employees, including 1030 croakers and 2063 nurses, it is the largest and oldest functioning sanitarium in the city and Piedmont Region of Italy. In terms of organizational overflows, this hospital is among the most complicated in Italy. In order to relate potential sources of threat for cases and understand failure modes and waste, the functionality of the advanced dispensary warning paradigm approach was specifically designed to examine the medical staff that the central pharmacy sends to the hospital wards. This was done in order to encourage development in the place of amenity generally.

The following procedure can be used to implement threat operations in a hospital pharmacy department. Recognizing the difficulty in finding the hidden traps that might impact the functionality of the pharmacy department is the first step. This may be accomplished through creative approaches such as performing a difficult judgment, looking back at previous occurrences and crimes, and getting input from workers and shareholders. Alcoholism, overdose reactions, a lack of available medications, and non-recommendatory adherence problems are just a few of the usual difficulties in the sanitarium pharmacy sector. Examine the dangers. The next phase is to evaluate the responsibility and effect of each hazard after the potential difficulties have been connected. This process aids in sorting out potential problems and identifying which bones require necessary treatment. For instance, a medicine mistake that might seriously harm an occurrence is a high-ultimatum situation that has to be addressed right now. Avoid the hazards. Applying actions to mitigate or reduce the legal responsibility and effect of associated hazards is the next step after identifying the potential problems. This process entails creating policies and procedures, educating employees, and implementing technical outcomes. As an example, using a barcode drug administration system can assist in lessening the legal consequences of drug offenses. Explain the dangers. The last stage is to handle the hazards in order to make sure that the jurisdiction procedures are successful and that any new difficulties are immediately connected and resolved. This stage entails continuing to keep an eye out for any problems, doing routine inspections and analysis, and getting input from shareholders and personnel [23, 24].

6.7 Future Scope

The following items are anticipated to be added to the future scope of the risk monitoring plan for the security and integrity of healthcare data.

6.7.1 Real-time monitoring

Risk monitoring used to be done often, like once every month or once every three months. However, the rising volume and velocity of healthcare data are making it more crucial to monitor data in real time. This will make it possible to identify threats and weaknesses more quickly and help guarantee that data is constantly protected.

6.7.2 Automated monitoring

Manual risk monitoring takes a lot of time and is prone to mistakes. Risk monitoring is anticipated to become more automated in the future. As a result, monitoring will be more effective and efficient, and human resources will be freed up to work on other projects.

6.7.3 Intelligent monitoring

Traditional risk management techniques frequently rely on fixed rules. However, risk monitoring is likely to get smarter in the future. This implies that it will be able to draw lessons from the past and recognize fresh dangers and weaknesses.

6.7.4 Collaborative monitoring

More and more healthcare organizations are exchanging data, which indicates that a team-based approach to risk monitoring is crucial. This will enable businesses to exchange information about threats and weaknesses and help ensure that data is safeguarded across various businesses [25].

6.7.5 Risk-based approach

Risk monitoring has frequently concentrated on a particular hazard or vulnerability in the past. However, it is expected to become more risk-based in the future. This means that it will concentrate on locating and minimizing the biggest threats to data confidentiality and integrity.

Broadening the scope of a risk monitoring plan can help healthcare organizations protect their data from unauthorized access, modification, or destruction. This will allow them to continue to deliver high-quality care while protecting the privacy of their patients.

6.7.6 Artificial intelligence (AI)

AI may be used to learn from the past, discover new dangers and weaknesses, and automate risk monitoring duties.

6.7.7 Machine learning

Algorithms that can recognize patterns in data and spot abnormalities that can point to a security threat can be developed using machine learning.

6.7.8 Blockchain

Healthcare data transfers can be recorded in a safe and impenetrable ledger using blockchain technology. This can help to safeguard the integrity of the data and prevent unauthorized access to it.

6.7.9 Cloud computing

Healthcare data can be processed and stored in the cloud in a safe and scalable setting. This can make risk monitoring less expensive and more effective.

Risk monitoring for medical data has a promising future. Healthcare organizations can contribute to the protection of their data against unauthorized access, modification, or destruction by implementing innovative technologies and methods. By doing this, healthcare organizations will be able to continue to deliver high-quality care while still protecting the privacy of their patients.

6.8 Conclusion

This essay offers a theoretical framework to direct the creation of strategies for addressing fairness in healthcare and health. Information can be a crucial component, even if it is not enough to achieve reduced health inequalities. Less privileged groups must be given careful consideration as we work toward more fairness, while the more significant category is likely to push back against comparable efforts. Scientifically accurate knowledge of health equity and specialized tactics for addressing equity must be included in a larger plan to confront the political barriers in order to overcome this opposition. When trying to gather, analyze, and disseminate information on equity, one needs to think about where, how, and who to include in order to intervene as effectively as possible against prevailing pressures. Positively, even though achieving less health fairness implies enormous obstacles, these obstacles will probably be less severe than if parity in money were the main goal because most cultures show far less tolerance for differences in health than in income. The unique difficulties in addressing health equality can be demoralizing, especially in light of the scarcity of population-based data sources that provide accurate data on socioeconomic groups and health recommendations that are most relevant in a particular context. While improved information and manner are required to address equality, more may be accomplished with existing data and straightforward styles in almost every nation – even the poorest countries with the most restricted data. This is provided that we have a clear understanding of what we want to address and why. Although tracking the medical domain is a technical endeavor, its elementary paragon is motivated by moral principles of distributive fairness and the pursuit of mortal rights, such as the right to health and non-discrimination.

References

[1] Rizwan M. et al., "Risk monitoring strategy for confidentiality of healthcare information," Computers and Electrical Engineering, vol. 100, p. 107833, May 2022, https://doi.org/10.1016/j.compeleceng.2022.107833.

[2] M. Sen, K. Sharma, S. Mishra, A. Alkhayyat and V. Sharma, "Designing a Smart and Intelligent Ecosystem for Autistic Children," 2023 4th International Conference on Intelligent Engineering and Management (ICIEM), London, United Kingdom, 2023, pp. 1-5, doi: 10.1109/ICIEM59379.2023.10166057.

[3] Braveman PA. Monitoring equity in health and healthcare: a conceptual framework. J Health Popul Nutr. 2003 Sep;21(3):181-92. PMID: 14717564.

[4] Arimbi, H.B., Puspasari, M.A., & Syaifullah, D.H. (2019). Hazard identification, risk assessment and risk control in a woodworking company. IOP Conference Series: Materials Science and Engineering, 505.

[5] Ni, H., Chen, A., & Chen, N. (2010). Some extensions on risk matrix approach. Safety Science, 48, 1269-1278.

[6] Gul, M., Ak, M.F., & Guneri, A.F. (2017). Occupational health and safety risk assessment in hospitals: A case study using two-stage fuzzy multi-criteria approach. Human and Ecological Risk Assessment: An International Journal, 23, 187 - 202.

[7] Popov, G., Lyon, B.K. & Hollcroft, B. (2016). Risk assessment: A practical guide to assessing operational risks. Hoboken, NJ: John Wiley & Sons.

[8] Schwarz, H., Koerts, T.T., & Hoercher, U.D. (2019). Semiquantitative Risk Analysis.An EPSC Working Group. Chemical engineering transactions, 77, 37-42.

[9] Korombel A, Tworek P. Qualitative risk analysis as a stage of risk management in investment projects: advantages and disadvantages of selected methods-theoretical approach. AD ALTA J Interdisciplinary Res. 2011;1(2):51–54.

[10] Spross J, Olsson L, Stille H (2018a) The Swedish Geotechnical Society's methodology for risk management: a tool for engineers in their everyday work. Georisk 12:183–189. https://doi.org/10.1080/17499518.2017.1416643.

[11] Strametz R. Requirements on clinical risk management systems in hospitals; 2017. Available from https://www.aps-ev.de/wp-content/uploads/2017/03/Clinical-Risk-Management-Systems-1.pdf. Accessed January 10, 2020. doi:10.21960/201707/E

[12] Vatanpour, S., Hrudey, S.E., & Dinu, I. (2015). Can Public Health Risk Assessment Using Risk Matrices Be Misleading? International Journal of Environmental Research and Public Health, 12, 9575 - 9588.

[13] Kaya GK, Ward J, Clarkson J. A Review of Risk Matrices Used in Acute Hospitals in England. Risk Anal. 2019 May;39(5):1060-1070. doi: 10.1111/risa.13221. Epub 2018 Nov 5. PMID: 30395689.

[14] Ramona, S.E. (2011). Advantages and Disadvantages of Quantitative and Qualitative Information Risk Approaches.

[15] D. Mehta, P. P. Das, S. Ghosh, S. Mishra, A. Alkhayyat and V. Sharma, "A Normalized ANN Model for Earthquake Estimation," 2023 2nd International Conference on Applied Artificial Intelligence and Computing (ICAAIC), Salem, India, 2023, pp. 151-155, doi:10.1109/ICAAIC56838.2023.10140242.

[16] Maimaris W, Paty J, Perel P, Legido-Quigley H, Balabanova D, Nieuwlaat R, McKee M. The influence of health systems on hypertension awareness, treatment, and control: a systematic literature review. PLoS Med. 2013;10(7):e1001490. doi: 10.1371/journal.pmed.1001490. Epub 2013 Jul 30. PMID: 23935461; PMCID: PMC3728036.

[17] Chiozza ML, Plebani M. Clinical Governance: from clinical risk management to continuous quality improvement. Clin Chem Lab Med. 2006;44(6):694-8. doi: 10.1515/CCLM.2006.127. PMID: 16729855.

[18] Briner M, Kessler O, Pfeiffer Y, Wehner T, Manser T. Assessing hospitals' clinical risk management: Development of a monitoring instrument. BMC Health Serv Res. 2010 Dec 13;10:337. doi: 10.1186/1472-6963-10-337. PMID: 21144039; PMCID: PMC3022874.

[19] M. Sen, K. Sharma, S. Mishra, A. Alkhayyat and V. Sharma, "Designing a Smart and Intelligent Ecosystem for Autistic Children," 2023 4th International Conference on Intelligent Engineering and Management (ICIEM), London, United Kingdom, 2023, pp. 1-5, doi: 10.1109/ICIEM59379.2023.10166057.

[20] Cagliano, A.C., Grimaldi, S., & Rafele, C. (2011). A systemic methodology for risk management in the healthcare sector. Safety Science, 49, 695-708.

[21] A. Srivastava, S. Samanta, S. Mishra, A. Alkhayyat, D. Gupta and V. Sharma, "Medi-Assist: A Decision Tree based Chronic Diseases Detection Model," 2023 4th International Conference on Intelligent Engineering and Management (ICIEM), London, United Kingdom, 2023, pp. 1-7, doi: 10.1109/ICIEM59379.2023.10167400.

[22] S. Mohanty, A. Behera, S. Mishra, A. Alkhayyat, D. Gupta and V. Sharma, "Resumate: A Prototype to Enhance Recruitment Process with NLP based Resume Parsing," 2023 4th International Conference on Intelligent Engineering and Management (ICIEM), London, United Kingdom, 2023, pp. 1-6, doi: 10.1109/ICIEM59379.2023.10166169.

[23] Swain, T., & Mishra, S. (2022, November). Evolution Of Machine Learning Algorithms For Enhancement Of Self-Driving Vehicles Security. In 2022 International Conference on Advancements in Smart, Secure and Intelligent Computing (ASSIC) (pp. 1-5). IEEE.

[24] Singh, A. K., & Patro, B. D. K. (2020). Elliptic curve signcryption based security protocol for RFID. KSII Transactions on Internet and Information Systems (TIIS), 14(1), 344-365.

[25] Mishra, N., Mishra, S., Tripathy, H.K. (2022). Rice Yield Estimation Using Deep Learning. In: Panda, M., et al. Innovations in Intelligent Computing and Communication. ICIICC 2022. Communications in Computer and Information Science, vol 1737. Springer, Cham. https://doi.org/10.1007/978-3-031-23233-6_28

7

Arduino-based Women's Safety Smart Device for Internet of Medical Things

Shweta Singh[1], Aditya Bhardwaj[2], Arun Kumar Tripathi[1], and Umesh Gupta[2,*]

[1]Department of Computer Applications, KIET Group of Institutions, India
[2]School of Computer Science Engineering and Technology, Bennett University, Gr.Noida, India-201310
E-mail: shweta.vidudi272@gmail.com; aditya.bhardwaj@bennett.edu.in; mailtoaruntripathi@gmail.com; er.umesh.gupta@gmail.com
*Corresponding Author

Abstract

Women's safety is a major societal problem, whether in rural or urban areas. Crimes against women have been in an alarming situation all this while. Changing the mindset of an individual is always a difficult task to accomplish, but we can provide ways to safeguard women from other perspectives. Various electrical and electronic devices android-based applications have been proposed earlier to protect women. Still, it is necessary to have more acceptable technology to cope with the current situation of women. In this study, we proposed an Arduino-based women's safety device for the Internet of Medical Things (IoMT) environment. The proposed device works based on functionality initiated through the panic button. In this, the user can begin an emergency message along with proof of the incident from the surroundings. The members from the pre-specified group will be sent an emergency message based on the seriousness of the situation, along with the database. The proposed device will provide safety features to women. Also, the device will help women maintain the evidence for the future since the proposed device will provide more aspects of women's safety and security.

DOI: 10.1201/9788770047395-7

The proposed invention will help women and females maintain their dignity and strengthen their inner souls to tackle various situations.

Keywords: Violence against women, women's safety, Internet of Medical Things (IoMT), Arduino, GSM, GPS module.

7.1 Introduction

Women have seen symbols of love, purity, and sacrifice. Hence, when a woman is happy and honored, society rises with peace and prosperity. People all around the world worship the goddesses bowing down. In the same house, many raise their hand at the actual goddess of their home. Crime against women is a crime against humanity. Violence against women (VAW) is increasing these days, and it [1] is understood as a violation of human rights. The VAW is a form of discrimination against women and shall mean all acts of gender-based violence [2]. This violence is likely to result in physical and psychological suffering for women. VAW is one of the crucial social mechanisms by which women are forced into subordinate positions compared to men.

VAW is usually perpetrated from two perspectives, i.e., by individuals and the community. VAW individuals will include domestic violence, traditional practices such as dowry violence, etc. VAW perpetrated by the community can consist of sexual violence, violence by authoritative personnel, etc. As per the reports maintained by the National Crime Record Bureau (NCRB) [3], it is found that approximately 63% [3, 4] of the total crimes in India are related to crimes against women. Further, NCRB has also reported that crime against women has increased to 4% since 2017. With the gradual increase in crimes or violence worldwide, women are the victims of many crimes. These crimes mainly include physical, sexual, psychological, and economic harm and suffering. Statistics of crime against women in India are shown in Figure 7.1. Thus, it threatens women's lives, which may result in coercion or arbitrary deprivation of liberty and the deepest levels of depression. Further, according to the NCB report [5], crimes against women are expected to increase.

Figure 7.1 describes the statistics collected through the NCRB in 2019 of crimes committed against women. The statistics show that crime against women has been increasing over the years, an alarming situation. Furthermore, crimes can grow gradually in the coming years, from 2017 to date. As depicted in Figure 7.1, it is inferred that the crimes committed by relatives

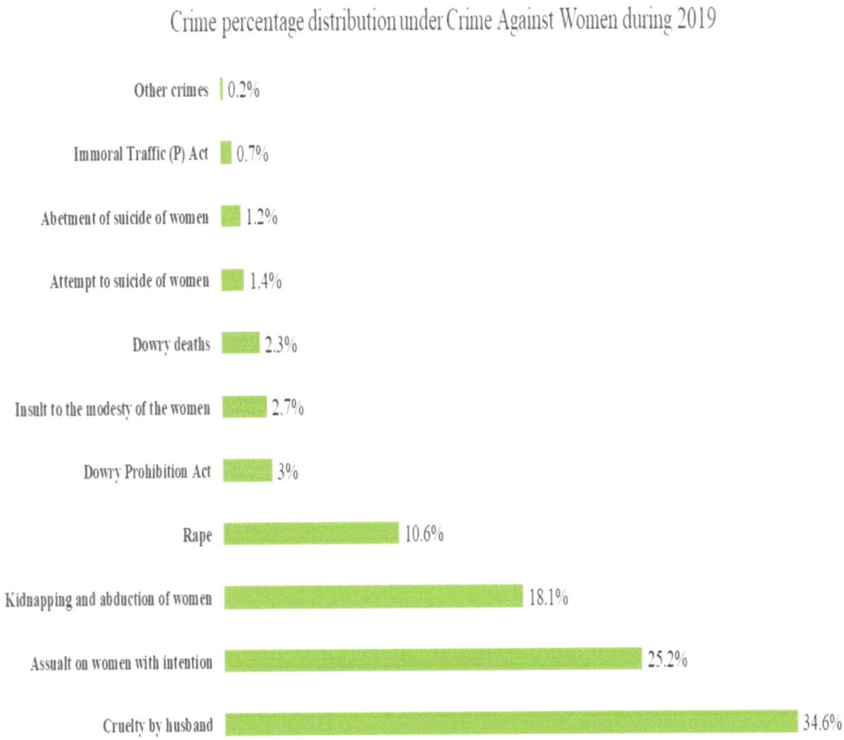

Figure 7.1 Statistics of crime against women in India [5].

and known women are 34.6%. Hence, there is a need for smart devices to ensure women's safety and security against violence in their lives.

IoMT [4] is one of the most vital forms of technology nowadays. For IoT, everything is to be connected and controlled via the internet. Thus, the day-to-day tasks can be performed efficiently. In existing studies [6], the authors proposed an IoMT-fog-cloud-based healthcare system to address the issue of COVID-19 outspread. Some studies [7, 9–10] also suggested that IoT-enabled hardware devices provide security for women. These studies provide a solution for the environment where women can be susceptible to crime. However, the solution proposed in these existing studies needs to consider evidence collection for the future, working with voice input, etc. To address these issues, we proposed an Arduino-based women's safety device for an IoMT-enabled environment in this chapter. Our proposed model will help provide security to all women across the globe who feel insecure moving out of any place. The main contributions of this study are summarized as follows:

- We explored security challenges regarding women's safety in the IoMT environment.
- She proposed an Arduino-based IoMT-enabled women's safety device.
- We conducted an experimental setup to identify and analyze the components used for Arduino-based IoMT-enabled women's safety devices.

The remainder of this chapter is organized as follows. Section 7.2 presents a state-of-the-art, existing, relevant related work. The proposed model for Arduino-based women's safety devices in the IoMT environment and its methodology are discussed in Section 7.3. Section 7.4 presents the comparison of the proposed approach with the existing solutions. Finally, research issues and challenges, followed by concluding remarks, are presented in Section 7.5.

7.2 Related Work

Regarding the gradual increase in violence cases against women, various refined and consistent technological gears have already been introduced. Several options are still available that help provide ways to attain safety and security. Various equipment have already been introduced to the market, each with some integrated feature. An essential factor to consider in this scenario is building up security and safety for an individual. With this, women can perform their day-to-day tasks efficiently without any fear in their minds.

For women's safety devices, various technologies-based solutions exist in the literature with a set of features such as triggering emergency calls [7] or messages [7–10], GSM facility [7–10], Wi-Fi [8], etc. Some of these existing solutions are explained in the following.

Venkatesh et al. [7] proposed a prototype regarding women's safety. Their prototype comprises a buzzer, LCD screen, touch sensor, Bluetooth and GPS, and GSM modules. The device works along with the user's Android phone. The device is supposed to be connected to the Android device to initiate emergency messages for the known user. The device can trigger an emergency alarm in the form of a buzzer so that people around the woman can come to the rescue. This prototype fails to collect evidence for future reference, and it does not trigger an emergency message to the government helplines.

Reddy et al. [8] proposed an automatic device focusing on women's safety. The device comprises a vibration sensor, camera, and pulse rate sensor.

It usually activates based on the threshold received via the pulse rate sensor and vibration sensor. The device can collect evidence for the future. This proposed device has limitations, such as the intruder's ability to easily see the camera. Users also need to accumulate different sensors for different body parts.

Kishore et al. [9] proposed a microcontroller focusing on women's security. The device is integrated with modules such as a pulse sensor, GPS, GSM module, three buttons, pulse sensor, and vibration sensor. The device is basically for females below 30 years of age. The women can initiate the emergency call-based seriousness, i.e., whether to send the content to family/friends or not. The proposed device needs to be clarified. In a panic situation, users may need clarification about which button must be pressed. Also, no such technique helps preserve evidence for future perspectives.

Hyndavi et al. [10] also explored women's safety issues with modules such as ATmega8, LCD, GSM, and GPS accelerometer sensors. The device is supposed to be activated based on readings recorded via an accelerometer sensor. Furthermore, the GSM module will activate to trigger an emergency SMS to the known user. The device underlines an advantage that women need not find buttons to press; the user can tap her ankle when required. The major limitation of having such a device is that users need to wear the parts of the device at different body parts. Also, there needs to be a method to capture the evidence for the future.

Apart from the above-discussed solutions regarding women's safety, various other solutions have been proposed. However, these existing solutions [7–10] need more evidence collection for the future, connectivity with family/friends, and working with voice input. In the chapter, to address the issues of existing work, we have proposed an Arduino-based IoMT-enabled device that can be used to provide women safety and security. The existing work could be more efficient in collecting evidence related to an emergency that has occurred in terms of speed, connectivity with family members, etc.

7.3 Proposed Arduino-based Women Security Device for IoMT-enabled Environment

This section discusses the proposed Arduino-based women's safety device for an IoMT-enabled environment. This device can provide safety and security to women and will address more aspects of women's security and safety. Women are prone to tragic situations where they feel helpless or emergency services are not arranged in time. The proposed Arduino-based IoMT-enabled device will help them achieve more convenient ways to safeguard themselves in situations.

7.3.1 Components used in the Proposed Work

The components used in our proposed Arduino-based IoMT-enabled women's safety device framework are shown in Figures 7.2 and 7.3. As shown in Figure 7.2, an Arduino Mega 2560 R3 is used, onto which several components are integrated under the proposed device. The modules integrated into the proposed device are the HC-05 Bluetooth serial module, micro SD Card memory shield module, microphone module, quadband GPRS-GSM module, and panic button.

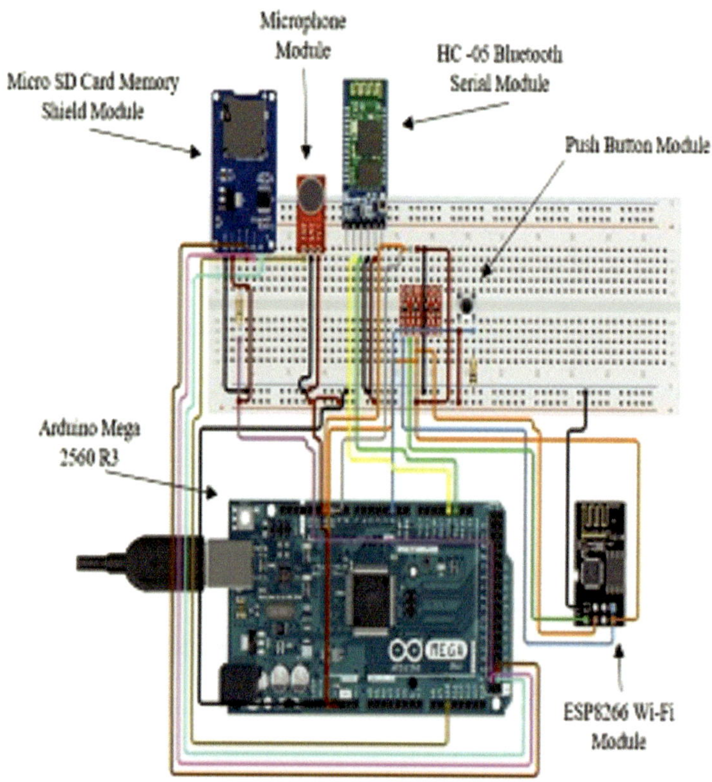

Figure 7.2 Configuration of hardware setup for proposed Arduino-based IoMT-enabled women's safety device.

The proposed device includes the following set of features.

7.3.1.1 Microphone

Usually, in an emergency, the user has no proof of the mishap. With a microphone embedded into the proposed Arduino-based IoMT-enabled device, one can record conversations in the surroundings. These recordings will help in finding the intruder of mishappening.

7.3.1.2 Panic button

The user will be given a panic button embedded into the proposed device. The panic button will be utilized; if the case user finds something unfair, the user can trigger an emergency call. The panic button will initiate this emergency call to the specified contact details.

7.3.1.3 Bluetooth

The HC-05 Bluetooth Serial Module is integrated for Bluetooth connectivity. The proposed Arduino-based IoT-enabled device will always stay connected to the user's Android phone. The user can initiate an emergency call to the contact details using the Android device [14].

7.3.1.4 GPS module

A quadband GPRS-GSM module is integrated to enable the GPRS and GSM features in the proposed device. The GPS module will help family and friends find a user's location in an emergency. Tracing the user's place after an emergency call is triggered becomes essential. The GPS module will communicate through the nearest base station (BS) [11] over the cloud [12–13, 15–19] based on critical parameters such as family, government helpline, etc., provided in the database set.

7.3.1.5 GSM module

GSM module will be one way to communicate with family contacts. It is utilized to send emergency messages and emergency calls to the details of family members in the database provided at the initial for a particular individual [16, 17].

7.3.1.6 Arduino with Wi-Fi module

Arduino is a core module that can be used. The Arduino Mega 2560 R3 module integrates other modules into the proposed device. The sensors, Wi-Fi, and modules listed above will be embedded in Arduino. Based on the initial source code, Arduino will work accordingly on the inputs received via various components used herein [18].

7.3.1.7 Memory card module

Micro SD card, memory shield module, is integrated into the proposed device so that the database can be maintained and sent based on the seriousness of the emergency call initiated by the user.

Figure 7.3 shows the three primary entities involved in Arduino-based IoMT-enabled women's safety devices: the embedded system, the user, and the hardware device. The embedded system comprises utilizable modules in an Android device. The hardware device comprises the components embedded in Arduino, and the user is supposed to carry the proposed device.

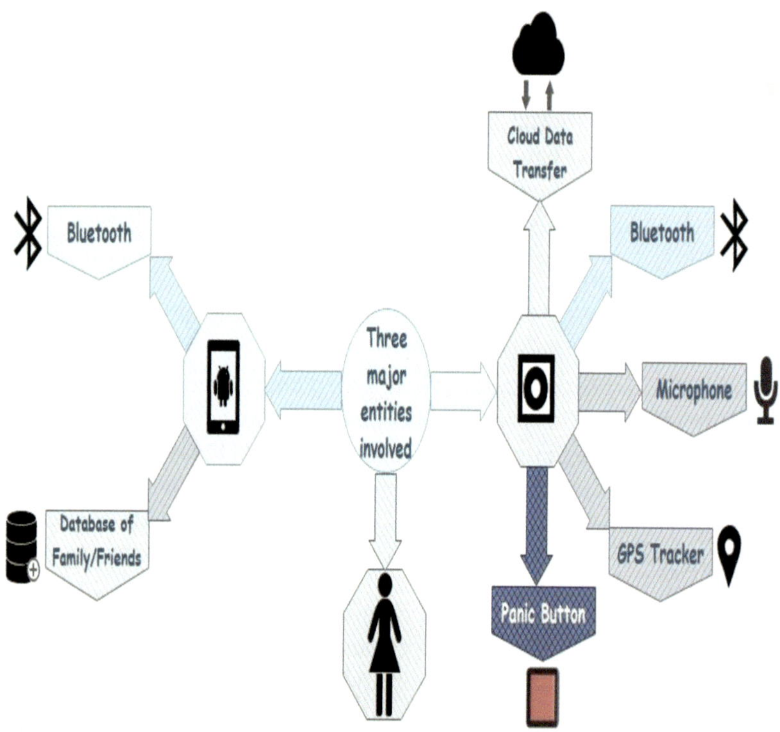

Figure 7.3 Components used in the proposed women's safety device.

7.3.2 Working methodology

This section describes a working methodology for our proposed Arduino-based IoMT-enabled women's safety device. The following steps are to be considered in implementing the proposed device:

Step 1. The user is to carry our proposed device.

Step 2. The device should always be connected via Bluetooth to the user's Android device.

Step 3. If the user senses some unfair atmosphere to resist, the user can initiate an emergency call by pressing the panic button provided within the proposed device.

Step 4. As soon as the panic button is pressed, an emergency call will be initiated accordingly (as depicted in Figure 7.2). The types of the emergency call will be decided based on the number of times the button is pressed, such as:

a. ***Single click:*** An emergency call will be initiated to the family or friends, along with the data (including the current location).
b. ***Double-click:*** An emergency call will be initiated to the family or friends, along with the data (including the current location and audio recording).
c. ***Long press:*** An emergency call will be prompted to the family/friends and government helpline along with the data (current location and audio recording).

Figure 7.4 diagrammatically represents the key points discussed, i.e., what sub-process the device will initiate and how it will be performed while triggering.

The proposed Arduino-based IoMT-enabled device will comprise panic buttons, a microphone, a GPS tracker, and a database. Figure 7.5 represents the modules to be included in an embedded system. These modules are to be utilized in case of any panic situation, along with various sub-processes. Whenever any user feels uncomfortable with the surroundings or the condition worsens, she can press the button. A proper operation will be initiated based on the intensity of the button pressed (depending on multiple functionalities).

A separate database will be maintained for the last 10-minute audio from the surroundings and sent to the respective members from the list. Data will be sent more securely via cloud-based technology. Depending on the functionality chosen by the user, a pre-defined operation will be initiated.

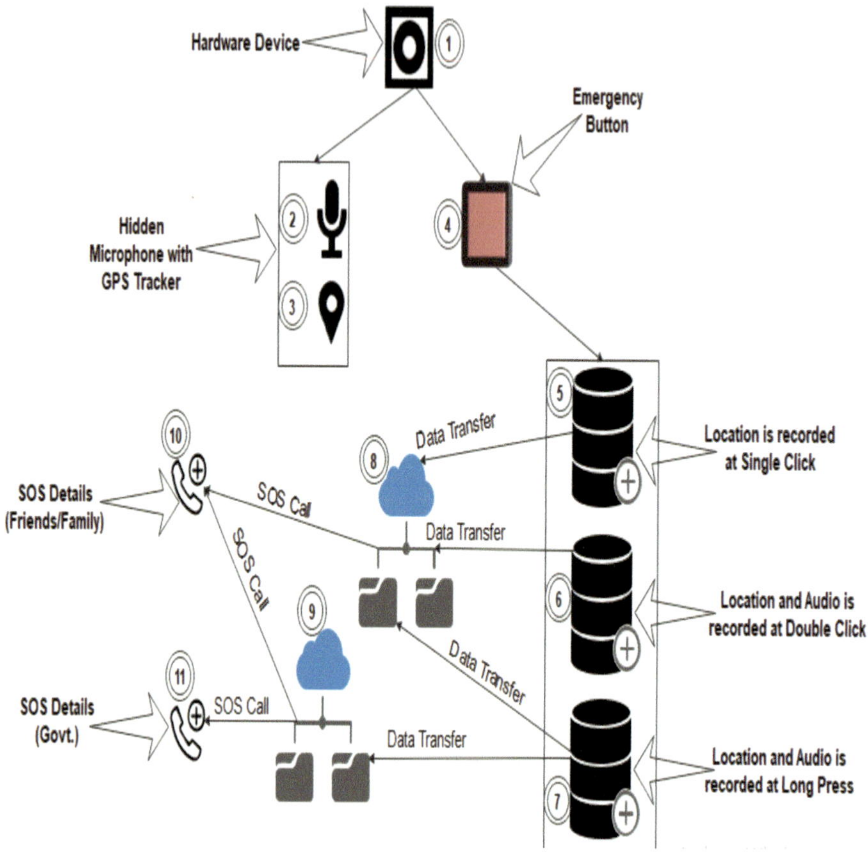

Figure 7.4 Working steps of our proposed Arduino-based IoT-enabled women's safety device.

Anyone from the list of family/friends can trigger an emergency SOS for the victim to the government personnel as and when required, to involve the government authorities promptly. So, Government personnel will handled before the situation get worse. Also, relevant evidence can be collected directly by government personnel regarding incidents that may occur with women.

Figure 7.5 represents the necessary processes to perform in a dedicated Android device. The proposed device will communicate with an Android device comprising features, mainly Bluetooth, a microphone, GPS tracker,

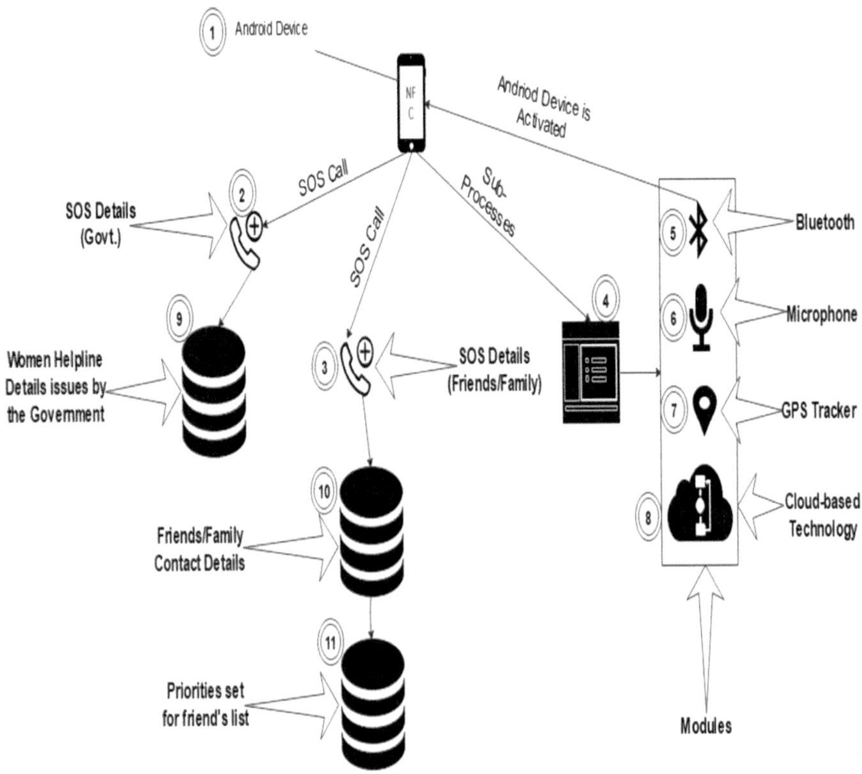

Figure 7.5 Key processes that will be triggered through the proposed device.

cloud-based technology, and various sub-processes, including a database (containing details of friends/family and a government helpline for women's safety). From Figure 7.5, the Android device (denoted by 1) is supposed to implement the list of sub-processes (marked as 4). The sub-processes will include functionalities related to Bluetooth (indicated by 5), microphone (shown by 6), GPS tracker (indicated by 7), and cloud-based technology (denoted by 8). Depending on the functionality chosen by the user, an emergency SOS will be triggered (indicated by 2 and 3). Separate databases are maintained for contact details of both the family/friends and the government helpline (denoted by 9, 10, and 11).

7.4 Comparison of the Proposed Arduino-based IoMT-enabled Device with the Existing Work

The proposed device banks on four factors, mainly W, D, F, and G. Here, W is concerned with the woman or girl child carrying the proposed device with her. D is involved with the embedded device that will always stay connected to the women's Android device via Bluetooth. F is concerned with the family/friends of the women, who will receive the triggered emergency call along with the database via cloud-based technology [20]. Finally, G is involved with the details of the government helpline.

Table 7.1 Comparison between existing and proposed Arduino-based IoMT-enabled women's safety device solutions.

S. No.	Feature	Existing women's safety devices	Proposed Arduino-based IoMT-enabled women's safety device
1	Cost	Expensive (numbers of modules are integrated)	Economic (inexpensive and refined modules are embedded)
2	Ambiguity	Ambiguous with other activities in the background	Unambiguous to other noise in the background
3	Speed and connectivity with family	Low	Improved (high-end and refined network connectivity is established)
4	Works on voice input	No	Yes (records the surround sound for evidence collection)
5	Database to be sent on triggering a panic button	Only location, along with the emergency message or call	Location, voice recording, emergency call, emergency message
6	Multiple functionalities (single press, double press, and long press)	One or two	All three are included
7	Evidence recording	Few devices are equipped with evidence-recording	Yes
8	Linked with Government helpline	Only emergency calling	Includes emergency calling with database
9	Application installation required	Few devices require the installation of various applications	No (works via Bluetooth)
10	Shaking required	Few devices require shakes to trigger an event	No (panic button is to be pressed)

Our proposed device focuses on protecting women inside and outside their houses from tragic and sudden emergencies. Table 7.1 compares existing and our proposed Arduino-based IoMT-enabled women's safety device.

7.4.1 Experimental setup

Figure 7.6 shows the experimental setup of our proposed Arduino-based IoMT-enabled device. The proposed device includes a micro SD card memory shield module, HC-05 Bluetooth module, quadband GPRS-GSM Sim800L module, microphone module, ESP8266 Wi-Fi module, and push-button module. These components must be assembled using an Arduino Mega 2560 R3 module, a breadboard, and jumper wires to establish connectivity with the modules. The functionality of each element is shown in this section.

The ESp8266 Wi-Fi module facilitates the cloud computing environment, where data is transferred securely. The micro SD card memory shield module is incorporated with the microphone module to maintain the database. The database will consist of audio recordings from the surroundings with the

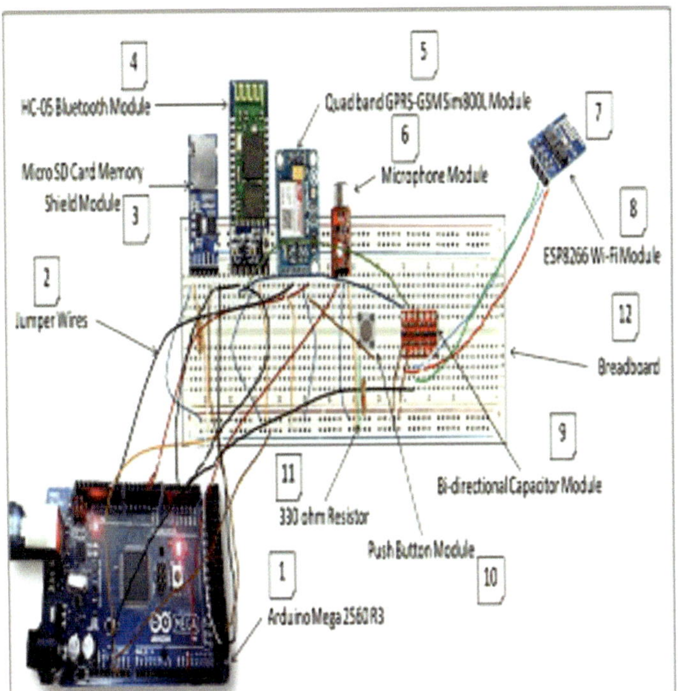

Figure 7.6 Experimental setup of the proposed Arduino-based women's safety device.

slightest noise input. A 330-ohm resistor is also used to maintain a voltage balance while flowing signals.

7.4.2 Experimental results and discussions

This section underlines the results generated from the proposed device's physical implementation. The proposed device's outcome is an emergency message that the user has to trigger for either family members or government personnel. The proposed device's analysis is performed comparatively with the existing solutions on various factors.

Figure 7.7 shows the clipping of an emergency message received by one of the user's family members. The proposed Arduino-based IoT-enabled device triggers the notification. Every message started by the proposed device may include the user's name, geographic location, longitude and latitude measurement, and an audio recording. The contents of the message triggered will depend on the functionality chosen by the user in any panic situation.

Figure 7.8 concludes the overall analysis of the proposed device with the existing solutions. A comparative study was conducted based on the

Figure 7.7 An emergency message was received on the family member's phone.

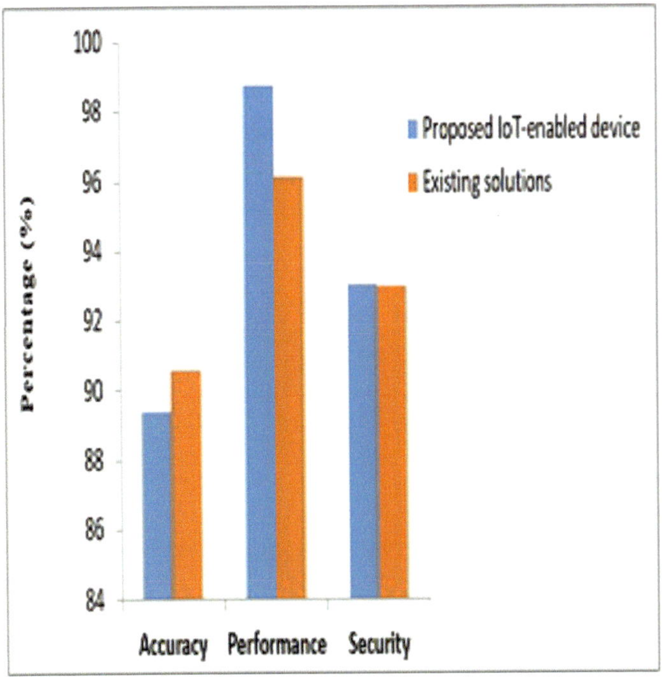

Figure 7.8 Comparative analysis of proposed and existing work with respect to accuracy, performance, and security.

literature review of existing solutions for the physical implementation of the proposed device. Figure 7.8 represents an average comparative analysis based on performance-based parameters, such as accuracy, performance, and security. From Figure 7.8, it can be concluded that the proposed device has met the acceptance criteria for all the parameters. The proposed device is more secure than the existing solution [7–10] as one of the reliable encryption techniques [14] is implemented.

Figure 7.9 concludes the average comparative analysis of the proposed device with the existing solution regarding non-performance-based parameters. If inexpensive and refined modules are integrated, the proposed device is more economical to use in terms of cost than the current solution [7–10]. It is also more reliable in terms of usability functionalities when compared with existing solutions [7–10, 19]. The proposed device is dedicated to multiple functionalities that may be chosen to be performed depending on the situation.

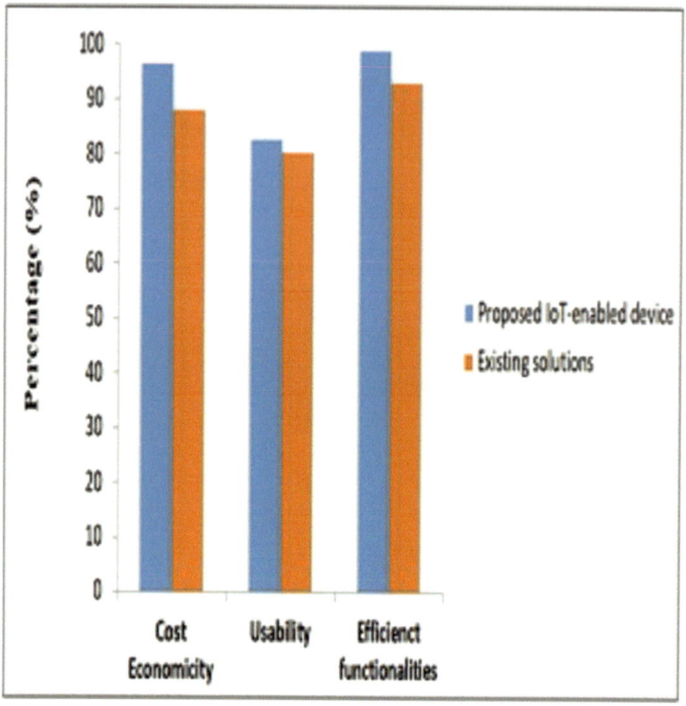

Figure 7.9 Comparative analysis of proposed and existing work with respect to cost, usability, and functionalities.

The proposed scenario will underline the following possible outcomes.

7.4.2.1 Accuracy

More accurate readings can be drawn from the proposed device, whether to measure the altitude and attitude for location searching or create the database from the readings from embedded modules.

7.4.2.2 The improved mental health of women

A healthy state of mind will be achieved for all the women who will be carrying this device along with them. They will feel secure every time and everywhere, as they will always be connected to their near and dear ones. Because, at times, it is not always possible for a user (in a panic situation) to interact with the family via mobile phone. A more reliable device can be utilized in such situations rather than interacting via mobile phone.

7.4.3 Stay connected

Women traveling outside their house or while staying inside will always be connected to their family/friends whom the user trusts. Users can trigger an emergency call to confront any panic situation.

7.4.3.1 Crime control

With the proposed Arduino-based IoT-enabled women's safety device, crime rates will also be managed efficiently, as the intruder can be held in time, and violence can be reduced to a level.

7.4.3.2 Speed and connectivity

Since everything is to be operated via the internet and services related to the internet, things can be managed (through cloud-based technology), and speedy actions can be made.

7.4.3.3 Evidence collection

It becomes challenging to find the intruder guilty. Sometimes, recording evidence or proof of the mishap was impossible. The proposed device will help collect shreds of evidence for the future as and when required.

7.4.3.4 Trustworthy

The database created can be trusted as it is generated via one of the finest modules. Further actions (whether to trigger an emergency call or send a database along with it) are to be drawn based on the user's activities. A measure of trust can be attained with the family/friends and women (carrying the device) regarding the proposed technology.

7.4.3.5 Economic

The estimated cost for the proposed Arduino-based IoT-enabled device is very reasonable and highly economical. It cuts the cost of extra equipment, and one of the finest modules is embedded. These modules are inexpensive and highly reliable. Our proposed Arduino-based IoT-enabled women's safety device will cut the costs (concerning the existing ones) by 20%. This is possible if fewer but refined modules are incorporated with the system rather than many modules.

7.4.3.6 User friendly

The proposed Arduino-based IoT-enabled women's safety device is highly user-friendly. It requires no applications to install with. It can be utilized with a minimum of settings made with the women's Android phone. This setting is to be made once only.

7.5 Conclusion

Women are a vital part of society, and it is the right of every individual to live with a positive state of mind anywhere around the world. However, it is seen so far that intruders at various levels of life make women a target. In this chapter, an Arduino-based IoMT-enabled women's safety device has been proposed. The proposed device will help women to provide a leased solution when they are in unsafe situations. The proposed device is offered with evidence collecting for the future that is both affordable and trustworthy. In the end, it will be easier for government officials to determine the modesty of women with this information. As a result of this method's potential to prevent fraud, the suggested gadget will assist women in enhancing their mental health.

Further, the proposed device will help society reduce the intensity of crime rates against women. Also, intruders can be caught easily through speech recognition technology by government officials in future investigations. In the future, the proposed invention shall be added with certain features related to safeguarding women, such as small weapons that can be used to combat a particular situation.

References

[1] World Health Organization. "Violence against women prevalence estimates, global, regional and national prevalence estimates for intimate partner violence against women and global and regional prevalence estimates for non-partner sexual violence against women", pp. 1-52, 2021.

[2] Villardón-Gallego, L., García-Cid, A., Estévez, A., & García-Carrión, R, "Early educational interventions to prevent gender-based violence: a systematic review," In Healthcare, Multidisciplinary Digital Publishing Institute, vol. 11, no.1, pp. 142, 2023.

[3] Raj, P., & Rahman, M. M, "Revisiting the economic theory of crime A state-level analysis in India," Cogent Social Sciences, vol. 9, no. 1, 2023.

[4] Razdan, S., & Sharma, S, "Internet of medical things (IoMT): overview, emerging technologies, and case studies,". IETE technical review, 39(4), pp. 775-788, vol. 39, no 4, 2022.

[5] National Crime Records Bureau, Available at: https://ncrb.gov.in/en/crime-india,accessedon10April2023.
[6] Ahanger T.A., Tariq U., Nusir M., Aldaej A., Ullah I., Sulman A, "A novel IoMT-fog-cloud-based healthcare system for monitoring and predicting COVID-19 outspread," J Supercomputing, pp, 1–24, 2021.
[7] Venkatesh, K., et al. "IoT based Unified approach for Women safety alert using GSM." IEEE 3rd International Conference on Intelligent Communication Technologies and Virtual Mobile Networks (ICICV), 2021.
[8] Reddy, V., Konguvel, E., Sumathi, G., & Sujatha, R, Emergency Alert System for Women Safety using Raspberry Pi, IEEE Second International Conference on Next Generation Intelligent Systems (ICNGIS), pp. 1-4, 2022.
[9] Kishore, K. Hari. "An Application on Women Safety Using Embedded Systems and IoT." Turkish Journal of Computer and Mathematics Education (TURCOMAT), pp. 65-73, vol. 11, no 5, 2021.
[10] Hyndavi, V., Nikhita, N. S., & Rakesh, S., "Smart wearable device for women safety using IoT," IEEE 5th International Conference on Communication and Electronics Systems (ICCES), pp. 459-463, 2020.
[11] Mishra, A., Singh, S., & Tripathi, A. K, "Comparison of MANET routing protocols," Int. J. Comput. Sci. Mob. Computing, vol. 8, pp. 67-74, 2019.
[12] Bhardwaj, A., & Krishna, C. R, "Impact of factors affecting pre-copy virtual machine migration technique for cloud computing," Materials Today: Proceedings, vol.18, pp. 1138-1145, 2019.
[13] Aditya., & Rama C., "Improving the performance of pre-copy virtual machine migration technique,." In Proceedings of Springer 2nd International Conference on Communication, Computing, and Networking: ICCCN, NITTTR Chandigarh, India, pp. 1021-1032, 2019.
[14] Olutola, Agbelusi, and Matthew Olumuyiwa. "Comparative Analysis of Encryption Algorithms." European Journal of Technology, vol. 7, no.1, pp 1-9, 2023.
[15] Cui, M., Baek, S. S., Crespo, R. G., & Premalatha, R, Internet of things-based cloud computing platform for analyzing the physical health condition. Technology and Health Care, vol. 29, no. 6, pp. 1233-1247, 2021.
[16] Razdan, S., & Sharma, S. "Internet of medical things (IoMT): overview, emerging technologies, and case studies," IETE technical review, vol. 39, no. 4, pp. 775-788, 2022.

[17] Gupta, D., Choudhury, A., Gupta, U., Singh, P., & Prasad, M. (2021). A computational approach to clinical diagnosis of diabetes disease: a comparative study. Multimedia Tools and Applications, 1-26.

[18] Gahlot, A., & Gupta, U. (2016). Gaze-based authentication in cloud computing. International Journal of Computer Applications, 1(1), 14-20.

[19] Singh, S., Bhardwaj, A., Budhiraja, I., Gupta, U., & Gupta, I. (2023). Cloud-Based Architecture for Effective Surveillance and Diagnosis of COVID-19. Convergence of Cloud with AI for Big Data Analytics: Foundations and Innovation, 69-88.

[20] G. Koutitas, P. Demestichas, 'A review of energy efficiency in telecommunication networks', Proc. In Telecomm. Forum (TELFOR), pp. 1-4, Serbia, Nov. 2009.

8

Integrating Digital Twin Technology and an Intelligent Transportation System for IoMT

Ajay Dureja[1], Aman Dureja[2], Varun Kumar[3], and Mahesh Kumar[1]

[1]Department of Information Technology, Bharati Vidyapeeth's College of Engineering, India
[2]Department of Information Technology, Bhagwan Parshuram Institute of Technology (BPIT), India
[3]Department of Management, Mangalmay Institute of Management and Technology, India
E-mail: ajaydureja@gmail.com; amandureja@gmail.com; varun.management@gmail.com; maheshmalkani@gmail.com

Abstract

Digital twin technology and intelligent transportation system (ITS) are two related technologies that are transforming the transportation industry. Digital twin technology is a virtual replica of a physical object or system, including transportation infrastructure and vehicles. It allows for present and actual time supervision or monitoring, analysis, and reconstruction of the work behavior of the actual physical system. In transportation, a digital twin can be used to model and monitor traffic flow, vehicle performance, road conditions, and other factors that impact the transportation system. The Internet of Things is a collection of millions of interconnected devices that work seamlessly with each other. Its rapid emergence and evolution are some of the main factors that have raised the bar for creating truly innovative applications. In terms of artificial intelligence and IoE, the existence of the digital era based on IoT can enhance the work–life balance of people or respective users. It can also be used to rationalize the use of their resources. Intelligent transportation system (ITS) with IoT-enabled devices is a way to reduce

DOI: 10.1201/9788770047395-8

traffic congestion. ITS can be defined as a transportation system that uses improved technologies. The major purpose and objective of an intelligent transportation system (ITS) is to evaluate, create, carry out analytical work, and integrate new technologies or innovations and try to achieve the target of traffic efficiency, improvement in environmental factors like quality, saving energy, saving time, and ensuring safety and security. This framework allows one to create and implement diverse scenarios where the various components of an overall Big Data system are integrated as IoE or sensors. This case study describes the various components of the Internet of Things platform, which allow for a flexible and dynamic setup.

Keywords: Internet of Things, machine learning, deep learning, support vector machine, Internet of Everything, digital twin technology, real-time monitoring, traffic flow, Internet of Medical Things.

8.1 Introduction

One of the important parameters for measuring the development process of any nation or country is increasing the number of vehicle owners. However, this vehicle ownership indirectly affects traffic congestion. In the past decade, India has seen a mass improvement in ownership, which has resulted in road blockages and traffic congestion in the metro cities. The primary reasons for traffic congestion in any city are the lack of road space and the lack of adequate infrastructure. So, there is a need for intelligent transportation systems in smart cities. With new means of transportation, in the earlier days, mobility allowed society to move in a free manner, and due to the rapid increase of urbanization across the world, mobility is driving progress and growth. Intelligent transportation system (ITS) with IoT-enabled devices is a way to reduce traffic congestion. ITS can be defined as a transportation system that uses improved technologies. The main objectives of an intelligent transportation system (ITS) are to evaluate, develop, analyze, integrate, and synchronize with new technologies and concepts to achieve traffic efficiency, improve environmental quality, save energy, conserve time, and enhance safety and comfort for drivers, pedestrians, and other traffic groups [29–31].

Digital twin technology and intelligent transportation systems (ITS) are two interconnected components of IoE-based smart cities. Digital twin technology is a virtual representation of a physical object or system that allows for real-time monitoring, analysis, and simulation of its behavior. In the context of ITS, a digital twin could be used to model and monitor transportation infrastructure and vehicles, including traffic flow, road conditions, and vehicle performance.

Intelligent transportation systems (ITS), on the other hand, use advanced technologies such as sensors, communication networks, and data analytics to improve the safety, efficiency, and sustainability of transportation systems. ITS can leverage the data collected from digital twin models to optimize traffic flow, reduce congestion, and improve safety [18].

In an IoE-based smart city, digital twin technology and ITS work together to create a more intelligent and responsive transportation system. By using real-time data from digital twins, ITS can make more informed decisions about traffic management, route planning, and public transportation services, ultimately improving the quality of life for residents and visitors alike. The intelligent transportation system in smart cities requires smart traffic planning and innovative ideas for public transportation systems. In the earlier days, transportation with fewer traffic jams and fewer emissions has been demonstrated to reduce the negative effects on the quality of life and environment in smart cities, resulting in an increase in positive habits among the population. Due to the development of IoT and IoE technologies, it is possible to drive sustainable ecosystems in smart cities. Advancements in IoT upgrade the quality of life [1]. The above situation provides a new relevant structure that belongs to different things, peoples, and the development of urban areas, especially metropolitan cities. The idea of the Internet of Things (IoT) was introduced in parallel to WSNs. Kevin Ashton coined the term Internet of Things. It refers to identifiable objects and their representations in an "internet-like" structure. IoT objects may range from buildings, cars, planes, and traffic lights to human beings, plants, and animals. IoT is a fast-developing area throughout the entire existence of areas. It is expected that 50 billion gadgets will have been produced by the end of 2021 [3, 4]. We can say that IoT is "a dynamic global network infrastructure with self-configuring capabilities based on standard and interoperable communication protocols where physical and virtual 'Things' have identities, physical attributes, and virtual personalities and use intelligent interfaces, and are seamlessly integrated into the information network" [5] or "a global infrastructure for the information society enabling advanced services by interconnecting (physical and virtual) things based on, existing and evolving, interoperable information and communication technology" [6].

Therefore, digital twin technology and ITS can work together to create a more intelligent and responsive transportation system. By using real-time data from digital twins, ITS can make more informed decisions about traffic management, route planning, accident information, and public transportation services. The integration of digital twins in smart mobility systems and IoMT devices generates a significant amount of sensitive data related to transportation patterns, patient health records, and medical diagnostics. Ensuring the privacy of this data is essential to prevent unauthorized access, misuse, or breaches that can compromise individuals' sensitive information.

The organization of this chapter is as follows. Section 8.1 describes the introduction with related work. The Internet of Everything (IoE) architecture model is described in Section 8.2. The relation between IoT and digital twin technology is presented in Section 8.3. Section 8.4 describes the relationship between the Internet of Medical Things and digital twin technology. Section 8.5 presents AI-based transportation systems and digital twin technology: a future vision as a prospect of the use of transportation systems in IoMT. Section 8.6 presents challenges and solutions related to security and privacy in IoMT using digital twin technology. Section 8.7 presents the conclusion of this chapter.

8.2 Internet of Everything (IoE) Architecture

The real world is composed of IoT devices like mobile pagers, smart watches, etc. These devices can communicate with each other through built-in sensor devices. Some special IoT devices work as aggregators or distributors and form an IoT Edge. The data generated from these IoT devices are received by an actuator, which in turn defines some logic for producing IoT solutions. IoT App acts as an interface between the IoT Edge and IoT Cloud infrastructure. IoT-related gadgets or devices provide more virtual and digitalization ability and may be available in core as individual or small single-board computers (i.e., Raspberry PI). These types of devices or computers can be openly linked to a wired network through a relevant, powerful link, using a small quantity of more energy, and can be established or installed where far-off or emote powering is available.

IoT edge devices can be smartphones, tablets, or any handheld devices like pagers, etc. In IoT Cloud infrastructure, the main component is the Cloud, which gathers all the related fixed data or information and actual data from the outside world through the special API known as Smart City API. Smart City API can receive and provide the microservices that are directly connected to the IoT App present in the IoT solution. Figure 8.1 shows the framework or architecture of the IoT solution.

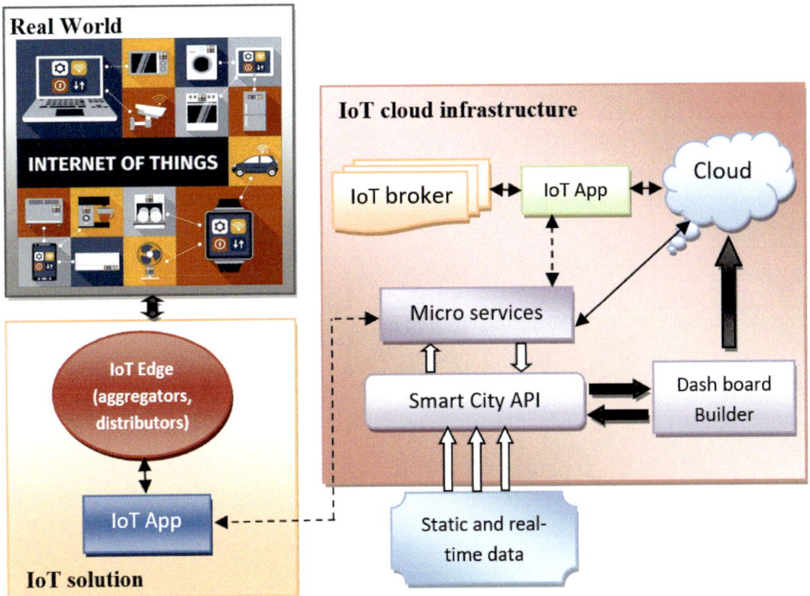

Figure 8.1 Internet of Everything (IoE) architecture.

8.2.1 IoE and digital twin technology based smart city: A future vision

The PLEEC program or project works on bringing initiatives for energy efficiency, especially for urban development [15]. It is totally focused on imagination relevant to technology, structure (in the form of the development structure and also of governance structure), and people's behavior, developing the three elements that impact energy requirements, energy demand or consumption, and emissions of cities or urban areas.

Consequently, in the Planning for Energy Efficient Cities (PLEEC) program, or extended in collaboration with six medium-sized cities (Eskilstuna, Sweden; Jyväskylä and Turku, Finland; Tartu, Estonia; Stoke-on-Trent, United Kingdom; Santiago de Compostela, Spain), the major areas of energy-efficient urban development, along with their respective domains, were identified through two web-based surveys (Figure 8.2). The yield consists of five major key variables with a particular number of most imperative range domains.

Based on the overcategorization and classification, the possibility or capacity for a more vitality-productive upgrade had been found in the shape

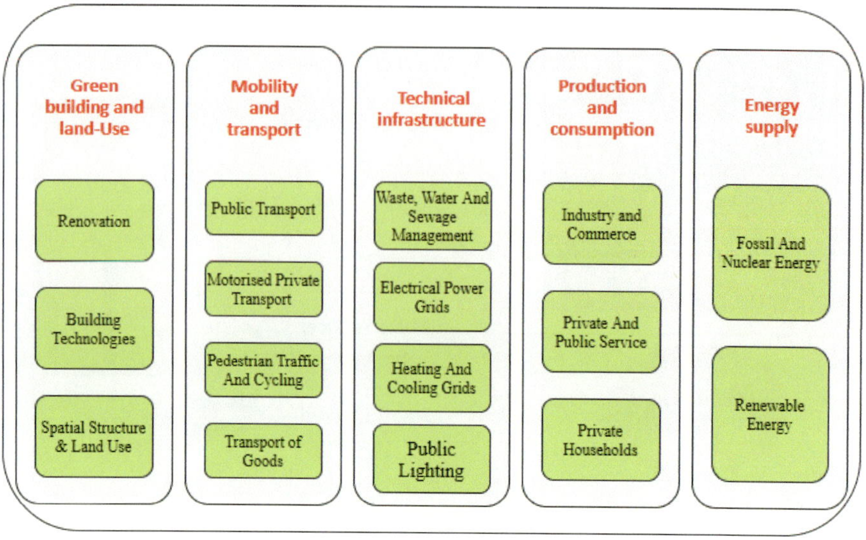

Figure 8.2 Major area domain in PLEEC project (Source: [15]).

of a vitality shrewd city profile by nearby citizens of their residential and domestic city.

8.3 Internet of Things and Digital Twin Technology

The Internet of Things (IoT) makes a difference in people's lives, works smarter than without IoT, and also controls and maintains their lives [17]. Enhancement of the digital market, including smartphones, leads to an automatic world and the development of robotized homes; IoT gives the basics to industry, commerce, and business. IoT gives businesses within the stipulated time the opportunity to see their frameworks truly work, providing the best experience in the whole thing, from the implementation of the work process and equipment to supply chain and coordination in operations.

IoT authorizes and boosts companies, firms, etc., to automate forms and diminish input costs. It additionally reduces the cost of waste and enhances the service delivery system, making it less costly to produce and provide products in economical delivery and providing straightforwardness in customer or buyer dealing transactions. Figure 8.3 shows the integration of IoT and digital twin technology.

Figure 8.3 illustrates the concept of digital twin (DT) as a virtual counterpart of IoT devices, enabling device-as-a-service. The main asset of a DT is to

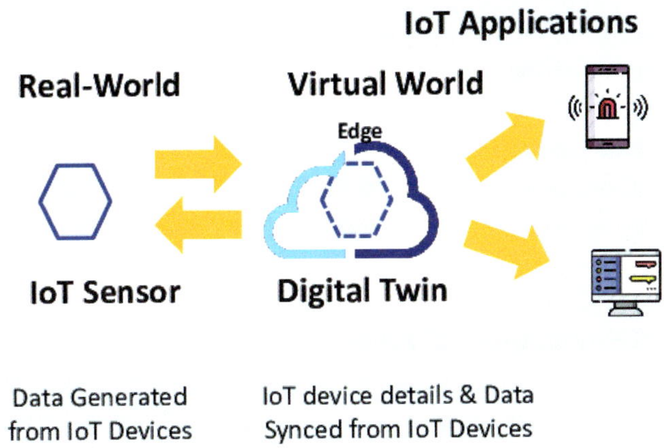

Figure 8.3 Integration of IoT and digital twin technology [16].

implement an abstraction layer that allows IoT applications to communicate with devices continuously. The main goal of a DT is to pursue the lifecycle and integrate the data with the device. DTs enable features like device simulation during development, their characteristics, behaviors in time, and integration of analytics.

8.3.1 Pros and cons of IoT

Some of the merits of IoT include the following:

- With the help of IoT, get data from any place at any time on any electronic device.
- Enhanced communication systems between associated electronic devices also provide a synchronization facility.
- Transferring information data over an associated network saves time and money.
- Automating everyday jobs can improve the quality of a business's administration and decrease the requirement for human efforts and intervention.

Some demerits or drawbacks of IoT include the following:

- As the number of connected and associated smart devices increases day by day and mass information in the form of data is shared and synchronized between electronic devices, the potential for a hacker to take secret data also increases.

- Enterprises may eventually have to deal with large numbers – perhaps millions – of IoT smart devices, and collecting and overseeing the information from all those smart devices will be challenging.
- If there are viruses or bugs within the framework, it is likely that each associated gadget will become corrupted.
- Since there is no worldwide standard of compatibility for IoT, it is troublesome for gadgets from diverse producers to communicate with each other.

8.3.2 Digital twin technology

Digital twin technology involves creating an online replicated version of a tangible or physical object, system, or process. It uses actual and real-time information from sensors, IoT devices, and other sources to model and simulate the behavior, performance, and characteristics of the physical counterpart. Some of the important features of digital twin technology are as follows.

Virtual model representation: In digital twin technology, a virtual model is created that behaves like a reflection of a physical object. This virtual model representation provides a basis for analysis, monitoring, and optimization in the real world.

Real-time data integration: In digital twin technology, physical components are connected with sensors and IoT devices to collect data like the status, condition, and performance of physical objects. This real-time data is incorporated into the digital twin to ensure that the virtual simulation accurately reflects the object's current state.

Examining and analysis: In digital twin technology, real-time data is examined using a virtual model, which can then be used to study performance issues and generate improvements, which can then be applied back to the physical object.

Predictive measurement: Digital twin technology can utilize advanced analytics and machine learning algorithms to make predictions and forecasts. This will enable the maintenance of physical object operations.

Simulation: Digital twin technology uses simulation, machine learning, and reasoning to help with decision-making. Digital twins can run any number of simulations to realize multiple processes of physical objects.

Remote monitoring and control: Digital twin technology provides remote monitoring and control of physical objects. Virtual models of physical objects can enable remote access to the performance, analysis issues, and control operations, which results in no need for physical presence near physical objects.

Optimization and decision support: Digital twins provide a platform for optimization and decision support. By analyzing data and simulating various scenarios, stakeholders can identify inefficiencies, optimize processes, and make data-driven decisions to improve performance, reliability, and sustainability.

Lifecycle management: Digital twins can be used throughout an asset or system's lifecycle. From design and development to operation and maintenance, they provide insights and support decision-making at every stage, leading to better efficiency, reduced costs, and improved outcomes.

8.4 Internet of Medical Things and Digital Twin Technology

The Internet of Things makes a difference in people's lives, works smarter than without IoT, and controls and maintains their lives. Enhancement of the digital market, including smartphones, leads to an automatic world and develops robotized homes; IoT gives basic to industry, commerce, and business. IoT gives businesses within the stipulated time the opportunity to see their frameworks truly work, providing the best experience in the whole thing, from the implementation of the work process and equipment to supply chain and coordination in operations.

IoT authorizes and boosts companies, firms, etc., to automate forms and diminish input costs. It additionally reduces the cost of waste and enhances the service delivery system, making it less costly to produce and provide products in economical delivery and providing straightforwardness in customer or buyer dealing transactions.

The IoMT refers to the network of interconnected medical devices, sensors, and healthcare systems that collect and exchange data for the purpose of monitoring patient health, delivering personalized care, and improving healthcare outcomes [23]. IoMT devices can include wearable devices, remote monitoring systems, implantable devices, and other medical sensors. These devices generate valuable data that can be utilized for real-time health monitoring, preventive care, and predictive analytics. Figure 8.4 shows such

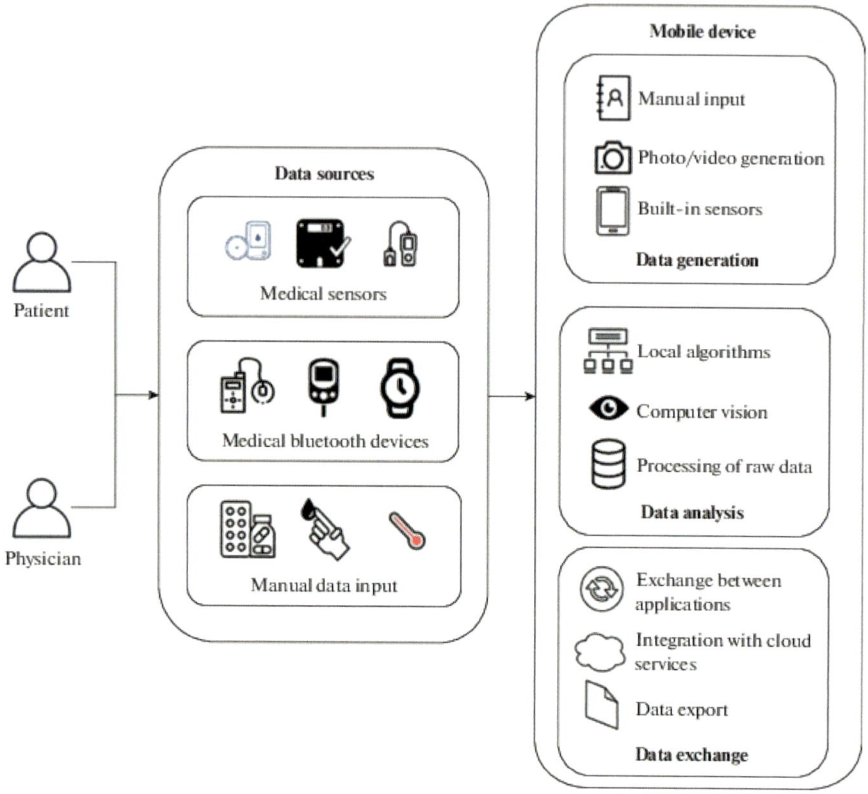

Figure 8.4 Integration of IoMT and digital twin technology [19].

integration of IoMT and digital twin technology. It includes technologies related to mobile applications and technologies of the Internet of Things, peripheral devices, computer vision, and telemedicine.

A digital twin can be assumed to be a digital replica of an object in the physical world. A digital twin is a computer program that uses real-time data and can help in the analysis, simulation, and optimization of physical objects. Digital twin technology can provide an inclusive view of physical systems, remote monitoring, predictive analytics, and performance optimization.

In terms of the healthcare ecosystem, digital twin technology can play a crucial role in the Internet of Medical Things.

Improved remote monitoring in IoMT environment: Digital twin technology can help us in the IoMT environment. A virtual replica of a patient can provide a real-time view to check the health status [19]. Healthcare providers can monitor patients from a remote location, analyze the collected data, and provide individualized care using the knowledge acquired from the digital twin.

Real-time feedback and iterative improvement: The integration of digital twin technology with IoMT devices enables a closed-loop feedback system. Real-time data from IoMT devices can be fed into the digital twin models, which can provide feedback to healthcare providers or patients. This feedback loop allows for iterative improvements in treatment plans, device performance, and healthcare interventions.

8.5 AI-based Transportation System and Digital Twin Technology: A Future Vision

By incorporating cutting-edge technologies into numerous facets of transportation, AI-based transportation solutions completely transform how we travel. These systems use artificial intelligence to improve safety, lessen environmental impact, and optimize traffic flow. Machine learning algorithms use predictive analytics to minimize commute times by optimizing route planning, anticipating traffic, and managing traffic lights. AI is also essential to autonomous cars since it allows them to communicate, navigate, and make decisions in real time for safer and more effective travel. AI-driven transportation solutions are developing along with smart infrastructure, paving the way for a time when mobility is not just comfortable but also sustainable and technologically sophisticated.

8.5.1 Benefits of transportation technology

The benefits of AI generation and the advantages they create for transportation inside a smart metropolis are the following:

- **Smart transportation is more secure:** Smart transportation based on AI does not get diverted, exhausted, emotional, or exciting. A self-reliant transportation system has very few chances of injuries and accidents as it has fewer human components. It is totally based on machine learning with IoT and 5G services, which create or develop self-dependent transportation systems.
- **Smart transportation is more controlled:** Smart transportation means an AI-based transportation system that is more capable of being controlled than traditional transportation systems.

- **Smart transportation is greener:** Artificial intelligence systems lead to an eco-friendly environment. So, IoT-based transportation systems are greener or more eco-friendly than traditional transportation systems.
- **Smart transportation is value-effective:** Artificial intelligence or IoT systems can help maximize the utilization of available resources. This can reduce costs or prices by conserving fuel, energy, etc., and lowering electricity consumption. In other words, a smart public transportation system is more cost-effective than private vehicles for individuals and society as well.
- **Smart transportation provides fast insights:** Specially, in Cities, Smart transportation systems provide better information sharing among traffic control facilitators related to problem spots or accidental locations, etc. This leads to public protection and provides a better management system for traffic control routes, etc.

8.5.2 AI vision for accident prevention

According to the CDC, approximately 1.35 million people become sufferers of motor vehicle accidents every year, with approximately 300 daily avenue coincidence deaths. A massive bite of these deaths every year includes pedestrians, cyclists, and motorcyclists. Such injuries arise because of a number of things, such as poor visibility, driving force fatigue, a lack of focus, and technical failure, among different motives. Smart transportation entails an IoT network that includes facts receptor sensors mounted on highways and busy streets in addition to motor automobiles. These sensors, along with PC imaginative and prescient-powered CCTV cameras, can offer timely statistics to automobile drivers about how near their vehicles are to pedestrians, static structures, or different motors in any given example. In a hyper-connected smart town, this fact is first captured autonomously by means of smart cameras. Then, it can be sent to linked cars. As soon as a motive force receives the records in their car's infotainment gadget, they could sluggish down or take an alternative course. The algorithms in laptop imaginative and prescient structures can expect the ability to coincide structures earlier to lessen avoidable mishaps.

These days, dynamic image capturing and processing are crucial components of automobiles. Cars in smart cities need laptop vision tools for occupant and pedestrian safety. Moreover, the visible facts accrued and analyzed by way of laptop imaginative and prescient applications may be used by municipalities and different public corporations for developing clever network tasks.

As with any computer imaginative and prescient or AI-primarily based era, smart transportation programs continue improving with time. So, the visual records receptors improve in identifying highway symbols and functions, lane markings, limitations, and other street-related information. Additionally, such structures end up markedly better at detecting gadgets and potential collisions and relaying information to car drivers and pedestrians through smartphone apps or wearable eras.

Safety technology that includes intuitive emergency braking, lane centering, blind-spot protection tracking, collision alert systems, adaptive cruise management, smart velocity edition systems, nighttime imaginative and prescient structures, pedestrian and avenue sign popularity systems, closely rely upon digital image-taking pictures, and cognitive information processing facilitated by means of laptop vision structures. Within the modern-day age of massive records, laptop vision makes it possible to analyze uncooked records on the fly through algorithms performing several million probability-based calculations and generating precious insights and forecasts to optimize avenue safety.

Clever transportation additionally boosts the sustainability factor of smart cities. For instance, device gaining knowledge of devices in public delivery cars allows transport agencies to recognize the routes with the very best variety of travelers [20]. This fact permits the organizations to lessen the range of automobiles in regions in which the variety of vacationers is usually low. As a result, gas and car usage may be managed. Clever towns, along with Amsterdam, actively prioritize sustainability and citizen protection while making city improvement plans. In addition to safety and sustainability, PCs, imaginative and prescient, can enhance mobility in clever towns through clever site visitors' management.

8.5.3 AI vision for traffic management

As implied in advance, smart transportation is not solely related to vehicle-based gear and applications. The idea also entails the optimization of street networks in a clever metropolis. Smooth mobility is an important factor for gauging the livability, workability, and sustainability of any clever town. As an example, if there is a medical emergency and a man or woman desires to be rushed to the clinic, having a mobile transportation community may be life-saving in this sort of scenario. Comparable examples of mobility being useful for enhancing the sustainability and workability of clever towns may be witnessed on an everyday foundation, too. So, how exactly does computer vision assist in traffic management and, by extension, enhance mobility in smart cities?

Traffic automation mechanisms that cannot be computerized normally generally tend to have numerous errors. So, in the era of unexpectedly growing daily commuters, shortened or slim roads, and globalization, visitor tracking has become a place of concern for nearby directors in any region. Smart towns feature some of the busiest highways and an extremely large range of automobiles, increasing the concern degree.

Laptop imaginative and prescient-powered clever transportation tools, at the side of IoT community gadgets, facilitate autonomous site visitors' monitoring and communication. Clever site visitors' lights, smart parking, and traffic guidance structures use computer imagination and prescient IoT to support drivers' approximately available lanes, which can make them reach their destination in less time. Automobile-setup information receptors and linked cell apps supplement laptop vision-based clever transportation applications for this motive.

Smart roads and highways are also part of a metropolis's clever transportation network. These standards function as IoT and AI-based total programs in roads and motors to control the rate limit of vehicles on all sorts of roads. Such programs constantly and autonomously monitor the waft of traffic and send indicators to drivers and police employees if vehicles are located crossing the velocity limit. This feature of clever transportation is mainly beneficial for police authorities as it prevents them from being crushed by the high visitors and velocity in clever towns.

Geospatial traffic steering structures, also part of laptop vision-powered clever transportation networks, use GPS, GIS, and radiofrequency devices for precise traffic tracking. Such equipment works in unison to provide 3D spatial and geographical information to site visitor controllers and drivers regarding car proximity, visitor density, upcoming impediment-related alerts, and site visitor inflows on unique routes.

One example of smart-town-based traffic management can be found in the town of Darmstadt, Germany.

8.5.4 AI vision for autonomous driving

Over the last few years, almost all fundamental carmakers have dipped their toes into the driverless car market. The range of autonomous cars is slated to grow over the next few years. Such motors will represent the following technology of smart transportation in smart cities. What's more, such vehicles additionally feature a plethora of generation, along with computer vision packages, that will affect their mobility, occupant, and pedestrian protection, and gas performance-related elements.

Self-sufficient vehicles depend upon several smart cameras for object reputation – for example, as it should be figuring out pedestrians, visitors lights, or other motors even in moderate to low visibility – with the purpose of regulating protection features such as airbags and automated brakes. Moreover, such vehicles also depend on laptops that are imaginative and prescient for three-D mapping for higher selection-making concerning course selection, using speed and parking – this outcome in a good lesser number of injuries in related clever cities.

Further to this, computer vision, IoT, and AI also make self-sustaining vehicles more "connected," which means they can "speak" autonomously with other clever motors and with smart transportation devices and applications. So, as an example, two independent automobiles in a slim lane can foresee an accident because of a car rushing toward them from the alternative aspect. The usage of IoT and laptops is imaginative and prescient; each vehicle can either pull over to protection or alternate lanes in ideal sync to keep away from a collision and the consequent vehicular pile-up. This is the most fundamental instance of what connected clever automobiles can do.

Clever transportation genuinely would not exist without PC vision, AI, IoT, blockchain, and a few different clever metropolis technologies. Computer imagination and prescient, in particular, are instrumental in studying dynamically captured statistics and using them across vehicles and transportation law gadgets. In this way, it says with certainty that computer vision plays its element in making smart cities extra livable, sustainable, and viable.

Metropolitan cities, which mean active cities, require smart transportation systems or AI-based network systems that provide smooth functionality. Artificial intelligence or IoT systems, which lead to digital platforms, provide metropolitan cities with the opportunity to achieve objectives without any hassle.

There must be three attributes in smart cities: livability, workability, and sustainability. Livability focuses on an easy and healthy life balance with environment, work, routine work, etc. Also, I aim to develop a healthy and sound work–life balance in a smart city. Workability is relevant with a sound and healthy working environment with good opportunities for employment. Finally, sustainability is a major component of the development of any smart city. Sustainability enables the proper usage of technology while decreasing energy consumption, pollutants, and accidents.

Already, AI vision can be used in countless unique programs in smart towns. One of the essential software areas is wise transportation. AI, IoT, and laptop, imaginative and prescient, convey their unique competencies to the desk to transform transportation networks and motors in smart cities in more than one method.

8.5.5 AI-based transportation systems integrated with digital twin technology

AI-based transportation systems integrated with digital twin technology are revolutionizing the way we plan, manage, and optimize transportation networks [21]. By harnessing the power of artificial intelligence and creating virtual replicas of physical assets and systems, these intelligent transportation systems are unlocking unprecedented capabilities. Through real-time data collection from IoT devices, AI algorithms can analyze and interpret the information within the digital twin, enabling predictive analytics, optimization, and informed decision-making [22].

The benefits of integrating AI-based transportation and digital twin technology include real-time traffic monitoring, traffic congestion management, optimized traffic route prediction, and improved user experiences. These intelligent systems have the power to drastically improve the effectiveness, security, and sustainability of transportation networks, resulting in a future mobility environment that is smarter and more interconnected.

8.6 Security and Privacy in IoMT using Digital Twin Technology and Intelligent Transportation System: Challenges and Solutions

The notion of "smart mobility," which entails utilizing linked devices, sensors, and data analytics to improve transportation systems, is explored in this chapter, which explores merging digital twin technology with intelligent transportation systems. Similar to this, IoMT employs networked medical systems and gadgets to enhance healthcare services. IoMT and smart mobility both rely on networked systems and data sharing, raising security and privacy issues. Here, the following difficulties are covered:

Data gathering, transmission, and storage are essential components in both data privacy and protection scenarios. Sensitive data on travel habits, patient health records, and diagnostics are produced in significant quantities as a result of the integration of digital twins in smart mobility systems and

IoMT devices. Ensuring the privacy of this data is crucial to avoid unauthorized access, abuse, or breaches that could jeopardize people's sensitive information.

Security threats and risks: The combination of IoMT devices and digital twin technologies could result in security flaws. Smart mobility systems, which rely on connected networks and sensors, are prone to cyberattacks that might impede transportation or jeopardize user safety. The IoMT environment is susceptible to assaults aimed at patient data, healthcare networks, or medical equipment. Addressing these security threats is imperative to ensure the efficiency and integrity of these systems.

Access control and strong authentication: Both fields require strong access control and strong authentication procedures. To implement smart mobility, it is crucial to make sure that only authorized parties can control crucial transportation infrastructure. Similar to this, the IoMT requires strict access control measures to safeguard patient data and stop illegal access to medical equipment or systems.

Data integrity and encryption: Encryption techniques can be used to safeguard data during transmission and storage to maintain its security and privacy in both domains. To avoid tampering or illegal adjustments, it is equally important to ensure the integrity of the data.

Regulatory and ethical considerations: Regulations and guidelines have been established by regulatory agencies in response to security and privacy problems in smart mobility and the Internet of Medical Things. To preserve user data and uphold ethical standards, compliance with rules such as the Health Insurance Portability and Accountability Act (HIPAA) for healthcare data and the General Data Protection Regulation (GDPR) for privacy is crucial.

Strong security measures, data protection mechanisms, and regulatory compliance are essential to safeguarding the integrity of these interconnected systems.

8.7 Conclusion

Many industries like manufacturing, healthcare, energy, transportation, smart cities, etc., use digital twin technologies. Consequently, there is an increase in efficiency, cost savings, and revolution. Better asset management, predictive maintenance, process optimization, and informed decision-making are some characteristics of the digital twin technology. In order to enhance environmental elements like quality, optimize traffic flow, save energy and time, and ensure public safety and security, the intelligent transportation system (ITS) was primarily created to examine, develop, analyze, and integrate new technologies and innovations.

To sum up, the integration of digital twin technology and IoT enables real-time monitoring, predictive analytics, remote management, and collaboration. By integrating IoT data to build a thorough and dynamic picture of physical assets and systems, digital twins increase operational efficiency, maintenance practices, and decision-making processes in a range of sectors.

The fusion of digital twin technology with ITS has vast applications for changing smart transportation. By combining real-time data, predictive analytics, and decision-making abilities, this integration can revolutionize the transportation network's operation and offer several benefits for customers, communities, and transportation authorities.

Integrating digital twin technology with ITS makes real-time monitoring and visualization of transportation systems possible. Digital twins gather data from numerous sources, such as traffic sensors, GPS devices, and weather stations, to provide a thorough picture of traffic conditions, congestion hotspots, and system performance. Using this real-time information, stakeholders are better equipped to make wise choices and take preventative action to improve traffic flow, reroute vehicles, and effectively handle emergencies.

Additionally, the integration of digital twins with ITS makes simulation and predictive analytics possible. Digital twins can forecast traffic trends, optimize routes, and foresee congestion by using historical and real-time data. This makes it possible for transportation authorities to proactively control traffic, increase the efficiency of the entire system, and optimize the schedules for public transportation. In order to make the best decisions, stakeholders can test various scenarios and assess the effects of prospective modifications or interventions using the simulation capabilities provided by digital twins.

References

[1] Dastjerdi, A. V.; Buyya, R. Fog Computing: Helping the Internet of Things Realize Its Potential. Computer (Long. Beach. Calif).2016, 49 (8), 112–116.

[2] Yan, Z.; Zhang, P.; Vasilakos, A. V. A Survey on Trust Management for Internet of Things. J. Netw. Comput. Appl.2014, 42, 120–134.

[3] D. Evans. The Internet of Things: How the next evolution of the Internet is changing everything.CISCO white paper.2011, 1, 1-11.

[4] Ray, S.; Jin, Y.; Raychowdhury, A. The Changing Computing Paradigm with Internet of Things: A Tutorial Introduction. IEEE Des. \& Test2016, 33 (2), 76–96.

[5] Van Kranenburg, R. The Internet of Things: A Critique of Ambient Technology and the All-Seeing Network of RFID; Institute of Network Cultures, 2008.

[6] TSSO, I. T. U. Next Generation Networks-Frameworks and Functional Architecture Models. Int. Telecommun. union Tech. Rep.2012.

[7] Abomhara, M.; Køien, G. M. Cyber Security and the Internet of Things: Vulnerabilities, Threats, Intruders and Attacks. J. Cyber Secur. Mobil.2015, 65–88.

[8] Serpanos, D. The Cyber-Physical Systems Revolution. Computer (Long. Beach. Calif).2018, 51 (3), 70–73.

[9] Bertino, E.; Islam, N. Botnets and Internet of Things Security. Computer (Long. Beach. Calif).2017, 50 (2), 76–79.

[10] Zhang, L.; Zhang, L.; Du, B. Deep Learning for Remote Sensing Data: A Technical Tutorial on the State of the Art. IEEE Geosci. Remote Sens. Mag.2016, 4 (2), 22–40.

[11] Levine, J.; Underwood, S. E. A Multiattribute Analysis of Goals for Intelligent Transportation System Planning. Transp. Res. Part C Emerg. Technol.1996, 4 (2), 97–111.

[12] Chowdhury, M. A.; Sadek, A. W. Fundamentals of Intelligent Transportation Systems Planning; Artech House, 2003.

[13] A Report to the ITS Standards Community ITS Standards Testing Program By Memorial Institute for US Department of Transportation (USDOT), Chapter 2.

[14] https://www.digi.com/blog/post/introduction-to-smart-transportation-benefits.

[15] https://smartcities.gov.in/.

[16] Shapna, Muralidharan & Yoo, Byounghyun & Ko, Heedong. (2020). Designing a Semantic Digital Twin model for IoT. 1-2. 10.1109/ICCE46568.2020.9043088.

[17] Kumar, S., Tiwari, P., & Zymbler, M. (2019). Internet of Things is a revolutionary approach for future technology enhancement: a review. Journal of Big data, 6(1), 1-21.

[18] Dureja, A., Sangwan, S. (2021). A Review: Efficient Transportation—Future Aspects of IoV. In: Singh, P.K., Noor, A., Kolekar, M.H., Tanwar,

S., Bhatnagar, R.K., Khanna, S. (eds) Evolving Technologies for Computing, Communication and Smart World. Lecture Notes in Electrical Engineering, vol 694. Springer, Singapore. https://doi.org/10.1007/978-981-15-7804-5_

[19] Volkov, I., Radchenko, G., & Tchernykh, A. (2021). Digital twins, internet of things and mobile medicine: a review of current platforms to support smart healthcare. Programming and Computer Software, 47, 578-590.

[20] Dureja, A., & Sangwan, S. (2022). Intelligent traffic management system using Ant Colony Optimization and Internet of Things. International Journal of Communication Systems, 35(13), e5248.

[21] Wu, J., Wang, X., Dang, Y., & Lv, Z. (2022). Digital twins and artificial intelligence in transportation infrastructure: Classification, application, and future research directions. Computers and Electrical Engineering, 101, 107983.

[22] Garg, A., & Singh, A. K. (2024). Authentication protocols for securing IoMT: current state and technological advancements. In Securing Next-Generation Connected Healthcare Systems (pp. 1-29). Elsevier.

[23] Majeed, F., Nazir, M., & Schneider, J. (2023, February). ISA: Internet of Medical Things (IoMT) in Smart Healthcare and its Applications: A Review. In 2023 3rd International Conference on Artificial Intelligence (ICAI) (pp. 129-135). IEEE.

9

Exploring the Potential of Explainable Artificial Intelligence for Medical Diagnosis: A Review of Current Approaches and Future Directions

Raj Gaurang Tiwari[1], Abeer A. Aljohani[2], Rajat Bhardwaj[3], and Vishal Jain[4]

[1]Chitkara University Institute of Engineering and Technology, Chitkara University, India
[2]Computer Science Department, Applied College, Taibah University, Saudi Arabia
[3]School of Computer Science and Engineering, RV University, India
[4]Department of Computer Science and Engineering, School of Engineering and Technology, Sharda University, India
E-mail: rajgaurang@chitkara.edu.in; aahjohani@taibahu.edu.sa; rajatbhardwaj.x@gmail.com; drvishaljain83@gmail.com

Abstract

Artificial intelligence (AI) and machine learning (ML) are increasingly being used in a variety of medical applications. Treatments using AI for both prevention and cure are very helpful, precise, and fruitful. Certain AI algorithms are not transparent, which raises concerns about potential risks, harm, and trust issues. The goal of the developing discipline of explainable artificial intelligence (XAI) is to make machine learning models more open and easier to understand. XAI has the potential to radically alter medical diagnosis by illuminating the process by which models make their predictions and provide practitioners with insights that may be used to improve patient care. Both model-agnostic and model-specific approaches to XAI in the medical sector are reviewed in this chapter, along with their benefits and drawbacks. We also

DOI: 10.1201/9788770047395-9

discuss the potential and threats facing XAI in healthcare, including the need to set assessment criteria and promote ethical AI usage. XAI has the potential to improve patient diagnosis and care by bridging the gap between data-driven insights and clinical decision-making. This chapter contributes to informed decision-making, promoting responsible and effective integration of XAI, thus advancing patient care and shaping the future of healthcare.

Keywords: Machine learning, artificial intelligence, XAI, deep learning, convolutional neural networks.

9.1 Introduction

In recent years, the rapid evolution of machine learning (ML) and deep learning (DL) has ushered in a new era of transformative possibilities in the healthcare sector. As vast amounts of medical data become increasingly accessible, the utilization of these advanced computational techniques holds immense promise for revolutionizing medical diagnostics, treatment strategies, and patient care.

9.1.1 Machine learning models

In machine learning, an algorithm is created to make a prediction. Instead of relying on human guidance, machine learning algorithms are taught entirely from the data. It was Arthur Lee Samuel [1] who invented the phrase "machine learning" back in 1959. Calibrating an existing model for a particular issue is known as training. Applying a model's learned patterns to fresh data with unknown inputs and producing an output based on training data is a generalization. The model's output may solve a classification or regression challenge. Despite being a subset of regression, classification has practical differences. In any scenario, the model's purpose is to get as close as feasible to the true value of any given input. "Ground truth" is a term for this value.

The learning process is supervised if the ground truth is known. With this new data, it is possible to calculate the model's performance using some measure to compare the gap between the model's forecast and the actual data. This is how the model's error is calculated. Learning is termed unsupervised if the underlying truth is unknown. For instances where the cost of labeling data is prohibitive, this is typically the case. Machine learning models may be used to conduct data clustering in these situations. All highly correlated data points must lie inside the same region. Hence, a decision boundary must be set. They may also reduce complexity [2–5].

9.1.2 Feature engineering

In machine learning, an algorithm is designed to make predictions. Machine learning is trained entirely on data, not human instructions as if learning on its own. A trained model is calibrated to address a problem. A model generalizes the patterns it learned from its training data to new data by accepting unknown inputs and creating an output. Classification and regression models both offer a label or value for a given input, depending on the problem. Classification is a subset of regression, except the model outputs an integer.

The model's purpose is to get as near to the true value as feasible for each given input. The ground truth is a value that is referred to as such.

A supervised learning process is defined as one in which the ground truth is known. To assess the difference between the model's prediction and the ground truth, we may use this extra information to compute the model's performance. The model's error function looks like this. Learning is deemed unsupervised in cases when the ground truth is not known. If the cost of labeling data is excessively high, this may be a common situation. To solve these issues, machine learning models may be used to cluster data. In other words, to draw a line connecting data points so that strongly connected data points are contained inside it. By performing dimensionality reduction, they may also be utilized to lessen the complexity of a problem.

9.1.3 Deep learning

If input and output are frequently linked in shallow learning, deep learning uses many processing layers to figure out how input and output are associated. Deep learning is the polar opposite of shallow learning. It is via this process that the model itself learns to extract and choose the characteristics from the input set automatically.

Deep learning algorithms are popular because they can represent complicated circumstances better than hand-crafted features [6–8].

Deep learning intermediate layers separate input and output layers. The complexity of a model increases linearly with the size and number of layers of a network's hidden layers. To learn them, you will need more data and computational power. Another reason for the recent surge in popularity of these models is the explosion in the amount of data that has been made accessible as a result of disciplines like Big Data [9].

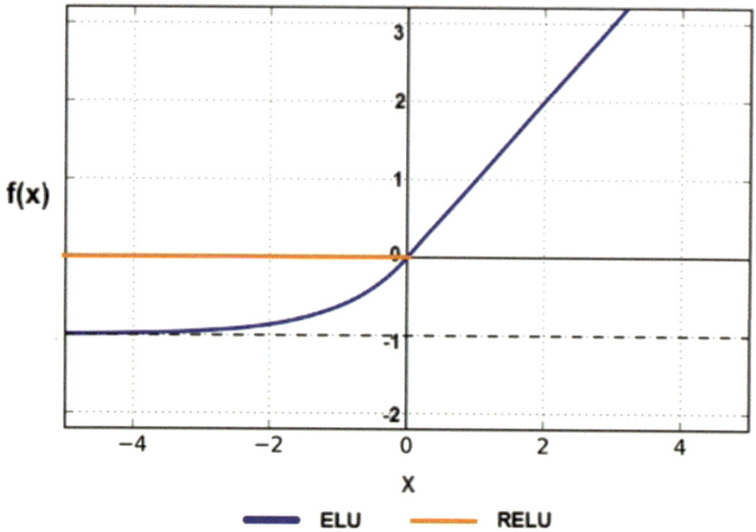

Figure 9.1 ELU and ReLU activation.

9.1.3.1 Activation function

An activation function modifies the neural network layer output. Activation functions translate a −1 to 1 result into a usable number. In buried layers, ReLU and ELU activations cause nonlinearity. Figure 9.1 shows nonlinear activation.

In classification problems, functions like Softmax, which compress output from 0 to 1, activate the output layer.

9.1.3.2 Overfitting and regularization

Machine learning models that have been overtrained to the point that they are no longer capable of accurately predicting new data are said to be overfitting. The size of the weights matrix becomes manageable, which pushes the decision boundary of the model too far in the direction of the training data.

It is common for models to get overfitted when they are given the same data repeatedly, resulting in weights being applied in the same direction repeatedly. Figure 9.2 provides a better illustration of the decision boundary of a model in three different scenarios: underfitting, desired, and overfitting.

Regularization methods prevent overfitting. By using regularization approaches, the model obtains more information that it can utilize to avoid getting too close to the optimal answer.

Figure 9.2 Overfitting visualization.

A data augmentation strategy may be employed to accomplish regularization. New data samples are created, but the label associated with them is preserved in the preprocessing of the dataset. In the case of picture data, it may be used to gently modify an image before feeding it to the model, causing the model's behavior on that image to change. Rotation, axis shift, cropping, axis flipping, and even image obfuscation are common operations performed on picture data, but there is a plethora of other options as well. While many operations may be applied to any dataset, rigorous pre-analysis is required to determine what information is being altered.

To train a model in deep learning, you need a lot more data than for other types of learning. Datasets are routinely given to models several times in the so-called training epochs because of this necessity. Additional regularization methods must be utilized to prevent overfitting.

Dropout [10] is a training technique that causes a layer of a network to arbitrarily eliminate the output of a neuron with a particular probability throughout the training process, setting that output to 0. Each sample training procedure is unique because of the unpredictability of the dropout, which implies that the neurons that are deleted are different for each sample. To avoid overfitting, the model is forced to depend on the actions of numerous neurons rather than a single neuron's prediction. The model becomes more resistant to overfitting as a result of higher dropout rates; however, this comes at the price of slower learning due to the fact that discriminative cell activations are less active during training. Dropout, much like other regularization strategies, is not activated until after the training phase of the model has been completed. Because the model uses all of its connections to evaluate unseen data, the performance of the model in testing is typically significantly higher than the performance of the model in training. This result, which may seem counter-intuitive to people who need to be made aware that this quality exists, is typical.

Batch normalization [11] is a newer kind of regularization for deep models. A layer of neurons is normalized over the training batch to prevent overfitting. As a result, connections with excessive weights will be moved toward the batch mean, preventing the model from making predictions based on their high weights. In addition, since the batches formed in each epoch should, for the majority of issues, be randomly generated, it also acts as a regularization. In other words, the batches supplied to the model are sometimes different. Therefore, the model can only learn a little about a certain weight since each batch is unique.

Early halting may also help avoid overfitting. Prior to overfitting the model, an early stopping technique is used. No progress in the model after a significant period of training is considered a failure. As a result, overfitting is prevented from occurring. Another negative of this method is that the model may need more time to attain its peak performance due to the stop condition being activated too early. The model will still overfit if the stop condition is defined too late and does not occur. The equilibrium between the two possibilities must be fine-tuned. Examples of training and validation error curves during model training are shown in Figure 9.3. When the two trajectories begin to diverge, it seems logical to make an early halt.

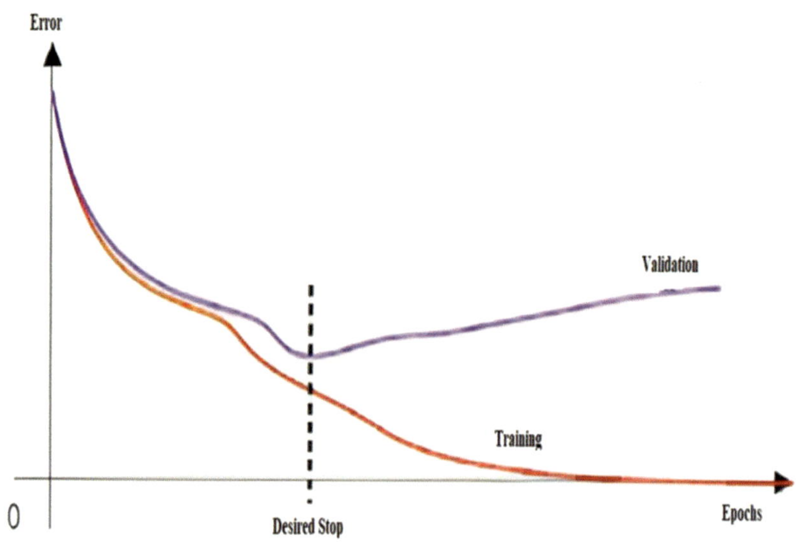

Figure 9.3 Early stopping visualization.

9.1.3.3 Convolutional neural networks

For example, there is a problem with the large dimensionality of image data, which makes it difficult for most algorithms to handle it effectively. Because of the very high number of connections that exist between neurons, neural networks struggle with both memory and computation. CNNs were designed to interpret visual input and have also been used for text and voice recognition. Convolution layers capture input attributes using local filters. So does deep learning. These filters, often called kernels, are more likely to link nearby pixels. Because each neuron in the next layer is not directly coupled to every other neuron in that layer, information is conveyed through convolutions, which repeatedly convolve around the picture in a predetermined window. Even in 3×3 pixel windows, these small-sized kernels are able to identify simple features such as edges and shapes in previously hidden layers. This is possible because these kernels can fit into smaller spaces. Following a few convolutional layers, the typical CNN design has a pooling layer. By reducing the number of dimensions in a picture, these layers save time by reducing the number of pixels in the image. As a second benefit, this pooling procedure enables the subsequent convolutions to examine information across a greater region of the picture, thereby allowing for the interpretation of more complicated aspects in an image. Using Keras and the MNIST dataset, Velickovic demonstrates how convolutional and pooling layers are implemented in a basic example model. Images of convolution effects are displayed in order to explain the process better.

9.1.4 Organization of the chapter

The remaining part of the chapter is organized as follows. Section 9.2 illuminates black-box models and white-box models. Section 9.3 focuses on the convolutional neural network, the base model in image classification. Section 9.4 discusses the model's interpretability. Section 9.5 reviews significant XAI-related works done in healthcare. Section 9.6 concludes with a remark.

9.2 Black Boxes and White Boxes

Black-box models and white-box models are two broad categories of models used to tackle machine learning challenges. The term "white-box" refers to a kind of model where the output may be examined to see how the input was transformed into the output. Humans can, for want of a better term, make sense of them. To humans, this is a valuable feature since it gives them a greater understanding of how the model works, as well as when it succeeds or fails in making accurate predictions. One of the most important qualities to have in any high-risk profession is the ability to take responsibility for one's actions and decisions.

Black-box models, on the other hand, are models that are invisible to visual inspection. Neural networks, for example, are deep learning models. They are quite difficult to examine. Due to the sheer number of variables involved, interpreting the model's output is impossible for the average person (the network used in this study has 13 million parameters and is relatively small). On the other hand, as processing power and memory become more readily available, deep learning classifiers are increasingly outperforming more classic models like decision trees. While this research is only one among several, it aims to narrow the gap.

9.3 The Convolutional Neural Network

To date, the highest-performing base model in the area of image classification is the convolutional neural network (CNN), thanks to the breakthrough that followed the launch of AlexNet [12]. It gained popularity and created new possibilities for image recognition research since it outperformed every other model when it was introduced in 2012 with a top-5 error rate of 17%. In 1998, Yann Lecun [13] suggested the idea. Lecun utilized the approach to classifying documents, not images. With the existing technology, a CNN-sized model could not be trained; therefore, the concept was abandoned until AlexNet. The AlexNet architecture may be seen in Figure 9.4.

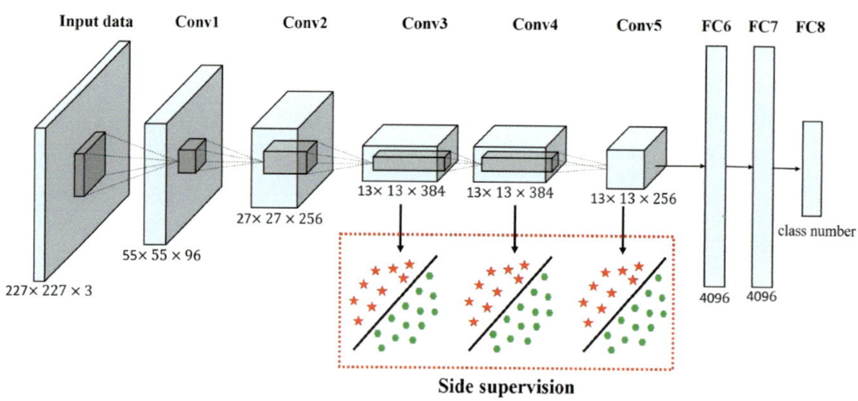

Figure 9.4 AlexNet architecture.

Based on the same CNN premise, the industry has seen explosive development since AlexNet was launched in 2012. ZFNet launched in 2013 with an error rate of 11.2% [14].

VGG NET [15], which achieved an error rate of just 7.2% by constructing basic but very deep structures, significantly improved state of the art for the communications petition the following year, in 2014. This chapter shows that increasing the depth of the network may overcome the optimization of hyperparameters that impact its design, such as kernel and padding size and the number of convolutional layers per pooling layer. Depth is necessary to capture hierarchical characteristics.

Both Google and Microsoft entered the fray in the following years with their versions of GoogLeNet and ResNet, respectively. In 2014, Google's GoogLeNet [16] also joined the competition, surpassing VGG by a slight margin with an error rate of 6.7%, which Google would improve to only 3.08% in 2016. There are 22 convolutional layers in this network, some of which are operating simultaneously, making it immensely more complex than VGG. It is only possible for researchers who have Google's resources to use this model because of its intricacy. GoogLeNet uses 1×1 convolutions as a type of dimension reduction while preserving convolutional layers' complicated feature maps. This enables the model to be incredibly efficient for its size. The potential of GoogLeNet's parallelism to be used in distributed computing makes it very valuable. It has been shown that non-sequentially stacked layers may even outperform stacked systems, ensuring the capacity to use distributed computing.

ResNet [17] from Microsoft joined the competition in 2015, winning it with a performance of 3.6%, a 50% decrease in prior records, as well as exceeding human error for the first time. It continues the VGG lineage with this network, which has 152 levels, proving that computational power can solve any problem. Even after two weeks of training on a system with eight graphics processing units, the network is still unable to match the results it achieved during the competition. In order to avoid overfitting in such deep architectures, a new technique must be introduced. This network does just that. As a byproduct of the convolutional + pooling layers, a residue is added to the input of this architecture. Instead of being entirely altered at each layer, this creates a new architecture that permits information to be transmitted along the tiers. Figure 9.5 provides a graphic depiction of the procedure.

The R-CNN combines picture segmentation and CNNs to enhance object detection [18]. R-CNN explains the learning process of CNNs in object identification by first employing image segmentation methods like Selective

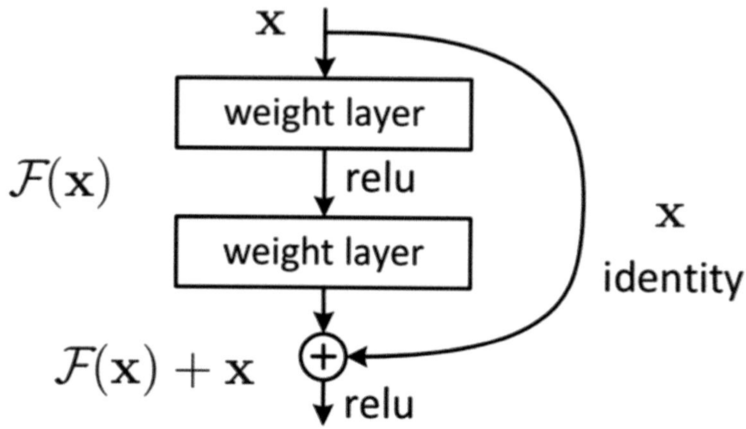

Figure 9.5 Residual block example.

Search to segment the picture into areas of interest, and then applying a CNN to those regions to determine whether an item is there. In 2017, Facebook researchers [19] introduced a technique for estimating an image's pixel-level mask for object recognition before feeding it to a CNN. It beat every single-model entry in the COCO challenge set for object identification.

9.4 Interpretability

A quality known as explainability or model interpretability is critical to the application of AI in a wide range of industries. To effectively improve a model, data scientists need to be able to see how it works in multiple situations. It has been difficult for us to keep up with how rapidly the models we are building are changing since we have yet to be able to grasp them as quickly as they have changed.

The first study on the subject was done in 2003, but it was not until the end of the decade that neural networks were widely used. There are two types of visualization approaches: decompositions (e.g., a Taylor series) and sensitivity studies (e.g., testing the model's sensitivity to changes in input).

Erhan et al. [20] make an effort at visualization. Each of the ten classes in the MNIST dataset is examined in their study, which is based on a current dataset that was accessible at the time. In this way, the numerous forms that activate the network at each layer may be represented graphically. Due to filtering and pooling procedures, this visualization approach cannot be used for more sophisticated models like the ones argued above since the original picture is transformed into forms that need to be more understandable to the human eye.

Decomposing a convolutional network is tough because of the various pooling procedures required.

Before AlexNet's release, academics studied ways to uncover deep convolutional models' inner workings. Visualize the model's feature and activation maps to understand its behavior. Zeiler and Fergus [21] published research applying deconvolution (the reverse of convolution) on a trained neural network's output. This provides heat maps showing which pixels are most commonly triggered by the network.

The first outcome of this research is the publication of LIME (local interpretable model-agnostic explanations) [22]. This innovative approach obfuscates the classifier's input image via image segmentation. To activate the classifier, the system must identify the most obscured sections. Since there are too many alternatives, the system uses an interpretable white-box model like a decision tree.

Simultaneously modifying input to get insight into model sensitivity is known as sensitivity analysis since it evaluates the model's response to a local change. A white-box model is used to process the original picture, making it simple to understand. When applied to a variety of models, this technique may provide the user with valuable information. Although the model is flexible, it is unable to provide information from inside the model's hidden layers – it only displays us an input–output link.

Despite this, the second publication from DARPA, aLIME for Anchor LIME [23], was released soon after. Using the so-called anchors, this method creates if–then rules for the model to employ as an extra explanation. Afterward, the model attempts to learn the shortest and most accurate rule set to describe a collection of photos. Because it is possible to create a rule set that is perfectly accurate to describe just one picture, this method aims to maximize rule set coverage while compromising the least amount of accuracy. For example, this provides for a clearer description of the procedure. Obviously, this has the drawback of necessitating the manual building of the anchors for each issue. In spite of the algorithm's model independence, each issue has its overhead.

Binder et al. [24] examine how pictures move through a convolutional network. These papers investigate various approaches to decomposing a convolutional network. In [25], a Taylor-series decomposition is used to arrive at the suggested technique. This breakdown makes it feasible to create a pixel-level heatmap of the activation of the inputs. Another published paper by the same team [26] explains the mathematical foundations for why this decomposition is viable.

According to Binder et al. [27], this approach may be further improved upon. Each layer's neuron receives a relevance score, which is propagated across the network and assigned to every pixel in the input picture. There previously needed to be a way to implement local renormalization layers as proposed in [24] using this method. The team constructs a measure for the importance of a pixel based on its sensitivity to changes in the input picture to validate that the findings produced are legitimate. Randomly assigning RGB values to pixels that are already projected to be of particular importance will generate more of a mess in the model's output than applying the same modification to other pixels. Similarly, a smaller drop in speed is to be predicted if just the least important pixels are altered. In line with this assumption, the reported findings show that the algorithm correlates to an effective network breakdown.

Hendricks et al. [28] researched photo explanations. Using a collection of bird images, an algorithm is being constructed to generate textual descriptions of an image's essential sub-components. Figure 9.6 illustrates the process output.

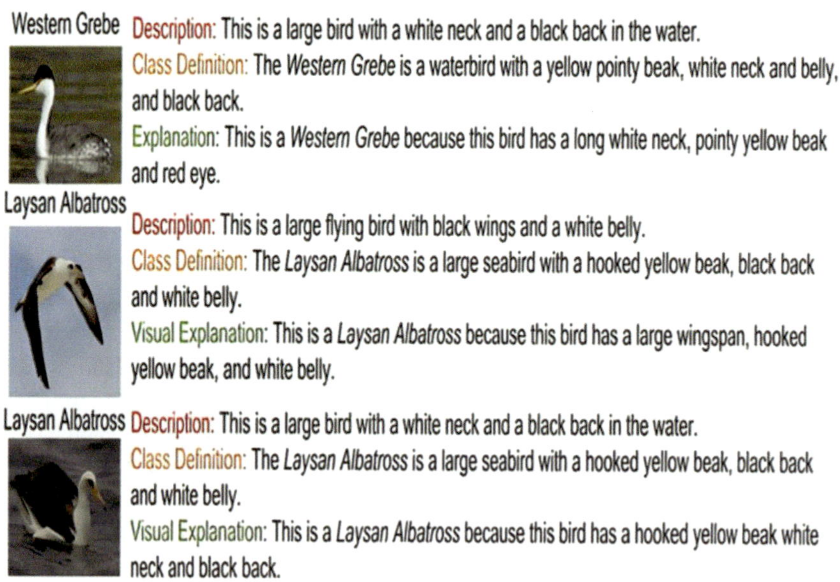

Figure 9.6 Birds explanation [28].

They used their dataset to train a long short-term memory (LSTM) generator model, which evaluated picture descriptions, class relevance, and explanation performance using a redesigned loss function and many new measures. The suggested metrics are aimed at evaluating how effectively an image description explains the information in the picture and how relevant it is to the class description. Since the same visual description (for example, dark bird with a large beak) applies to several bird classes, this is tough to do. Thus, measurements serve as a beginning approach to quantifying this accuracy.

9.4.1 Feature transferring

For the first time, researchers have attempted to quantify the extent to which layers may be applied to similar issues. No new models will be developed as a result of this research; instead, a well-known model's performance will be examined under various test settings to better understand its learning patterns. The objective is to find out how much of a model's weight can be transferred from another model, a process known as transfer learning.

ImageNet is used to compare the performance of two different models. One model is pre-trained on the same dataset, whereas the other has had its layers transferred from a separate dataset. These traits are examined in terms of how "transferable" or "generic" they are.

Both models are compared when they are trained on datasets with comparable super-classes (such as man-made items) against datasets that are different (such as unlabeled images) (not sharing the same super-classes, such as man-made objects versus natural objects).

9.4.2 Necessity of explainable AI

Convolutional neural networks (CNNs) should be able to perceive things like humans; however, Szegedy et al. [16] found otherwise. The authors applied learned disturbance to input image. The algorithm failed miserably in correct classification.

Kurakin et al. [29] revisit this difficulty to perform modest input modifications. To decrease the amount of model-specific knowledge needed to generate disturbance maps, Kurakin et al. [29] evaluate different techniques and design one that needs input–output matchings. The study shows that a model may fail with only one piece of data: its output in response to a given input. CNNs cannot be employed in major systems or domains in their present form.

9.4.3 Defining explainable AI

The next logical step is to figure out how to define these new, more explainable models. Trust, causality, transferability, and informativeness are four fundamental criteria for evaluating explainable theories. The degree to which an end-user may trust and rely on a model's output for a specific situation is a subjective criterion that relies on the model's job. Analysis of a model's causal links, transferability of its generalization capacity, and informativeness are all aspects of the model's usefulness to the user. If the model links to alternate data inputs that yield the same classification, it gives more information without disclosing the model's structure. Lipton's work also focuses on the ethical difficulties of machine learning. The expanding use of machine learning and AI in social arenas like crediting and screening employment applications raises concerns about bias elimination.

However, several definitions exist of what constitutes an "explainable" artificial intelligence (AI) model. A worldwide standard and measurements for this issue have not been established yet.

9.5 XAI in the Medical Domain

In the medical field, visualization is a helpful way to explain the model's prediction explanation to the end-users. We have seen a lot of interest in visualizing interpretability data. With the use of visualizations and radiological evidence highlighted, Warman et al. [30] suggested that a diagnosis for radiological review may be made using all labeled aspects in an interpretable decision tree. Researchers at Qiu et al. [31] used a color map overlay to the standard imaging modalities so that illness risk could be easily understood. There is also an innovative new clinically interpretable ConvNet architecture (EAMNet) suggested by Liao et al. [32], which gives a visual area of interest to assist the accuracy of their diagnostic choice. This study by Hao et al. [33] shows how anesthesiologists may benefit by visualizing the factors that contribute to their work.

Attention may be utilized as a standalone feature or as an extension of XAI. Shickel et al. [34] used self-attention to highlight key time steps in input time series for real-time prediction (DeepSOFA). Using attention models between the RNN encoder and 1D convolution layers, high-attention SSEs in proteins and atoms in compounds were found. When making medical choices, it is important to describe what you are doing in clear words.

To compensate for a shortage of training data, data augmentation methods like generative adversarial networks (GAN) were developed. Xiang et al.

[35] used mode data to train their GAN model for resilience. Fiosina et al. [36] benchmarked DL and random-forest-based metadata augmentation of tissue, age, and sex using short RNA (sRNA) expression profiles. This study suggests a tradeoff between prediction accuracy and algorithm transparency. Blended systems, like those developed by Kanda et al. [38], may be utilized to identify high-risk patients. Garg et al. [37] have identified the importance of IoT in the healthcare domain and have explored the related issues.

9.6 Conclusion

As a consequence, many of the best-performing strategies need to be more sophisticated (abstract) and explained in simple terms. In order to arrive at probabilistic judgments, these approaches must analyze high-dimensional input data in a nonlinear and hierarchical way. A clear understanding of what knowledge is required to make particular judgments, for example, needs to be clarified. As a consequence, these models are sometimes referred to as "black box" models since they lack transparency or openness. The presence of this mysterious figure hampers a variety of disciplines. For example, judgments concerning a patient's care in a hospital or a defendant's punishment in court should be able to be explained. The topic of explainable AI (XAI) has recently reappeared in an attempt to overcome this problem. Rather than discussing AI systems that have desired qualities that make them explainable, this chapter presents a reality-rooted approach illustrating what XAI can provide. There are further prospects for XAI research in the fields of ML with humans in the loop, DL robustness, and the tradeoff between accuracy and explainability. There is still a lot of room for advancement in the XAI field in terms of particular use cases, approaches, and techniques. Future research could delve into innovative XAI techniques that bridge interpretability and performance in medical contexts. Integrating diverse data modalities and leveraging domain knowledge could enhance explanations and decision support. By continuing to uncover novel approaches, the chapter's scope extends to shaping responsible, effective, and patient-centric AI-driven medical diagnosis.

References

[1] A. L. Samuel, "Some studies in machine learning using the game of checkers," IBM Journal of Research and Development, vol. 44, no. 1–2, pp. 207–219, 2000, doi:10.1147/RD.441.0206.

[2] S. Bhardwaj, S. Jain, N. K. Trivedi, A. Kumar, and R. G. Tiwari, "Intelligent Heart Disease Prediction System Using Data Mining Modeling Techniques," pp. 881–891, 2022, doi:10.1007/978-981-19-0707-4_79.

[3] Hassanien, A. E., Gupta, D., Singh, A. K., & Garg, A. (Eds.). Explainable edge AI: a futuristic computing perspective (Vol. 1072). Springer Nature. 2022.

[4] R. G. Tiwari, M. Husain, V. Srivastava, and K. Singh, "A hypercube novelty model for comparing E-commerce and M-commerce," 2011. doi:10.1145/1947940.1948068.

[5] R. G. Tiwari, M. Husain, V. Srivastava, and A. Agrawal, "Web personalization by assimilating usage data and semantics expressed in ontology terms," 2011. doi: 10.1145/1980022.1980133.

[6] H. Agarwal, P. Tiwari, and R. G. Tiwari, "Exploiting Sensor Fusion for Mobile Robot Localization," 2019. doi:10.1109/I-SMAC47947.2019.9032653.

[7] A. K. Agarwal, L. Rani, R. G. Tiwari, T. Sharma, and P. K. Sarangi, Honey Encryption: Fortification Beyond the Brute-Force Impediment. 2021. doi:10.1007/978-981-16-0942-8_64.

[8] R. G. Tiwari, A. Misra, V. Khullar, A. K. Agarwal, S. Gupta, and A. P. Srivastava, "Identifying Microscopic Augmented Images using Pre-Trained Deep Convolutional Neural Networks," 2021. doi:10.1109/ICTAI53825.2021.9673472.

[9] R. G. Tiwari, A. Pratap Srivastava, G. Bhardwaj, and V. Kumar, "Exploiting UML Diagrams for Test Case Generation: A Review," 2021. doi:10.1109/ICIEM51511.2021.9445383.

[10] N. Srivastava, G. Hinton, A. Krizhevsky, I. Sutskever, and R. Salakhutdinov, "Dropout: a simple way to prevent neural networks from overfitting," The journal of machine learning research, vol. 15, no. 1, pp. 1929–1958, 2014.

[11] S. Ioffe and C. Szegedy, "Batch normalization: Accelerating deep network training by reducing internal covariate shift," in International conference on machine learning, 2015, pp. 448–456.

[12] Ramesh, T. R., Umesh Kumar Lilhore, M. Poongodi, Sarita Simaiya, Amandeep Kaur, and Mounir Hamdi. "Predictive analysis of heart diseases with machine learning approaches." Malaysian Journal of Computer Science (2022): 132-148.

[13] Y. LeCun, L. Bottou, Y. Bengio, and P. Haffner, "Gradient-based learning applied to document recognition," Proceedings of the IEEE, vol. 86, no. 11, pp. 2278–2323, 1998, doi:10.1109/5.726791.

[14] M. D. Zeiler and R. Fergus, "Visualizing and Understanding Convolutional Networks arXiv:1311.2901v3 [cs.CV] 28 Nov 2013," Computer Vision–ECCV 2014, vol. 8689, no. PART 1, pp. 818–833, 2014, doi: 10.1007/978-3-319-10590-1_53.

[15] Lilhore, Umesh Kumar, M. Poongodi, Amandeep Kaur, Sarita Simaiya, Abeer D. Algarni, Hela Elmannai, V. Vijayakumar, Godwin Brown Tunze, and Mounir Hamdi. "Hybrid model for detection of cervical cancer using causal analysis and machine learning techniques." Computational and Mathematical Methods in Medicine 2022 (2022).

[16] C. Szegedy et al., "Going deeper with convolutions," in Proceedings of the IEEE conference on computer vision and pattern recognition, 2015, pp. 1–9.

[17] Z. Wu, C. Shen, and A. van den Hengel, "Wider or Deeper: Revisiting the ResNet Model for Visual Recognition," Pattern Recognition, vol. 90, pp. 119–133, Jun. 2019, doi:10.1016/J.PATCOG.2019.01.006.

[18] T. Yirtici and K. Yurtkan, "Regional-CNN-based enhanced Turkish sign language recognition," Signal, Image and Video Processing 2021 16:5, vol. 16, no. 5, pp. 1305–1311, Jan. 2022, doi:10.1007/S11760-021-020 82-2.

[19] K. He, G. Gkioxari, P. Dollar, and R. Girshick, "Mask R-CNN," Proceedings of the IEEE International Conference on Computer Vision, vol. 2017-October, pp. 2980–2988, Dec. 2017, doi: 10.1109/ICCV.2017.322.

[20] D. Erhan, Y. Bengio, A. Courville, and P. Vincent, "Visualizing higher-layer features of a deep network," University of Montreal, vol. 1341, no. 3, p. 1, 2009.

[21] M. D. Zeiler and R. Fergus, "Visualizing and Understanding Convolutional Networks arXiv:1311.2901v3 [cs.CV] 28 Nov 2013," Computer Vision–ECCV 2014, vol. 8689, no. PART 1, pp. 818–833, 2014, doi: 10.1007/978-3-319-10590-1_53.

[22] N. Barr Kumarakulasinghe, T. Blomberg, J. Liu, A. Saraiva Leao, and P. Papapetrou, "Evaluating local interpretable model-agnostic explanations on clinical machine learning classification models," Proceedings - IEEE Symposium on Computer-Based Medical Systems, vol. 2020-July, pp. 7–12, Jul. 2020, doi:10.1109/CBMS49503.2020.00009.

[23] M. T. Ribeiro, S. Singh, and C. Guestrin, "Nothing Else Matters: Model-Agnostic Explanations By Identifying Prediction Invariance," Nov. 2016, doi:10.48550/arxiv.1611.05817.

[24] S. Bach, A. Binder, G. Montavon, F. Klauschen, K. R. Müller, and W. Samek, "On Pixel-Wise Explanations for Nonlinear Classifier Decisions

by Layer-Wise Relevance Propagation," PLOS ONE, vol. 10, no. 7, p. e0130140, Jul. 2015, doi:10.1371/JOURNAL.PONE.0130140.

[25] S. Bach, H. H. I. Fraunhofer, A. Binder, E. D. U. Sg, and W. Samek, "Deep Taylor Decomposition of Neural Networks".

[26] G. Montavon, S. Lapuschkin, A. Binder, W. Samek, and K. R. Müller, "Explaining nonlinear classification decisions with deep Taylor decomposition," Pattern Recognition, vol. 65, pp. 211–222, May 2017, doi: 10.1016/J.PATCOG.2016.11.008.

[27] A. Binder, G. Montavon, S. Lapuschkin, K. R. Müller, and W. Samek, "Layer-wise relevance propagation for neural networks with local renormalization layers," Lecture Notes in Computer Science (including subseries Lecture Notes in Artificial Intelligence and Lecture Notes in Bioinformatics), vol. 9887 LNCS, pp. 63–71, 2016, doi:10.1007/978-3-319-44781-0_8/COVER/.

[28] L. A. Hendricks, Z. Akata, M. Rohrbach, J. Donahue, B. Schiele, and T. Darrell, "Generating visual explanations," Lecture Notes in Computer Science (including subseries Lecture Notes in Artificial Intelligence and Lecture Notes in Bioinformatics), vol. 9908 LNCS, pp. 3–19, 2016, doi: 10.1007/978-3-319-46493-0_1/FIGURES/8.

[29] A. Kurakin, I. J. Goodfellow, and S. Bengio, "Adversarial examples in the physical world," 5th International Conference on Learning Representations, ICLR 2017 - Workshop Track Proceedings, 2019.

[30] A. Warman et al., "Interpretable Artificial Intelligence for COVID-19 Diagnosis from Chest CT Reveals Specificity of Ground-Glass Opacities," medRxiv, p. 2020.05.16.20103408, May 2020, doi:10.1101/2020.05.16.20103408.

[31] S. Qiu et al., "Development and validation of an interpretable deep learning framework for Alzheimer's disease classification," Brain, vol. 143, no. 6, pp. 1920–1933, Jun. 2020, doi:10.1093/BRAIN/AWAA137.

[32] W. Liao, B. Zou, R. Zhao, Y. Chen, Z. He, and M. Zhou, "Clinical Interpretable Deep Learning Model for Glaucoma Diagnosis," IEEE Journal of Biomedical and Health Informatics, vol. 24, no. 5, pp. 1405–1412, May 2020, doi:10.1109/JBHI.2019.2949075.

[33] J. Hao, S. C. Kosaraju, N. Z. Tsaku, D. H. Song, and M. Kang, "PAGE-Net: Interpretable and integrative deep learning for survival analysis using histopathological images and genomic data," Pacific Symposium on Biocomputing, vol. 25, no. 2020, pp. 355–366, 2020, doi:10.1142/9789811215636_0032.

[34] B. Shickel, T. J. Loftus, L. Adhikari, T. Ozrazgat-Baslanti, A. Bihorac, and P. Rashidi, "DeepSOFA: A Continuous Acuity Score for Critically Ill Patients using Clinically Interpretable Deep Learning," Scientific Reports 2019 9:1, vol. 9, no. 1, pp. 1–12, Feb. 2019, doi:10.1038/s41598-019-38491-0.

[35] A. Xiang and F. Wang, "Towards Interpretable Skin Lesion Classification with Deep Learning Models," AMIA Annual Symposium Proceedings, vol. 2019, p. 1246, 2019, Accessed: Jun. 15, 2022. [Online]. Available: /PMC/articles/PMC7153112/

[36] J. Fiosina, M. Fiosins, and S. Bonn, "Explainable Deep Learning for Augmentation of Small RNA Expression Profiles," Journal of Computational Biology, vol. 27, no. 2, p. 234, Feb. 2020, doi:10.1089/CMB.2019.0320.

[37] Garg, A., Singh, A. K., Mohit, A., & Aleem, A. (2024). Forensics in the Internet of Medical Things. In Securing Next-Generation Connected Healthcare Systems (pp. 179-212). Academic Press.

[38] E. Kanda et al., "Application of explainable ensemble artificial intelligence model to categorization of hemodialysis-patient and treatment using nationwide-real-world data in Japan," PLOS ONE, vol. 15, no. 5, p. e0233491, May 2020, doi:10.1371/JOURNAL.PONE.0233491.

10

A Comprehensive Study on Securing Healthcare Systems using Futuristic Machine Intelligence

Apaar Vashishtha, Swastik Mohapatra, and Sushruta Mishra

Kalinga Institute of Industrial Technology, Deemed to be University, India
E-mail: 20051942@kiit.ac.in; 2005137@kiit.ac.in;
sushruta.mishrafcs@kiit.ac.in

Abstract

The growing use of technology in healthcare systems has led to concerns about the security of personal health information. Artificial intelligence has been proposed as a solution to improve the security of healthcare systems. This chapter offers a systematic examination of the current state of healthcare system security, focusing on the integration of emerging AI technologies. Artificial intelligence (AI) constitutes a branch of computer science dedicated to the development and understanding of intelligent entities, typically manifested as software programs. The review explores the different techniques used to secure healthcare systems and the applications of AI in healthcare security. This chapter also analyzes the challenges and limitations related to using AI in healthcare security and proposes future research directions. The review highlights the potential of AI in improving the security of healthcare systems, including detecting and mitigating cyber threats, monitoring access to sensitive health data, and enhancing authentication processes. The review also identifies the need for further research in developing AI-based healthcare security systems that can effectively detect and prevent security breaches while preserving patient privacy and confidentiality. Overall, this chapter provides an extensive analysis of the current state of healthcare security using AI technology and offers insights for future research and challenges in this

DOI: 10.1201/9788770047395-10

field. The study emphasizes the importance of addressing challenges as well as limitations associated with AI in healthcare security to protect patient data. Further research and development of effective AI-based healthcare security systems are needed for better healthcare outcomes and a secure healthcare environment.

Keywords: Artificial intelligence, healthcare, blockchain, security systems, machine learning, cybersecurity, deep learning, artificial neural network.

10.1 Introduction

Healthcare is an important aspect of our lives. Without health, we cannot do anything, no matter how much time, money, or other resources we have. Everyone needs a fit body and a fit mind.

The healthcare industry is experiencing a transformation in the way it views and uses artificial intelligence (AI) technology. This technology is bringing significant benefits such as better efficiency, access control, technological advancements, and protection of privacy and data security in healthcare data management. Artificial intelligence can be used in many fields of healthcare, such as detecting diseases rapidly, providing personalized treatment plans, and automating drug discovery and diagnostics processes. It also offers the promise of improving patient outcomes, enhancing safety, and reducing healthcare delivery costs.

However, effortless access to healthcare in technological aspects has its risks and vulnerabilities that can easily compromise and hinder the performance of smart healthcare systems. The healthcare industry needs help managing data from heterogeneous devices due to variations in data size, format, quality, and precision. Safeguarding this data from malicious individuals who aim to exploit it for personal gain is also a significant challenge. Consequently, intelligent healthcare systems are highly susceptible to a range of security risks and vulnerabilities, including hardware- and software-based attacks, system-level breaches, and network attacks, all of which possess the potential to endanger patients' lives in the most dire circumstances. Technological accidents inevitably occur when technology becomes complex and coupled with bad security measures, which leads to something going wrong in the system as a whole; they are called system breakdowns. Therefore, this chapter is written to make AI systems in the healthcare sector more secure.

The future of using AI in healthcare systems is extremely bright and filled with numerous possibilities for further innovation and research. Moving forward into an immensely linked digital world, artificial intelligence will undoubtedly become an indispensable asset that will definitely change how doctors and other professionals in the healthcare industry treat, diagnose, and cure patients. The potential for using artificial intelligence in healthcare is tremendous and offers a promising future that includes advancements, enhanced patient experiences, and, ultimately, better outcomes.

The data in the healthcare industry is becoming more and more complex, and the volume of data generated is also increasing exponentially, which means artificial intelligence (AI) will progressively be relevant within the field, which will benefit all the stakeholders and ensure efficient and smooth working for all. Payers, providers of care, and life sciences companies are already utilizing various types of AI. Presently, the primary utilization categories encompass diagnosis, treatment, patient involvement, and compliance, along with administrative functions within hospitals and various healthcare institutions. Despite the fact that AI has proven capable of performing various healthcare tasks equally or more effectively than humans, e.g., When AI powered robots do the procedures and review the test results, the results are usually better than the manual processes, thus increasing the accuracy, decreasing the chances of errors and improving the health of the patients. This transformative integration demonstrates how AI is changing the face of today's medical practices. The automation of healthcare professional jobs on a large scale is likely to face considerable obstacles related to the practical implementation of technology. These challenges may include issues related to the development of appropriate AI tools, data privacy, and security concerns, as well as the need for significant investments in infrastructure and staff training. These barriers are expected to impede the adoption of automation in the healthcare industry for the foreseeable future.

Furthermore, alongside these hurdles in implementation, it is imperative to consider significant ethical aspects when employing AI in healthcare. These issues may include questions related to patient privacy and autonomy, the accuracy and reliability of AI algorithms, and the potential for AI to exacerbate existing healthcare disparities. As such, it is important for healthcare professionals and policymakers to carefully consider these ethical concerns when developing and implementing AI solutions in healthcare. Historically, healthcare decisions have been made by humans, and utilizing AI to make such decisions presents concerns regarding accountability, transparency, consent, and confidentiality. Undoubtedly, AI is expected to assume a pivotal role in the future of healthcare, particularly through its application in machine learning (ML), which is a pivotal advancement for the field of precision medicine. While initial attempts at utilizing AI for diagnosis, treatment, and recommendations have posed significant challenges, it is expected that AI will eventually become proficient in these areas as well. With the rapid advancements in AI technology for image analysis, AI will probably likely be used to analyze the majority of radiology and pathology images at some point in the future. Figure 10.1 highlights the financial loss incurred due to cyberattacks in the medical domain.

When implementing AI in healthcare in a secure environment, there are many challenges too, like lack of standardization. Globally, there are no universally recognized standards for the application of artificial intelligence tools throughout the economic sectors, even in the field of medicine. The lack of such guidelines makes it difficult to ensure ethics, security, and uniformity in the implementation of AI. This is also very important in order to ensure the availability of the comprehensive requirements to be used in the application of AI without losing public confidence and allowing development in all areas. There is the need for continuous investment and development to overcome this challenge, and another huge challenge for inducing AI in healthcare is that there are already many legacy systems present as of now in healthcare industry and it is very difficult as well as burdensome to shift technology with all the database and other useful things present; also it will

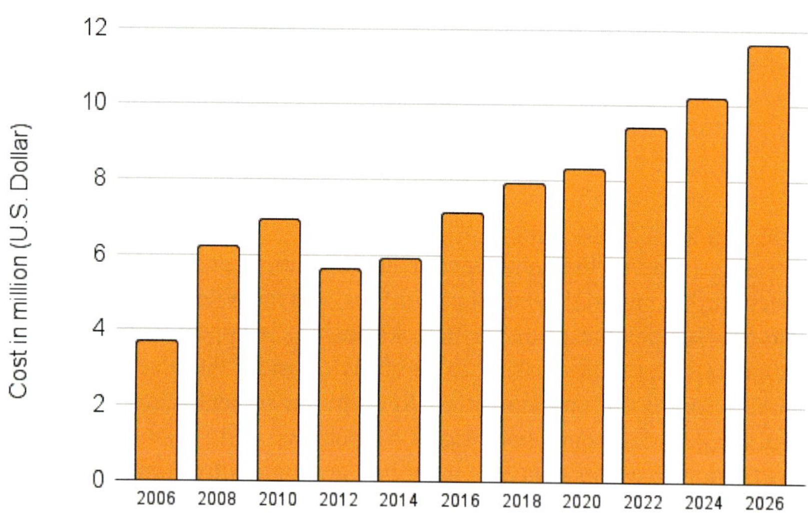

Figure 10.1 Total monetary loss due to cyberattacks on healthcare sector [2].

need lots of financial aid. Another challenge is that there is not much trust in artificial intelligence and its results among the common people of developing countries like Pakistan in the current times. Further implementing AI-based models and its technologies leads to very high functioning and operating costs, and despite the potential benefits that AI holds for transforming the healthcare industry, a crucial impediment to its widespread adoption is the lack of qualified personnel in the field. More individuals with the necessary skills to design and implement AI technologies for healthcare purposes are needed, presenting a significant concern. The need for more adequately skilled personnel poses a significant impediment to the incorporation of AI into the healthcare sector.

The chapter's structural layout is as follows. Section 10.1 discusses various aspects concerning securing healthcare entities and its issues. Section 10.2 highlights important related works and models in context to the work. Section 10.3 presents futuristic AI models for healthcare security. Finally, the chapter is concluded in Section 10.4.

The main objectives of this study are as follows:

- To identify the current security gaps and vulnerabilities in healthcare systems and assess how AI technology can address these issues and improve them.
- To investigate the potential of AI-based intrusion detection systems, threat intelligence, and access control mechanisms for making healthcare systems secure.
- To evaluate the accuracy, reliability, and scalability of artificial intelligence solutions in real-world healthcare settings and scenarios all around the globe.
- To develop and test AI algorithms that will detect and prevent cyberattacks, data breaches, and other security threats to healthcare systems.
- To investigate all the ethical implications and potential biases associated with the use of AI technology for healthcare security.
- To develop frameworks for integrating AI technology into existing healthcare security systems and protocols.
- To examine how AI technology has the capacity to improve patient privacy, uphold confidentiality, and bolster data protection within healthcare systems.
- To identify future research directions and potential collaborations to advance the use of AI technology for securing healthcare systems.

10.2 Related Works

Artificial intelligence and deep learning models have been widely used in image analysis to address a number of challenges in medical therapies. Deep learning might perform better when taught on a large amount of data. Patients, diagnostic labs, research organizations, and hospitals can collaborate to share important findings and enhance the AI algorithm. However, due to privacy and security issues, they have trouble sharing crucial data with outside parties. Consequently, a barrier to raising the caliber of AI-based healthcare systems is secure data exchange.

Kumar et al. [1] have suggested a strategy for improving lung cancer prediction using CT scan images. This strategy includes sharing regional models via blockchain. As a result, the collectively updated model assists in accurately diagnosing patients' illnesses, leading to enhanced therapy. By preventing real data sharing, privacy is maintained.

Kim et al. [2] have presented a blockchain algorithm that checks refined data.

Nguyen et al. [3] have suggested an intrusion detection system to safeguard data transmission in the healthcare cyber–physical system.

Khan et al. [4] investigated a wireless capsule endoscopy frame-based automated technique for identifying stomach infections. A convolutional neural network model is secured using a blockchain-based method to enable accurate identification of stomach conditions like ulcers and bleeding.

According to Shinde et al. [5], there are particular defense techniques for AI adversarial attacks and even adversarial training is an AI-based technique that is further vulnerable to various attacks. As a result, they have created a conceptual framework for AI-based healthcare apps using blockchain technology that takes into account the requirements of each NLP, computer vision, and acoustic AI application.

Shaheen et al. [6] concentrate on three emerging domains of AI-based healthcare: drug discovery, clinical trials, and patient care. According to their research, pharmaceutical companies have experienced advantages in healthcare due to AI by accelerating their drug discovery process and automating target identification.

Wahl et al. [7] described how AI is being used in the healthcare sector and also define the various types of AI and how each one is helping.

Radanliev et al. [8] produced a summary map of various issues, solutions, and anticipated outcomes from integrating functional AI in healthcare systems as a result of the study. This map was derived from the synthesis of COVID-19 knowledge and presented new insights in the form of a conceptual methodology that includes six phases for managing a future Disease X event.

Rahman et al. [9] thoroughly investigate the most exciting and advanced technologies in the field of intelligent healthcare, which include FL- and XAI-based AI approaches. The authors provide an in-depth discussion on the integration of these technologies into smart healthcare, emphasizing a decentralized approach. They provide comprehensive guidance to readers on developing innovative healthcare solutions utilizing FL and AI. Additionally, the research covers an extensive range of areas and identifies the potential of FL-based AI systems for the future of the healthcare industry. Overall, the study highlights the significance and benefits of implementing FL- and XAI-based AI approaches in healthcare.

Jiang et al. [10] work on the fact that with the increase in resources and data in the healthcare industry, analytic techniques are growing every day. It is a comprehensive approach to have a strong background review of artificial intelligence (AI) in healthcare in the past, present, and future. In this chapter, we can find the missing details to help us achieve the best outcome of AI in healthcare. We have presented the fact that a successful AI system in healthcare must possess the machine learning (ML) component, which is suitable for managing structured data such as images, genetic data, and EP data, while the natural language processing (NLP) component is adept at extracting information from unstructured texts.

Kayyali et al. [11] stated that the US federal government and other public stakeholders are making their extensive healthcare knowledge available, which includes clinical trial data and information on patients covered by public insurance programs. They also mentioned that many innovative healthcare data applications in the US are going beyond just reporting past events and are incorporating interventions and predictive capabilities.

Neill et al. [12] address and cover all the major challenges and advances of AI in the US healthcare structure, especially in the sphere of inpatient care, and also the mistakes in healthcare delivery that result in avoidable negative health outcomes are a significant concern. Over-treatment, inadequate implementation of care plans, and failure to follow recommended practices for preventing harm to patients can have a substantial impact on healthcare expenses and patient well-being. They covered the topic of answers in general patient care as well as abnormal pattern detection for inpatient care.

Zahid et al. [13] focused on developing energy-efficient communication solutions for body sensor networks (BSNs) to create cost-effective and self-sufficient healthcare platforms for patients. They proposed two innovative approaches: (i) adaptive transmission data rate (ATDR) algorithm, which adjusts the active time and packet sizes of the transmission to maintain the same energy consumption level for every transmission, and (ii) self-adaptive routing algorithm (SARA), which makes autonomous routing decisions to reduce energy consumption and improve the reliability of the system. These solutions aim to balance energy-saving, channel reliability, and battery lifetime extension during the transmission of vital sign signals in BSNs.

Raunak et al. [14] discussed a wide range of applications from the real-time systems to hybrid fault detection systems, catering to the needs of different stakeholders. This work focuses on the need for explainability of AI systems and algorithms in order to enhance trust over medical innovations. This article explores the field of explainable AI and ML in healthcare.

Yu et al. [15] conducted research on AI's impact on medical practice and concluded that AI is having a positive effect on the field. Recent advancements in data collection, machine learning, and computing infrastructure have enabled AI applications to expand into areas that were traditionally considered to be within the realm of human expertise. In their study, optometric physicians and computer engineers collaborated to develop and test an automated image categorization system capable of analyzing millions of retinal images from diabetic patients.

Ghosal et al. [16] conducted an extensive survey on the use of cloud-based IoT in healthcare and the application of machine learning for ensuring security. The study reviewed various machine learning techniques employed in cybersecurity and proposed a standard model. The authors also drew attention to a critical security concern, which relates to the potential risks that may arise from the gathering and processing of large volumes of data from wearable sensors in cloud-based IoT healthcare systems.

In their study, Alahmari et al. [17] presented a data-driven approach based on artificial intelligence (AI) called "Musawah," which automatically detects and identifies healthcare services that can be co-created by various stakeholders through social media analysis. The case study concentrated on cancer disease in Saudi Arabia, utilizing Twitter data analytics in the Arabic language.

Zhang et al. [18] analyzed phase-domain-deep patient ECG image learning for zero-effort smart health security. The model is a domain-deep patient ECG image learning framework to overcome biometric user identification challenges. The only threat was biometric user identification in ECG scenarios while evaluating the framework using two public databases and a deep convolutional neural network.

Zhang et al. [19] surveyed 203 participants to explore their perceptions and acceptance of patient-facing health systems driven by AI. The study aimed to investigate the factors that influence people's perceptions of using AI to access information about their diagnostic results. The findings revealed that despite the low awareness and experience of patient-facing AI systems among the participants, they generally held a positive attitude toward such systems. Most participants expressed a high level of comfort and willingness to use health AI systems, acknowledging their potential to help them understand diagnostic results. The study also highlighted the significant role played by intrinsic factors such as education and technology literacy in shaping people's perceptions of using AI to comprehend diagnostic results.

Gopalan et al. [20] presented a study and analysis of different classifications based on past survey papers and journal papers between 2014 and 2019. The study analyzed and highlighted on how AI can be used to tackle IoT security vulnerabilities in various healthcare situations.

Artificial intelligence (AI) has gained significant traction within the healthcare sector and is poised to continue its growth in the near future. With the increasing availability of vast datasets and advancements in machine learning algorithms, AI is transforming healthcare by enhancing patient outcomes, reducing costs, increasing efficiency, and elevating overall patient experiences. This literature review explores the current landscape of AI in healthcare, its applications, associated challenges, and potential future directions. One notable application of AI in healthcare is its role in clinical decision-making. AI systems process extensive datasets, including patient records, medical literature, and clinical guidelines, to generate recommendations for healthcare providers. These recommendations not only enhance diagnostic accuracy but also improve the effectiveness of treatments and patient outcomes. For instance, AI algorithms have been designed to predict patient outcomes in intensive care units and identify individuals in critical conditions. Another impactful use of AI in healthcare is the development of personalized treatment plans based on individual patient characteristics. By analyzing patient data, including genetic information, AI can identify the most suitable treatment options for each patient. This personalized approach can lead to improved patient outcomes and reduced healthcare costs. AI's involvement in medical imaging is another dimension that holds promise. AI algorithms can analyze radiology test results with exceptional accuracy, identifying abnormalities and potential diseases, such as tumors. This assists radiologists in making more precise diagnoses and reduces the necessity for invasive procedures involving instruments like endoscopes, catheters, scalpels, scissors, and various medical devices. Despite the numerous benefits of AI in healthcare, several key challenges exist.

Ethical and legal concerns are significant hurdles, especially regarding the use of AI in clinical decision-making. Transparency and interpretability issues in AI algorithms can lead to biased or incorrect recommendations, raising ethical concerns. Patient privacy and data security are also major considerations. Furthermore, the need for more standardization in AI development and deployment poses a challenge. Standardized data formats, algorithms, and evaluation metrics are essential to ensure the reliability and reproducibility of AI systems. AI has the potential to revolutionize the healthcare industry by enhancing patient outcomes, reducing costs, and improving operational efficiency. However, addressing challenges related to ethics, legalities, standardization, and data security is crucial. Future research should focus on resolving these challenges while developing AI systems that prioritize transparency, interpretability, and ethical responsibility.

10.3 Application Domains on Futuristic AI for Healthcare Security

This section discusses the role and impact of advanced AI models and systems on the security and privacy of healthcare data and modules.

10.3.1 Responsive artificial intelligence in healthcare

Responsive AI has risen a lot recently, and, hence, accuracy has increased in data-driven decisions. It is expected that the healthcare industry will see a rise in the use of machine learning/artificial intelligence in clinical decision-making, leading to more automation in the field. Large-scale systems' data are used to identify chronic illnesses before symptoms appear. These conditions include cancer, diabetes, cardiovascular conditions, etc. An exploratory analysis of responsive AI is illustrated in Figure 10.2.

The primary obstacle to implementing groundbreaking AI technologies, such as the widespread integration of artificial intelligence in the field of medicine, revolves around establishing trust among the public in AI systems [21]. Overcoming this challenge entails making the responsible utilization of AI accessible, repeatable, and achievable for all individuals who interact with these AI systems. Within the medical realm, doctors stand to gain numerous advantages from the application of artificial intelligence, spanning patient care and administrative tasks. Experts point to several factors that contribute

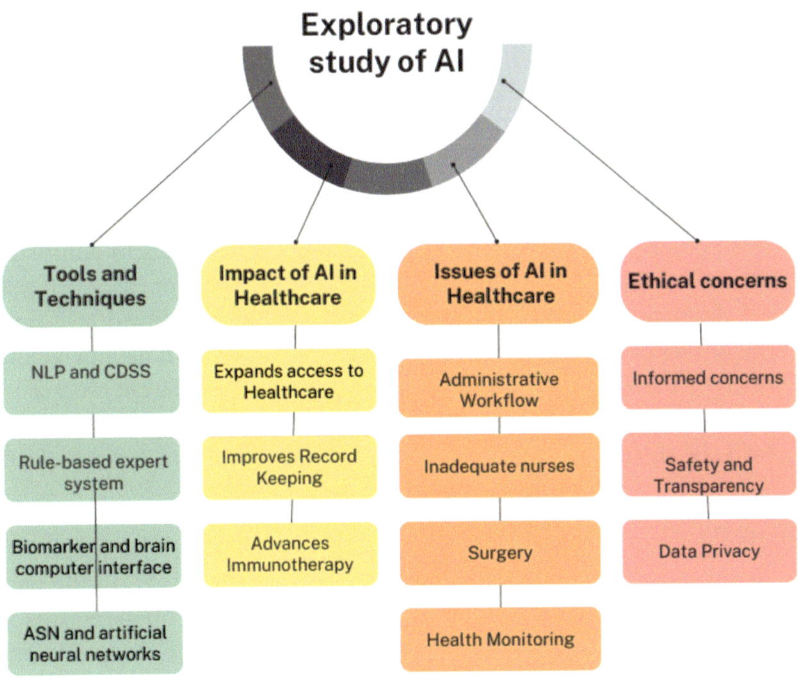

Figure 10.2 An exploratory study of responsive AI in healthcare.

to diagnostic errors, such as the ineffective coordination and integration of health information technology, breakdowns in communication between healthcare professionals, patients, and their families, and an insufficiently supportive healthcare work environment for diagnostic processes.

- **Natural language processing:**

Unstructured healthcare data for machine learning makes up nearly 80% of the data stored in electronic health record systems or locked data. Natural language processing (NLP) tools are frequently used in the healthcare industry to transform complex documents/reports that are readable by humans into data that is easier to use and analyze by machines. Today, it is possible to study and analyze a patient's record using NLP technology and gather important data elements like the patient's prescriptions, treatment approach, and medical issues. Most NLP systems use either speech recognition or text analysis, and then translation [22].

- **Rule-based expert systems:**

Expert systems built using different types of "if–then" regulations were the most popular artificial intelligence technology in healthcare during the 1980s and the following decades. One drawback of this system is that it can only apply the rules to a certain point. However, by using AI-based systems in this situation, we can circumvent these constraints.

- **Clinical decision support system (CDSS):**

The main objective of the clinical decision support system is to optimize the treatment of an illness by leveraging patient data from prior cases. Presently, clinical decision support systems are predominantly employed at the point of care, allowing clinicians to integrate their expertise with data or guidance furnished by the system. CDSS can be categorized into different groups based on the timing of their intervention and whether they are delivered actively or passively, distinguishing between knowledge-based and non-knowledge-based systems.

- **Biomarker:**

Biomarker testing is another valuable application area for AI. In the pursuit of providing patients with optimal care, biomarker testing, often referred to as molecular analysis, involves conducting a series of tests to detect molecular indicators of health. Machine learning algorithms assess numerous unbiased hypotheses based on input features derived from training data, devoid of any preconceived biases. These algorithms primarily fall under the category of classification algorithms, with some incorporating feature selection techniques. Gene expression data, typically obtained from human cell RNA sequencing information, is the primary data source employed with most of these algorithms.

- **Brain–computer interface:**

Within the healthcare sector, artificial intelligence (AI) is harnessed through the brain–computer interface, facilitating direct communication between the human brain and computer systems. This interface serves as a tool for observing activities in and around the central nervous system. Healthcare professionals employ the brain–computer interface to monitor brain activity and explore the characteristics of the brain that can be leveraged to enhance, replace, or improve human functions. The brain–computer interface is used in the healthcare system to measure brain activity and analyze the brain's features that replace, restore, and improve human functions. It is well known that the brain–computer interface can restore lost abilities, such as speech and movement, and that it has done so with excellent outcomes. The brain–computer interface measures the brain's activity using various AI techniques. The first method involves the use of electrical signals, which are discovered through the invasive application of charged electrodes carefully positioned close to the cortex's surface. There have reportedly been positive effects on healthcare despite the BCI's early stages.

- **Arterial spin labeling (ASL) imaging:**

Arterial spin labeling (ASL) imaging represents another automated system that integrates artificial intelligence into healthcare. ASL is a commonly employed non-invasive method for monitoring cerebral blood flow [23]. The software used for data analysis offers various operating modes, resulting in a significant improvement in diagnostic accuracy. The ASL system closely mimics the natural functioning of the brain and possesses the statistical capability to handle extensive datasets with exceptional precision.

- **Artificial neural networks:**

Another system in healthcare that uses artificial intelligence is called artificial neural networks (ANN). They are computer simulations with brain-inspired designs. With the use of artificial neural networks, this system has made huge progress in AI, such as the recognition of voice, images, and robots.

- **Robot-assisted surgery:**

There has been a growing adoption of robotics in healthcare on a global scale. Robots are particularly preferred in operating rooms primarily for their capacity to enable minimally invasive procedures. This is attributed to their ability to execute surgical tasks through small incisions, leading to decreased patient discomfort, reduced blood loss, and quicker recovery times. The precision of robotic surgeries also contributes to their less invasive nature compared to human-performed surgeries, where larger incisions are often required, leading to prolonged discomfort and healing periods.

- **Diagnosis and treatment applications – electronic health records:**

For the past five decades, the primary emphasis of AI in healthcare has been on disease diagnosis and treatment. While still in its early stages, certain electronic health record (EHR) software companies are starting to incorporate limited healthcare analytics features based on artificial intelligence into their product offerings. Healthcare providers utilizing standalone EHR systems must either undertake substantial integration endeavors independently or depend on external AI providers capable of interfacing with their EHR systems to harness the potential of AI in healthcare fully.

- **Expands access to healthcare:**

It is imperative to entrust the human body to a qualified expert to avoid deterioration of health or potential fatality due to inaccurate diagnosis, improper management, or biased care. Unfortunately, there are very few doctors in developing and underdeveloped countries. A consequence of AI is the development of diagnostic machines in these nations. The AI tools used in chest X-rays for tuberculosis diagnosis are examples of such devices.

- **Improves record keeping:**

Most hospitals opt for electronic health records (EHR) as the preferred method of record keeping due to its reliability and user-friendly nature, which surpass traditional manual data entry and storage techniques. Voice recognition and dictation AI technologies have significantly contributed to streamlining the documentation process and reducing user fatigue.

- **Advances immunotherapy:**

Leveraging artificial intelligence (AI) is pivotal in enhancing the efficacy of immunotherapy as a cancer treatment option. While a definitive cancer cure remains elusive, immunotherapy represents a promising avenue for treatment. It involves harnessing the body's immune system to combat diseases. Employing cutting-edge technology like artificial intelligence (AI), machine learning algorithms can adeptly assess intricate patient data to pinpoint individuals who may derive benefits from this treatment method [24].

The existing challenging issues in healthcare with responsive AI are as follows:

- **Administrative workflow:**

Doctors, nurses, and other workers in the healthcare sector spend the majority of their time working on laborious paperwork, which requires extreme accuracy. A medical officer who is in charge of treating patients should not be placed in such a situation. Due to this, they are more likely to experience burnout and occasionally become distracted while listening to patients. To make the workplace in the medical industry more employee-friendly, technology should be used to manage such voluminous paperwork.

- **Inadequate nurses:**

In many healthcare facilities, people wait in line for hours to see a doctor. Because of this, patients who are seeking these services feel guilty, anxious, and afraid to see a doctor. The pressure to treat every patient in a line as quickly as possible can also fall on the doctors and nurses.

- **Surgery:**

In general, all types of surgery must be performed after intricate procedures in a precise and adaptable manner. Because of this, surgeons spend more time in the operating rooms than they should, which lowers their expected productivity. They may also experience burnout and occasionally lose focus.

- **Health monitoring:**

As part of standard health monitoring procedures in several healthcare institutions, patients are frequently mandated to make regular visits to the hospital. They are also instructed to keep an eye on their physical condition and are required to report to the medical center when their health problems worsen. Therefore, using AI to address these problems is necessary.

- **Informed consent:**

AI finds extensive applications in the medical sector, encompassing areas like medical imaging, surgical procedures, and diagnostics, all of which significantly influence the patient–physician relationship. However, there remains to be clarity surrounding the circumstances under which AI should be employed in healthcare. There is a pressing need to establish guidelines for educating patients about the utilization of AI in the healthcare industry [25]. Furthermore, even for healthcare practitioners, some of these AI programs employ highly complex, less transparent techniques like black-box testing algorithms. An additional ethical dilemma revolves around determining what information should be conveyed to patients via chatbots. Certain critical medical notifications should be conveyed exclusively by healthcare professionals and not through DIY apps.

- **Safety and transparency:**

Safety in the healthcare sector should always remain a top priority. AI is extensively employed to review patient medical records and explore treatment alternatives. However, flawed or insufficiently trained algorithms can potentially generate unsafe and unreliable treatment suggestions. Moreover, there is a challenge associated with safeguarding intellectual property and securing AI against cybersecurity threats while also making these algorithms accessible to the public. Given that black-box testing is commonly employed in medical AI, establishing transparency in such cases presents a considerable challenge.

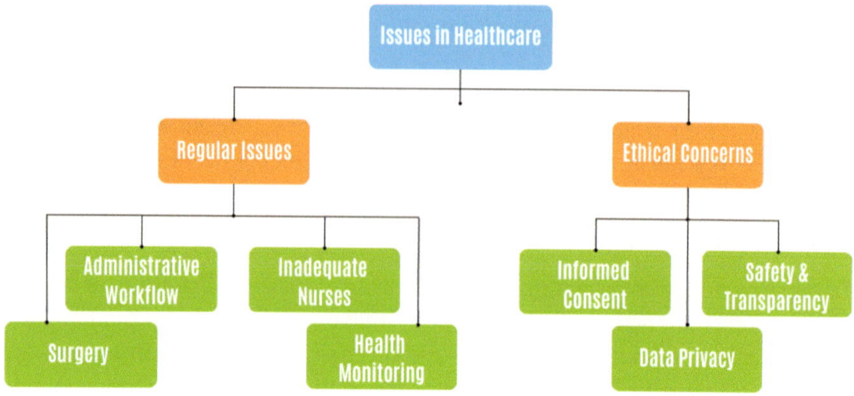

Figure 10.3 Issues in modern healthcare.

- **Data privacy:**

Maintaining the utmost privacy of patient health information is paramount, and strict regulations like HIPAA in the United States are designed to ensure this. Even a single medical record from a patient's file cannot be disclosed to a third party without informed consent. It is crucial to educate clinicians on how to trust and effectively integrate AI technologies into their medical practices. Ethical concerns arise when governments and healthcare organizations commercialize patient data, using it for profit. Occasionally, AI developers and their partners obtain approval to use patient data to train and test algorithms. Another significant concern revolves around the nature of the data and the extent of privacy intrusion. All these pertinent issues are highlighted in Figure 10.3.

10.3.2 Transformative artificial intelligence in healthcare

Transformative artificial intelligence (AI) is on its way to changing the scenario of healthcare. Data generation is at its peak, machine learning is taking place, and all computer infrastructure is doing its work. Earlier, it was considered that AI would not enter certain fields, but now we can see clearly that AI has proved its presence in almost every field possible.

In Aravind Eye Care, India, many ophthalmologists and computer scientists are testing and are about to deploy a first of its kind AI automatic system for classifying images that can be used to review millions of photographs of diabetic patients' retinas, which can help to give a solution to diabetic retinopathy (DR), which is one of the major causes of blindness in adults. However, it is difficult for ophthalmologists, and a group of scientists from Google and other partnered organizations are attempting to demonstrate that an artificial intelligence (AI) system, which is taught using various images, can attain the same level of accuracy as a doctor in detecting referable DR5, while also discovering any previously unidentified correlation between image patterns in the fundus photograph and cardiovascular risks. This study is being conducted in the United States and other Western nations [26].

Artificial intelligence (AI) has become a popular topic among scientists and the general public due to the frequent unveiling of new advancements and technologies by tech companies and researchers. Despite considerable advancements in the field in recent decades, an ongoing discussion persists regarding the exact definition of "true AI" due to its ever-evolving nature. This research endeavor seeks to investigate diverse facets of AI, encompassing its applications within the realm of medicine, including clinical practice, translational medical research, and fundamental biomedical research.

It is widely acknowledged that medical science was among the earliest and most reliable domains for the application of artificial intelligence. Earlier, the first generation of AI systems in healthcare was required to be managed by experts, and they made all the important decisions, but now it is not like AI systems are so robust nowadays that they can manage themselves with the help of classification, regression, and characterization. Various transformative challenges in healthcare are shown in Figure 10.4.

Machine learning methods can be utilized to carry out tasks such as classification, regression, and the characterization of similarity among instances that share common outcome labels. In contrast, unsupervised learning can unveil concealed patterns within unlabeled data, facilitating the detection of anomalies, the creation of reduced-dimensional representations, or the identification of subgroups. Machine learning techniques enable the development of artificial intelligence applications without the need to explicitly define decision rules or consider complex interactions among input features.

This also includes various layers of training models, which are used in deep learning models, as in deep neural networks, for better understanding and insights because they improve the results substantially. The core architecture of deep neural networks comprises an input layer, an output layer, and multiple intermediate hidden layers positioned in between. Some of the most basic designs of deep neural networks are the perceptron and feedforward neural networks. These networks operate straightforwardly, with input being fed into the network and output generated by the final layer, with various computations taking place in the hidden layers. Nowadays, deep learning models can have around 100 layers and hundreds and millions of parameters to optimize the results in every way possible, but this will require more input data, computation power, and advanced architecture.

With the current graphics processing units (GPUs) capable of handling more than 7 trillion floating-point operations, their integration with robust computational infrastructure, extensive datasets, and convolutional neural networks (CNNs) has become a reality. These networks utilize a unique layer called the convolutional layer to extract significant features by summarizing and modifying groups of pixels in images. Unlike conventional approaches, CNNs can process raw images and adeptly acquire pertinent features from training datasets [27].

A significant hurdle with deep learning algorithms lies in their substantial need for labeled data. Despite the recent surge in medical data availability,

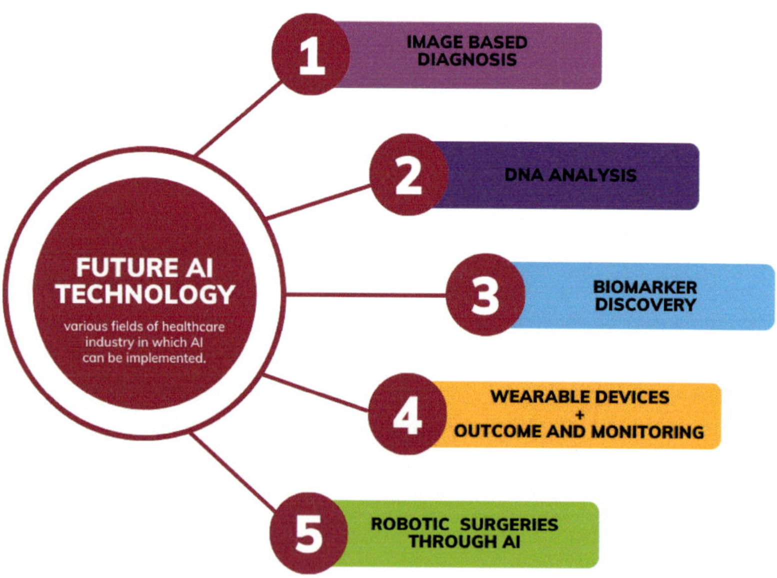

Figure 10.4 Numerous transformative AI technologies are used in the healthcare industry [15].

many large-scale studies have been hindered by this constraint. Nevertheless, the AI landscape has surged forward due to the accumulation of extensively annotated clinical data, the evolution of machine learning techniques, the accessibility of open-source machine learning toolkits, and the increased affordability and scalability of computational resources and cloud storage. AI systems have showcased performance levels that are on par with specialist expertise across various diagnostic tasks, outperforming clinicians in patient prognosis predictions and even offering assistance in surgical procedures. This potential can revolutionize medical practice and redefine the roles of healthcare professionals.

Image-based diagnosis:

- **Radiology:** In the field of radiology, diagnostic radiologists employ a range of medical imaging modalities, including X-ray radiography, computed tomography, magnetic resonance imaging (MRI), and positron–emission tomography, to detect and diagnose medical conditions. Computational approaches have been proposed and implemented to aid in radiological diagnoses, such as transfer learning, which can reduce the volume of training data needed to train a neural network with millions of parameters. To enhance the interpretability of neural network models, methods like saliency maps and gradient-weighted class activation maps are employed to provide visual insights into their decision-making processes. Additionally, activation maximization can generate images that optimally activate a selected neuron, and convolution filters can be visualized by generating synthetic input images that maximize filter responses. These techniques are aimed at rendering neural network models more interpretable in the context of radiological diagnoses.
- **Dermatology:** In the realm of skin lesion diagnosis, visual inspection plays a pivotal role, with dermatologists relying on established rules of thumb to distinguish between benign moles and malignant skin melanoma. Recent advancements in the field have seen convolutional neural networks (CNNs), trained on a substantial dataset of 129,450 clinical images, achieving diagnostic accuracy in identifying skin malignancies that rival that of dermatologists. Remarkably, in a comparison involving assessments by 21 dermatologists, the deep learning algorithm outperformed the average dermatologist in its predictions when analyzing a set of photographic and dermoscopic images. The resulting diagnostic model can potentially be employed on mobile devices,

thereby increasing the accessibility of expert-level skin lesion screening on a global scale.

- **Ophthalmology:** Fundus photography is a non-intrusive technique employing specialized retinal cameras to capture detailed images of the retina, optic disc, and macula. These images play a crucial role in the identification and ongoing monitoring of diseases such as age-related macular degeneration, retinal neoplasms, glaucoma, and diabetic retinopathy (DR). Clinical guidelines advocate for annual DR screening for diabetic patients with minimal or no retinal damage, whereas those with advancing DR require more frequent assessments. Nonetheless, the conventional method of reviewing and interpreting fundus photographs by ophthalmologists presents a bottleneck when it comes to scaling up to the vast number of diabetic patients at risk of developing DR and potentially sight-threatening complications.
- **Pathology:** The conventional approach for diagnosing various cancer types relies on histopathological assessment, which entails staining tissue slides obtained from biopsies or surgical samples with dyes. Nevertheless, inconsistencies among pathologists have been observed, and the process needs more scalability. AI has demonstrated its potential in detecting prostate cancer in biopsy specimens, recognizing breast cancer metastases in lymph nodes, and identifying mitotic figures in breast cancer cases. An automated system could effectively address these challenges by providing rapid and impartial evaluations of histopathology slides, ultimately enhancing the quality of cancer care. Nevertheless, the translation of research findings into practical clinical applications is a complex endeavor, albeit one with the potential to profoundly reshape current medical practices.

DNA analysis:

Genomic research heavily depends on high-throughput sequencing techniques, which produce vast volumes of raw data essential for advancing precision medicine. Traditional approaches to pinpointing disease-causing genetic variations and understanding the roles of non-coding DNA are gradually giving way to deep neural networks, demonstrating superior performance. As an example, a novel method that converts the genomic variant-calling challenge into an image classification problem has outperformed established tools like the Genome Analysis Toolkit. These computational techniques prove especially valuable in diagnosing intricate diseases rooted in genetics.

ML in biomarker discovery:

Omic technologies offer the capability to simultaneously measure thousands of genes and proteins, as well as millions of genomic and epigenomic variations. Machine learning approaches can identify molecular patterns associated with disease status and subtypes, capture intricate interactions among these measurements, and generate omic signatures for predicting disease characteristics. Biomarker panels derived from machine learning have demonstrated superior performance compared to those chosen by experts or conventional statistical techniques guiding treatment decisions. Nevertheless, the task of identifying robust biomarkers becomes methodologically challenging when the number of measurements or parameters significantly exceeds the sample size, and the reproducibility of certain biomarkers has come under scrutiny. With the establishment of standardized profiling methods, nationwide biobanks, and advanced machine learning techniques, we anticipate the emergence of more reliable and precise biomarkers.

Outcome and monitoring:

Electronic health records (EHRs) hold the potential to forecast clinical outcomes, including factors like readmission rates, mortality rates, and the duration of hospital stays, by analyzing patient attributes and health insurance claims. Furthermore, EHRs can be harnessed to predict how cancer patients will respond to chemotherapy and identify clinical factors that influence the prognosis of patients who have undergone thoracic organ transplantation. This capacity can aid both healthcare providers and patients in tailoring treatment plans to individual needs. Additionally, AI-driven alert systems can be developed to predict critical medical events such as cardiac arrests or transfers to the intensive care unit (ICU), while interpretable machine learning models can assist anesthesiologists in anticipating hypoxemia occurrences during surgical procedures.

Using AI in wearable devices:

Wearable devices can be valuable in identifying illnesses and deducing health states by monitoring heart rate, skin temperature, and ECG readings, among other things. However, their precision could be more consistent, and about 33% of the American customers discontinue their usage within six months. Further research is necessary to optimize the usefulness of wearables in promoting and sustaining good health.

Table 10.1 Comparative analysis of responsive and transformative AI.

Responsive AI in healthcare	**Transformative AI in healthcare**
AI is being increasingly used in healthcare to automate clinical decision-making and identify chronic illnesses before symptoms appear. However, building public trust in AI is the biggest challenge.	AI is transforming healthcare through machine learning and computer infrastructure. Automated image classification systems are being developed to screen diabetic patients for retinopathy.
Doctors can benefit from AI in patient care and office management, but diagnostic errors are caused by factors such as ineffective collaboration and communication breakdowns.	Deep neural networks with hundreds of millions of parameters can optimize results, but they require more input data and computation power. Artificial intelligence (AI) systems are capable of achieving expert-level accuracy in diagnosing medical conditions and can aid in surgical procedures. This can revolutionize the field of medicine and reshape the methods by which healthcare professionals perform their responsibilities.
Biomarker testing utilizes AI to identify molecular indicators of health in patients through unbiased hypothesis testing. Machine learning algorithms, including feature selection and classification, are commonly used with gene expression data from human cell RNA sequencing.	Omic technologies measure thousands of genes and proteins, enabling machine learning methods to identify disease-related patterns and predict disease outcomes. Biomarker panels derived from machine learning outperform conventional methods, but reproducibility challenges exist.
The use of robotics in healthcare has grown worldwide, particularly in operating rooms, where they are favored for their ability to facilitate minimally invasive procedures. Robotic surgeries are considered less invasive than human surgery, as they offer high accuracy rates and reduce the need for large, uncomfortable incisions that take time.	AI-controlled robots are used in assembly lines and labs, but adoption in medical interventions could be faster. Knot-tying robots and a supervised system for suturing have shown promise. It is anticipated that surgical robots, which are pre-programmed, guided by imaging, and capable of being operated remotely, will see increased use in medical settings.
The healthcare industry faces various challenges that can be addressed using AI. These include administrative workflow, inadequate nurses, surgery time, health monitoring, and ethical concerns related to informed consent, safety and transparency, and data privacy. The use of AI in healthcare holds promise for enhancing the results of medical treatment, but addressing these challenges is crucial to minimize potential risks and ensure equitable access to AI-powered healthcare technologies.	The rapid growth of AI in healthcare presents technical, socio-economic, and legal challenges. A key technical challenge is developing accurate algorithms while protecting patient privacy and security. Socio-economic challenges include ensuring equitable access and addressing job displacement concerns. Legal issues such as liability, data ownership, and regulatory compliance must also be addressed to maximize most of AI's benefits in healthcare while minimizing potential risks.

Robotic surgeries:

AI-controlled robotic systems are already being employed in biomedical labs and assembly lines, but their integration into medical procedures has been slower. However, recent advancements include the development of autonomous robots capable of tying knots and a supervised robotic system that was able to suture an intestinal anastomosis with greater precision than human surgeons. Future innovations are expected to include pre-programmed, image-guided, and teleoperated surgical robots that will become a routine part of surgical practice.

Technical, socio-economic, and legal challenges:

The utilization of artificial intelligence (AI) in the healthcare industry is rapidly growing, but it is challenging. One of the main technical challenges is developing algorithms that can accurately analyze vast amounts of medical data while maintaining patient privacy and security. Additionally, there are socio-economic challenges, such as ensuring equitable access to AI-powered healthcare technologies and addressing concerns about job displacement for healthcare workers. From a legal standpoint, issues such as liability, data ownership, and regulatory compliance must also be addressed as AI becomes increasingly integrated into healthcare systems. Addressing these challenges will be crucial in realizing the full potential of AI in improving healthcare outcomes while minimizing potential risks, and it will eventually be beneficial for all stakeholders. Table 10.1 highlights the differentiating factors between the two AIs in the context of healthcare.

10.4 Conclusion

The potential for transforming healthcare through the adoption of advanced AI technology in the future is significant. It could revolutionize patient care and disease management. Thanks to the progress in machine learning and natural language processing, AI algorithms can proficiently examine extensive volumes of patient data, discern patterns, and forecast outcomes with an unprecedented level of precision.

AI can provide significant benefits in healthcare, particularly in enhancing patient results and reducing expenses. By utilizing AI-powered tools to monitor patient health and identify early symptoms of illness, healthcare providers can adopt a proactive approach to care that may result in improved health outcomes and long-term reduction of healthcare costs.

Furthermore, AI technology can empower healthcare providers with previously challenging or unattainable insights, aiding them in making more informed decisions. For example, AI-powered tools can assist with diagnostic decision-making by analyzing medical images and identifying subtle patterns that human clinicians may have missed. Consequently, this has the potential to result in timelier and more precise diagnoses, ultimately enhancing the overall outcomes for patients.

It should be acknowledged that incorporating AI into healthcare raises ethical and regulatory issues that require attention and resolution. Issues such as data privacy, bias, and accountability must be considered when developing and implementing AI-powered healthcare tools. Furthermore, it is crucial to ensure that AI technology does not replace the human touch in patient care but rather serves as a tool to augment and support healthcare providers.

In summary, the integration of AI technology into healthcare holds the promise of revolutionizing our approach to patient care and disease management. Harnessing the capabilities of machine learning and natural language processing, AI-driven tools can enhance patient results, curtail healthcare expenses, and support healthcare professionals in making well-informed choices. Nevertheless, it is vital to approach this technology thoughtfully, addressing ethical and regulatory aspects to guarantee the secure and efficient utilization of AI-powered healthcare tools.

In the first case study, we discussed some tools and techniques related to AI/ML that can help the healthcare sector in many ways, like X-rays, prescriptions, chatbots, etc. Then, we also saw some demerits of using those technologies, which can cause serious problems in the healthcare sector. We got to analyze how NLP, robot-assisted surgery, and artificial neural networks can help. After that, we saw how AI can impact healthcare systems in a good way as well as a bad way. In the end, we also discussed how AI can affect the future of this sector.

In the second case study, we looked at and explored how things are changing in developing nations and how situations are changing rapidly around the healthcare industry just because AI and ML are getting upgraded at a very fast pace. We got to know various fields, the part of artificial intelligence in them, and the various imperfections of the same. It was seen how image-based diagnosis can be done by artificial intelligence, and it was discovered that with a large dataset and correct computation power, it can slowly replace the professional in the near future.

References

[1] Rajesh Kumar, WenYong Wang, Jay Kumar, Ting Yang, Abdullah Khan, Wazir Ali, Ikram Ali, An Integration of blockchain and AI for secure data sharing and detection of CT images for the hospitals, Computerized Medical Imaging and Graphics, Volume 87, 2021, 101812, ISSN 0895-6111, https://doi.org/10.1016/j.compmedimag.2020.101812.

[2] Kim, T.M.; Lee, S.-J.; Chang, D.-J.; Koo, J.; Kim, T.; Yoon, K.-H.; Choi, I.-Y. DynamiChain: Development of Medical Blockchain Ecosystem Based on Dynamic Consent System. Appl. Sci. 2021, 11, 1612. https://doi.org/10.3390/app11041612

[3] Gia Nhu Nguyen, Nin Ho Le Viet, Mohamed Elhoseny, K. Shankar, B.B. Gupta, Ahmed A. Abd El-Latif, Secure blockchain enabled Cyber–physical systems in healthcare using deep belief network with ResNet model, Journal of Parallel and Distributed Computing, Volume 153, 2021, Pages 150-160, ISSN 0743-7315, https://doi.org/10.1016/j.jpdc.2021.03.011.

[4] M. Attique Khan, I. Mashood Nasir, M. Sharif, M. Alhaisoni, S. Kadry *et al.*, "A blockchain based framework for stomach abnormalities recognition," *Computers, Materials & Continua*, vol. 67, no.1, pp. 141–158, 2021.

[5] Shinde, Rucha & Patil, Shruti & Kotecha, Ketan & Potdar, Vidyasagar & Selvachandran, Ganeshsree & Abraham, Ajith. (2022). Securing AI-based Healthcare Systems using Blockchain Technology: A State-of-the-Art Systematic Literature Review and Future Research Directions. 10.48550/arXiv.2206.04793.

[6] Mohammed Yousef Shaheen. Applications of Artificial Intelligence (AI) in healthcare: A review. *ScienceOpen Preprints.* 2021. DOI: 10.14293/S2199-1006.1.SOR-.PPVRY8K.v1

[7] Wahl B, Cossy-Gantner A, Germann S, et al. Artificial intelligence (AI) and global health: how can AI contribute to health in resource-poor settings?BMJ Glob Health 2018;3:e000798. doi:10.1136/ bmjgh-2018-000798

[8] Radanliev, P., De Roure, D., Maple, C. *et al.* Methodology for integrating artificial intelligence in healthcare systems: learning from COVID-19 to prepare for Disease X. *AI Ethics* 2, 623–630 (2022).

[9] Rahman, A., Hossain, M.S., Muhammad, G. *et al.* Federated learning-based AI approaches in smart healthcare: concepts, taxonomies, challenges and open issues. *Cluster Comput* (2022).

[10] Jiang F, Jiang Y, Zhi H, et al. Artificial intelligence in healthcare: past, present and future. Stroke and Vascular Neurology 2017;2: e000101. doi:10.1136/svn-2017-000101

[11] Basel Kayyali, David Knott and Steve Van Kuiken article on The big-data revolution in US health care: Accelerating value and innovation(McKinsey)

[12] D. B. Neill, "Using Artificial Intelligence to Improve Hospital Inpatient Care," in IEEE Intelligent Systems, vol. 28, no. 2, pp. 92-95, March-April 2013, doi: 10.1109/MIS.2013.51.

[13] Noman Zahid, Ali Hassan Sodhro, Usman Rauf Kamboh, Ahmed Alkhayyat, Lei Wang. AI-driven adaptive reliable and sustainable approach for internet of things enabled healthcare system[J]. Mathematical Biosciences and Engineering, 2022, 19(4): 3953-3971. doi: 10.3934/mbe.2022182

[14] M. S. Raunak and R. Kuhn, "Explainable artificial intelligence and machine learning [Guest Editors' introduction]," in Computer, vol. 54, no. 10, pp. 25-27, Oct. 2021, doi: 10.1109/MC.2021.3099041.

[15] Yu KH, Beam AL, Kohane IS. Artificial intelligence in healthcare. Nat Biomed Eng. 2018 Oct;2(10):719-731. doi:10.1038/s41551-018-0305-z. Epub 2018 Oct 10. PMID: 31015651.

[16] P. Ghosal, D. Das and I. Das, "Extensive Survey on Cloud-based IoT-Healthcare and Security using Machine Learning," 2018 Fourth International Conference on Research in Computational Intelligence and Communication Networks (ICRCICN), Kolkata, India, 2018, pp. 1-5, doi: 10.1109/ICRCICN.2018.8718717.

[17] Alahmari, N.; Alswedani, S.; Alzahrani, A.; Katib, I.; Albeshri, A.; Mehmood, R. Musawah: A Data-Driven AI Approach and Tool to Co-Create Healthcare Services with a Case Study on Cancer Disease in Saudi Arabia. Sustainability 2022, 14, 3313. https://doi.org/10.3390/su14063313

[18] Zhang Q. Phase-domain Deep Patient-ECG Image Learning for Zero-effort Smart Health Security. Annu Int Conf IEEE Eng Med Biol Soc. 2019 Jul;2019:2622-2628. doi:10.1109/EMBC.2019.8856515. PMID: 31946434.

[19] Zhang, Z, Genc, Y, Xing, A, Wang, D, Fan, X, Citardi, D. Lay individuals' perceptions of artificial intelligence (AI)-empowered healthcare systems. *Proc Assoc Inf Sci Technol.* 2020; 57:e326.

[20] S. S. Gopalan, A. Raza and W. Almobaideen, "IoT Security in Healthcare using AI: A Survey," 2020 International Conference on Communications, Signal Processing, and their Applications (ICCSPA), Sharjah, United Arab Emirates, 2021, pp. 1-6, doi:10.1109/ICCSPA49915.2021.9385711.
[21] M. Sen, K. Sharma, S. Mishra, A. Alkhayyat and V. Sharma, "Designing a Smart and Intelligent Ecosystem for Autistic Children," 2023 4th International Conference on Intelligent Engineering and Management (ICIEM), London, United Kingdom, 2023, pp. 1-5, doi:10.1109/ICIEM59379.2023.10166057.
[22] Cagliano, A.C., Grimaldi, S., & Rafele, C. (2011). A systemic methodology for risk management in the healthcare sector. Safety Science, 49, 695-708.
[23] A. Srivastava, S. Samanta, S. Mishra, A. Alkhayyat, D. Gupta and V. Sharma, "Medi-Assist: A Decision Tree based Chronic Diseases Detection Model," 2023 4th International Conference on Intelligent Engineering and Management (ICIEM), London, United Kingdom, 2023, pp. 1-7, doi:10.1109/ICIEM59379.2023.10167400.
[24] S. Mohanty, A. Behera, S. Mishra, A. Alkhayyat, D. Gupta and V. Sharma, "Resumate: A Prototype to Enhance Recruitment Process with NLP based Resume Parsing," 2023 4th International Conference on Intelligent Engineering and Management (ICIEM), London, United Kingdom, 2023, pp. 1-6, doi:10.1109/ICIEM59379.2023.10166169.
[25] Swain, T., & Mishra, S. (2022, November). Evolution Of Machine Learning Algorithms For Enhancement Of Self-Driving Vehicles Security. In 2022 International Conference on Advancements in Smart, Secure and Intelligent Computing (ASSIC) (pp. 1-5). IEEE.
[26] Mishra, N., Mishra, S., Tripathy, H.K. (2022). Rice Yield Estimation Using Deep Learning. In: Panda, M., et al. Innovations in Intelligent Computing and Communication. ICIICC 2022. Communications in Computer and Information Science, vol 1737. Springer, Cham. https://doi.org/10.1007/978-3-031-23233-6_28.
[27] Mohapatra, S. K., Mishra, S., & Tripathy, H. K. (2022, November). Energy Consumption Prediction in Electrical Appliances of Commercial Buildings Using LSTM-GRU Model. In 2022 International Conference on Advancements in Smart, Secure and Intelligent Computing (ASSIC) (pp. 1-5). IEEE.

11

Artificial Intelligence and Machine Learning Approaches for Intrusion Detection in the Internet of Medical Things – Opportunities and Future Directions

S. Jothimani, S. N. Sangeethaa, and M. Karthiga

Department of Computer Science and Engineering, Bannari Amman Institute of Technology, Sathyamangalam, India
E-mail: jothimanis.phd@gmail.com; dr.snsangeethaa@gmail.com; karthigam@bitsathy.ac.in

Abstract

As a result of developments in information and communication technology (ICT), the traditional model of how computers are used has been upended. These developments have made it possible for a variety of new forms of communication, including the Internet of Things (IoT). The Internet of Medical Things (IoMT) is a subset of IoT in which individual medical devices are able to talk to one another and exchange private information. These developments allow for enhanced patient engagement and care in the healthcare sector. There are various security and privacy concerns with them as well, including replay, man-in-the-middle, impersonating, privileged-insider, remote hijacking, password cracking, denial of service (DoS), and malware assaults. Each of these assaults on sensitive data raises the risk that permitted data may be lost to the attacker or altered in a way that makes it useless to authorized users and consumers. The intrusion detection system (IDS) relies heavily on machine learning techniques for real-time network and host attack detection and classification. The accurate identification of an anomaly has been the focus of several algorithms developed by academics in the fields of machine

DOI: 10.1201/9788770047395-11

learning and data mining. Yet, the primary difficulty in IDS models is building a scalable system that can manage the dynamic and unpredictable behavior of harmful assaults. Since network activity and attack methods evolve at a breakneck pace, researchers have been able to evaluate the growing mountain of data by using a variety of dynamic methods.

Furthermore, the diverse nature of medical equipment's connectivity, as well as its limited computational, storage, and energy capacity, makes it difficult to incorporate traditional security techniques like cryptography. When it comes to stopping modern, zero-day assaults, these safeguards are equally worthless. It is crucial to implement stringent safety protocols to safeguard data during its collection, transport, storage, and analysis. An additional security solution tailored to the peculiarities of IoMT systems can be provided by intrusion detection systems (IDS) built on machine learning (ML) and deep learning (DL). This research thus explores how ML-based IDS might resolve security and privacy concerns in IoMT networks. Lastly, the work provides a direction for future research by discussing the difficulties and restrictions of applying ML-based IDS to each layer of IoMT.

Keywords: Internet of Medical Things (IoMT), intrusion detection system, machine learning, security, healthcare sector.

11.1 Introduction

Because of the coronavirus (COVID-19) pandemic, there has been a big drop in international relations [1, 2]. Because the pandemic is so complicated, cutting-edge technological innovations in healthcare are needed to help people who are locked up and stop the disease from spreading. At the same time, IoMT is expected to let doctors stay away from their patients and treat them from afar, which is needed to deal with the pandemic [3]. As Internet of Things (IoT) technology has improved, IoMT has become more popular as a way to build smarter healthcare systems and give patients faster, more effective healthcare services. In order to save lives during the uncertain pandemic crisis, many countries have set up IoMT to improve rapid diagnosis through real-time patient monitoring [4].

IoMT, also called healthcare IoT, connects a wide range of medical devices to electronic health records so that patients can get more personalized care. Because of IoMT, patients now have more ways to get high-quality medical care without having to leave the comfort of their own homes. Reducing avoidable hospital visits and lengths of stay can also lower costs [6]. Also, turning many hospital-based services into telemedicine practices has lessened the burden on the medical staff. IoMT has many advantages, in addition to the fact that it greatly enhances both diagnostic and therapeutic accuracy. Providers hope IoMT will allow them to remotely monitor and treat multiple patients at once without expanding their healthcare infrastructure in the event of a pandemic [3].

Smart blood pressure monitors, smart glucometers, smart bands, smart pacers, smart pulse rate monitors, etc., are only a few examples of the new generation of linked medical equipment that is part of the Internet of Medical Things (IoMT) [7–9]. Through the gateway, these private records are transferred to the appropriate recipient in the cloud. The architecture of the IoMT is depicted in Figure 11.1, and it links and communicates with numerous smart medical equipment and professionals in order to provide effective support and treatment. Cloud computing allows for data to be stored remotely and made available to end users via an alternate portal. Hackers are inspired by technological progress and innovation to break into databases containing private information. These intelligent medical gadgets are susceptible to a wide variety of threats. If an attacker takes over a smart pacemaker, for instance, he may potentially kill the patient with a jolt. These new dangers pose a serious risk to the IoMT ecosystem and must be dealt with immediatel [10].

The rest of the chapter will be structured as follows. In Section 11.2, we will talk about how AI helps with IoMT intrusion detection. In Section 11.3, we define and discuss the taxonomy of IDS. In Section 11.4, we will go into

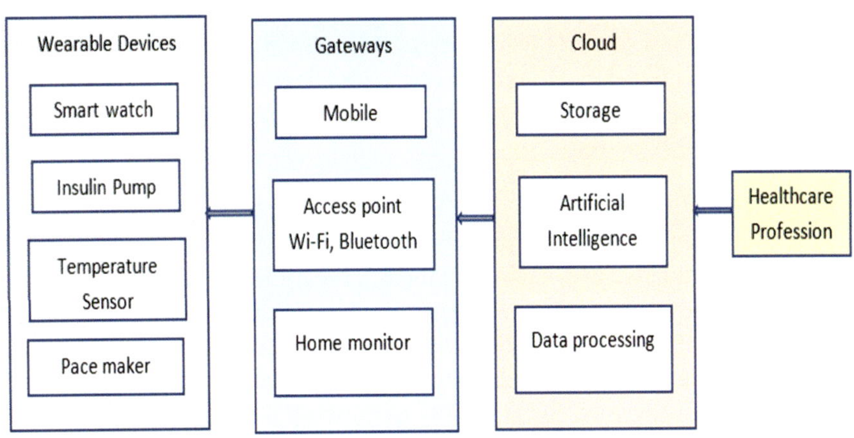

Figure 11.1 IoMT architecture.

further detail about the IDS that relies on AI and ML. We wrap off this chapter in Section 11.5.

11.2 Artificial Intelligence in Intrusion Detection of IoMT

The Internet of Medical Things (IoMT) is a rapidly growing field that uses networked medical equipment and sensors to collect and analyze health data in real time. Although the IoMT has the potential to improve healthcare, it also poses serious safety concerns. Patient privacy and safety are in danger if unauthorized parties gain access to their information, making this a top priority.

Intrusion detection systems (IDS) can be used to keep an eye on IoMT networks and notify security staff whenever something suspicious happens. Machine learning and deep learning are used to find outliers and trends in network data. This will help intrusion detection systems (IDS) work better. Misuse IDS and anomaly IDS are the two primary types of IDSs that may be found in the literature [11]. The first technique detects assaults by comparing them to known parameters and signatures, but it cannot keep up with evolving threats. In another method, unusual transactions are identified. Information that is both sensitive and crucial is always a target for hackers and is at risk of being compromised. Intrusion is the process of gaining unauthorized access to a computer system or network with the intent of stealing, altering, or corrupting data belonging to another user. When an attacker gains access to a server or system, they can exploit a number of flaws, including weak passwords, incorrect settings, and improper use. The sheer scale of a network, with its many gigantic servers and myriad online services, makes it an attractive target for hackers who can use their superior intelligence to break in and steal sensitive data. To protect connected devices from cybercriminals, there is a pressing need for an effective and insightful intrusion detection model in the IoMT setting.

Detection of intrusions over a range of fields:

Artificial intelligence (AI) techniques, including machine learning and deep learning, find valuable applications in the Internet of Medical Things (IoMT). They are employed to analyze the vast amounts of data generated by medical devices, identifying anomalies and potential security concerns. Machine learning models utilize predefined parameters like packet size, protocol type, and port number to assess the normality of network traffic. These models can learn to distinguish between normal and abnormal network behavior through exposure to labeled datasets. Intrusion detection within IoMT networks also benefits from deep learning methods, such as convolutional neural networks (CNNs) and recurrent neural networks (RNNs). CNNs are proficient at analyzing raw network data, including packet payloads, while RNNs excel in evaluating sequences of network traffic over time.

In addition to making intrusion detection systems (IDS) more accurate, machine learning and deep learning can also be used to automate the detection and mitigation of possible security risks. An intrusion detection system (IDS) is primarily divided into two categories, misuse IDS and anomaly IDS [5], and machine learning models can be used to prioritize warnings based on severity and the likelihood of being an actual threat. The first technique detects assaults by comparing them to known parameters and signatures, but it cannot keep up with evolving threats. In another method, unusual transactions are identified. Information that is both sensitive and crucial is always a target for hackers and is at risk of being compromised. Intrusion is the process of gaining unauthorized access to a computer system or network with the intent of stealing, altering, or corrupting data belonging to another user. When an attacker gains access to a server or system, they can exploit a number of flaws, including weak passwords, incorrect settings, and improper use. The sheer scale of a network, with its many gigantic servers and myriad online services, makes it an attractive target for hackers, who can use their superior intelligence to break in and steal sensitive data. To protect connected devices from cybercriminals, there is a pressing need for an effective and insightful intrusion detection model in the IoMT setting.

We decided to look into ML's potential for application in IoMT intrusion detection because of its many benefits.

1. Machine learning can make the IoMT system smarter and more suited to meet their security needs. Thus, these techniques may be superior to more conventional forms of access restriction during crises.
2. The volume, velocity, and variety of information produced by IoMT and IoT systems qualify it as big data. These records are useful for security purposes since they can be mined for insights into typical behavior and utilized to spot anomalies before they cause significant harm.
3. Unlike conventional ML methods, which necessitate a separate extraction step before classification can be performed, DL algorithms can automatically extract the relevant attributes.

Contrary to threat signature-based approaches, those based on ML can identify zero-day threats and previously unknown vulnerabilities.

11.2.1 Security requirements of IoMT

Changes in frameworks, architectures, and communications that are adaptable, versatile, secure, and inevitable without being meddlesome [12] are necessary for the IoT to be realized. Ethics, information insurance, specialized design, distinguishing evidence of structured articles, and administration are just a few of the areas where specialists anticipate the IoMT's technological breakthroughs to make fundamental enhancements. Potential security is essential, as is a robust connection with feedback management and information since more and more smart technologies are connected to the internet. A fundamental part of facilitating the widespread adoption of IoMT technology improvements and applications is resolving the security concerns (assurance of information protection) that may arise during data collection, transmission, and exchange. IoMT healthcare's rapid development poses threats to privacy and safety. Hence, it is essential to design and implement effective universal detection systems to safeguard patient confidentiality in the healthcare setting. Many publications [13–19] have been written to help reduce and comprehend security and privacy risks in healthcare apps. Unwanted security concerns for patients could result from the misuse of such sensitive information [20].

Thus, small smart sensors need safe methods to transfer recorded information at high speeds to guarantee that they can send data to a central server for analysis and interpretation at any time. Specialized arrangements, such as encryption, ID management, and security improvement innovations, should not be the exclusive means of ensuring privacy. For IoMT communication systems to be useful in healthcare applications, interoperability may be required. This would allow for a wider range of devices to work together to provide the desired outcome. If an intervention is to be effective in an emergency, it must be granted a degree of laziness and trustworthiness within reasonable bounds. When exchanging important information as depicted in Figure 11.2, authentication, security, privacy, and respectability are required.

Strong and practical verification methods are required to safeguard the data being generated, amassed, and shared via networked devices. Some of the information received could be sensitive, and patients may not want to discuss it with anybody (including their primary care physicians), for fear of repercussions. Smart devices may, therefore, record, store, and send patient data to a cloud server; this necessitates safe methods of transmitting recorded data at quick speeds to ensure individual records can never be compromised.

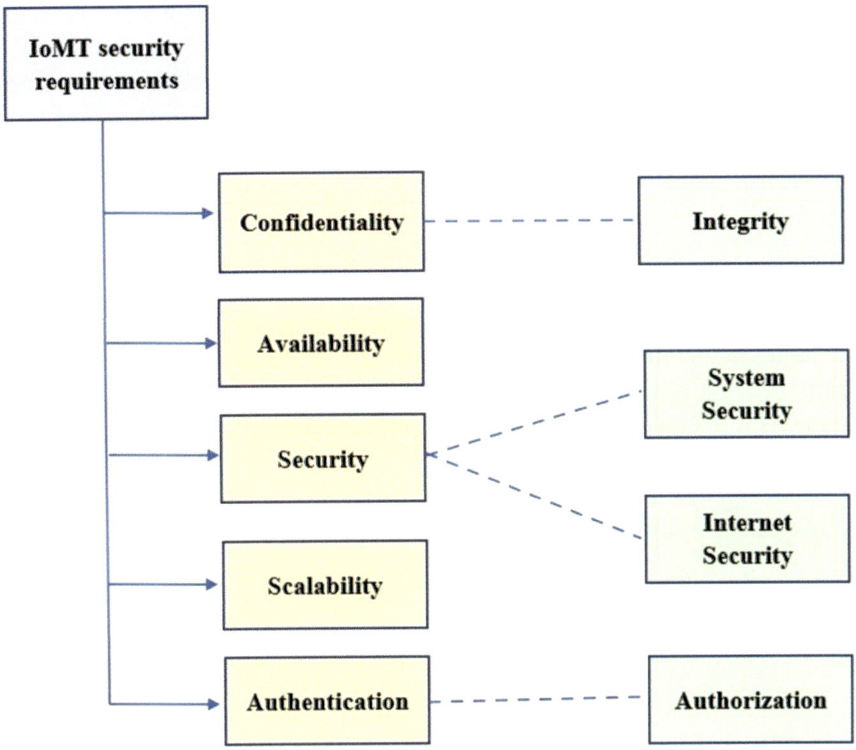

Figure 11.2 Security requirements of IoMT.

Planned consideration of data security, privacy, and assurance is essential. In conclusion, healthcare should fully integrate security, beginning with the device and continuing through the system and into the server.

11.2.2 Security threats for IoMT

Improved patient outcomes and lower healthcare costs are only two of the many advantages of the IoMT. Nevertheless, the IoMT also brings security difficulties and possible threats. Personal information about patients, such as their medical history, diagnoses, and treatment plans, is collected and shared through the IoMT. Individuals' health records could be compromised in the event of a data breach, which could lead to identity theft, insurance fraud, or other criminal activities. Hackers might obtain access to the system, disrupt or modify patient data, or even seize control of medical devices, potentially putting patients in danger if they were to exploit weaknesses in IoMT devices. Malware assaults on IoMT devices could impair crucial medical activities like medicine distribution or vital sign monitoring. When healthcare personnel who have access to IoMT devices and systems misuse or mishandle patient data, they represent a risk to patient privacy and data security.

Security and privacy of patient information require strict adherence to healthcare rules such as HIPAA (Health Insurance Portability and Accountability Act). There may be monetary and legal repercussions for disobedience. Financial loss, reputational injury, and compromised patient safety are just some of the potential outcomes of these security vulnerabilities. In light of the importance of protecting IoMT systems and patient data from security threats, as shown in Table 11.1, healthcare organizations must implement stringent security measures, including encryption, access control, and frequent vulnerability assessments.

Here is Table 11.2 listing some common layer-wise attacks in the Internet of Medical Things (IoMT) along with examples:

Table 11.1 List of security threats of IoMT.

Security threats	**Impacts**
Unauthorized access to sensitive information	Personal information can be stolen, resulting in identity theft or financial loss
Malware or viruses	Malicious software can damage the device, compromise data, or steal information
Distributed denial of service (DDoS) attacks	Can render IoMT devices or networks unusable, potentially putting patient health at risk
Insider threats	Authorized personnel may misuse or steal sensitive information
Lack of encryption	Data transmitted over the network can be intercepted and read by unauthorized parties
Weak passwords	Easy-to-guess or default hackers can exploit passwords to gain access to devices or networks
Physical security breaches	Devices can be stolen, tampered with, or accessed by unauthorized individuals
Vulnerabilities in third-party software	It can be exploited to gain access to the device or network
Lack of software updates and patches	Attackers can exploit unpatched vulnerabilities
Interoperability issues	This can result in data breaches or other security vulnerabilities when different systems are not compatible
Lack of user awareness and training	Users may inadvertently introduce security risks by not following best practices or by falling for phishing scams

Table 11.2 List of layer-wise security attacks with examples in IoMT.

Layer	Attack type	Description	Example
Physical	Tampering	Manipulating the hardware	Physically modifies a device to steal patient data
	Theft	Stealing devices	Steals a device containing patient information
	Destruction	Destroying or damaging devices	Destroys a medical device to harm patients
Network	Man-in-the-middle	Intercepting and altering communication	Steal patient data
	Denial of service	Overwhelming a network with traffic	Prevent medical devices from communicating with each other
	Eavesdropping	Monitoring network traffic	Obtain patient data
Transport	Replay	Intercepting and retransmitting data	Impersonate the device
	Injection	Injecting malicious code	Malicious code into a medical device to gain control of it
	Modification	Altering data in transit to disrupt	Manipulate patient data
Application	Remote code execution	Executing malicious code on a device remotely	Remotely executes malicious code on a medical device
	SQL injection	Exploiting vulnerabilities	Unauthorized access to patient data
	Cross-site scripting	Injecting malicious scripts into web pages	Injects malicious scripts into a web application
Data	Leakage	Disclosing sensitive data	Leaks patient data
	Breach	Unauthorized access	Vulnerability in a server

It is important to note that this is a partial list of all possible attacks, and new attack methods are constantly being developed. Implementing appropriate security measures at each layer of the IoMT architecture can help mitigate these risks.

11.3 Taxonomy and Definition of IDS

An IDS defines an intrusion as any effort to obtain data from a computer system illegally or to cause harm to the functioning of a computer system. An intrusion detection system (IDS) is an application designed to identify security breaches, both external (such as attempted break-ins) and internal (such as system penetration and misuse). IDSs are primarily used for host and network monitoring, network and system behavior analysis, alert generation, and incident response. IDSs are often installed close to the protected network nodes, as they detect related domains and channels (e.g., the switches in major network segments). Both detection-based and data-source-based approaches can be used to categorize IDS systems. Misuse detection and anomaly detection are two types of detection-based methodologies used by IDSs. IDSs can be broken down into host-based and network-based approaches among data-source-based methods. This study utilizes both types of IDS classification approaches, prioritizing the data source and giving less weight to the detection method.

In IoMT, the taxonomy and idea of IDS consist of the following.

11.3.1 Network-based intrusion detection system (NIDS)

In order to identify prospective assaults, a network is monitored by a network-based intrusion detection system (NIDS). IoMT makes use of NIDS to keep tabs on all the data flowing between various sensors, equipment, and systems in the medical industry. In the context of the IoMT, a network-based intrusion detection system (NIDS) is a security solution meant to monitor and analyze the network traffic of linked medical devices. Connected medical devices in the IoMT allow for remote monitoring, control, and management of things like insulin pumps and pacemakers, as shown in Figure 11.3. Patient safety and privacy may be at risk if unauthorized individuals gain access to these interconnected devices.

By monitoring network activity for signs of unusual or malicious activity, a network intrusion detection system (NIDS) in IoMT can aid in the detection

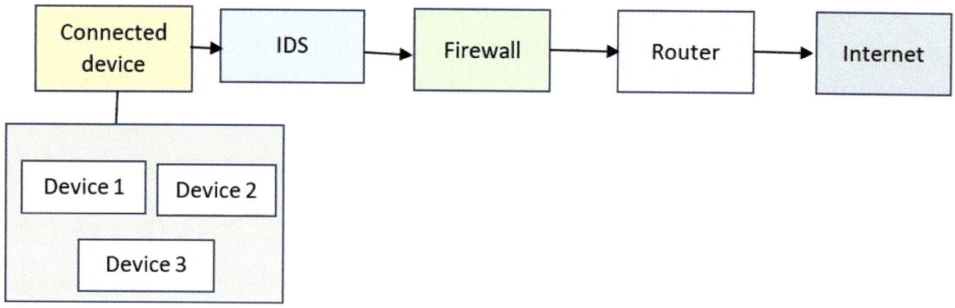

Figure 11.3 Network intrusion detection system (NIDS) in IoMT.

and prevention of such assaults. Usually, a mix of signature-based and anomaly-based detection methods is used for this purpose. In order to identify malicious behavior on a network using signature-based detection, data is compared to known patterns of harmful activity or attack signatures. Nevertheless, anomaly-based detection focuses on network activity that seems out of the ordinary. An NIDS may monitor network activity in real time and notify security staff of any suspicious activity by combining these methods. This can ensure the safety of patients using the IoMT by reducing the likelihood of cyberattacks on medical devices.

11.3.2 Host-based intrusion detection systems (HIDS)

Host-based intrusion detection systems (HIDS) detect intrusions by watching the behavior of specific hosts. In IoMT, HIDS can be used to monitor the functioning of various medical sensors and equipment to spot irregularities.

The Internet of Medical Things relies heavily on host-based intrusion detection systems (HIDS) for security (IoMT). HIDS are built to keep a close eye on and analyze the behavior of specific devices or hosts in order to spot any intrusion attempts or other unusual behavior. Medical devices, including infusion pumps, pacemakers, and blood glucose meters, can all benefit from HIDS monitoring and anomaly detection in the IoMT. Because of their widespread internet and network connectivity, these gadgets are typically the targets of malicious hacking attempts. With HIDS, healthcare facilities can detect attacks and take measures to avoid or lessen their severity. The data created by a device, such as system logs and system calls, are analyzed by HIDS to look for signs of malicious activity. A host intrusion detection system (HIDS) may monitor for suspicious activity like tampered files or altered settings. If an HIDS picks up on something fishy, it can either notify human security staff or take preventative measures on its own. Using an HIDS in the IoMT is beneficial since it can help keep an eye out for any dangers in real time. As a result, healthcare institutions will be better prepared to deal with future assaults and protect patient information. After an attack has occurred, HIDS can be used to gather forensic data that can be analyzed to learn more about what happened.

11.3.3 Signature-based IDS

The signature-based IDS compares network traffic to a library of known attack signatures to identify malicious activity. Signature-based intrusion detection systems (IDS) can be utilized in the IoMT to identify common threats against healthcare infrastructure. Signature-based intrusion detection systems (IDSs) in IoMT compare incoming network traffic to a database of known attack signatures. An intrusion detection system (IDS) alerts security staff when network traffic fits a signature, suggesting an attack is in progress. Signature-based IDS can quickly and accurately detect known attacks, which is an advantage. It is only useful for spotting attacks that fit specific patterns known in advance. As a result, it might not protect you from assaults that you have not seen before or that do not fit a particular profile. Organizations can get around this shortcoming by using anomaly-based IDS or behavior-based IDS, which look for unusual patterns of behavior that could point to an attack. To guarantee the system is always ready to defend against new threats, it must be constantly monitored and updated, including the signature database.

11.3.4 Anomaly-based intrusion detection systems

Anomaly-based intrusion detection systems rely on machine learning algorithms to spot out-of-the-ordinary activities that may foreshadow an attack. Anomaly-based intrusion detection systems (IDS) are useful in IoMT because they can identify attacks that have never been seen before. Anomaly-based intrusion detection systems (IDS) are widely deployed in the field of information security to identify uncommon actions or behaviors that may suggest a security breach or assault. To prevent harm from being done to medical equipment, networks, and systems across the Internet of Medical Things (IoMT), anomaly-based intrusion detection systems can be implemented.

To capture and communicate patient health data to healthcare professionals and other authorized entities, the IoMT makes use of networked medical devices like sensors, wearables, and other smart gadgets. Yet, there is a risk of cyberattacks jeopardizing patient privacy and safety due to the widespread adoption of these devices. In order to detect security breaches, anomaly-based IDS in IoMT constantly monitors the activity of medical devices and network traffic. These systems scan massive amounts of data with machine learning algorithms and statistical analysis methods to spot red flags that could warn of an impending attack. Early identification of security threats, less chance of data breaches, and enhanced patient safety are just some of the many advantages of employing anomaly-based IDS in IoMT. These technologies can also aid compliance with data privacy and security regulations like HIPAA and GDPR. Challenges, such as the requirement for specialized expertise and the possibility of false positives or false negatives, can arise while deploying anomaly-based IDS in IoMT. That is why it is crucial to weigh the pros and cons of these systems and figure out how to include them in your organization's larger security plan.

11.3.5 Hybrid intrusion detection systems

Hybrid intrusion detection is a valuable addition to enhancing security by combining signature and anomaly-based approaches. In the context of the Internet of Medical Things (IoMT), these hybrid IDS systems play a crucial role in identifying both known and emerging threats to medical equipment and systems. By using predefined patterns or signatures, they can recognize familiar threats, while anomaly-based detection is employed to identify deviations from standard network behavior, which could indicate a potential attack. Moreover, the integration of machine learning algorithms allows for the detection of previously unseen threats within the data.

Beyond their role in identifying and preventing cyberattacks, hybrid IDS systems in IoMT offer additional functionalities, including real-time monitoring, alerting, and support for post-attack forensic analysis. As a result, hospitals and clinics will be better prepared to deal with the effects of cyberattacks on patient confidentiality and safety. In conclusion, hybrid IDS in IoMT is a significant step in protecting patient safety and privacy in the era of connected healthcare by ensuring the security and integrity of medical devices and networks.

11.4 Artificial Intelligence and Machine-Learning-Based IDS

In alignment with the current deep learning techniques for attack detection [21] and adhering to the classification presented in prior studies [22, 23], we can broadly classify them into three categories: unsupervised, supervised, and hybrid methods. A detailed breakdown of this categorization is illustrated in Figure 11.4. Many improvements in attack detection approaches may result from implementing various deep learning algorithms. Accuracy is typically good when using a supervised-learning-based approach because of the wealth of data available from manually labeled samples. Unsupervised-learning-based methods typically perform poorly because they need the necessary knowledge from labeled data. Unfortunately, labeling by hand is a laborious process, especially for sophisticated attacks. The complexity of actual network attacks makes it such that some situations defy easy categorization.

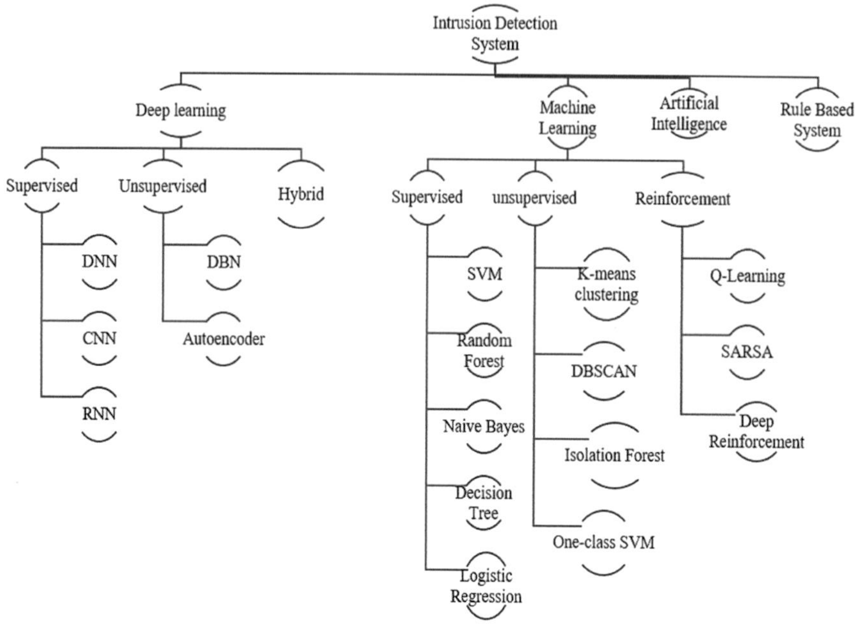

Figure 11.4 Artificial intelligence and machine-learning-based IDS.

Consequently, it is clear that there is an advantage to using approaches based on unsupervised learning, as they may perform effectively even without any prior knowledge of attacks. Hybrid approaches are well-suited for handling varied attack scenarios because they reduce the required number of training samples while maintaining a relatively high level of performance. Unfortunately, its widespread implementation is hampered by its complex structure and lengthy computation requirements.

IoMT (Internet of Medical Things) systems now have a strong tool at their disposal: deep learning. In IoMT, image-based detection is commonly performed using convolutional neural networks (CNNs). Anomalies in medical imaging like X-rays and CT scans can be indicators of an impending attack, and CNNs can spot them. Time-series data, such as measures of vital signs or electrocardiograms, can be analyzed effectively with the use of recurrent neural networks (RNNs) (ECGs). RNNs are able to recognize irregular patterns and record the data's temporal connections. RNNs with long short-term memories (LSTMs) may recall past data for a longer period.

Long short-term memories (LSTMs) can aid in the detection of attacks that unfold over time, such as the manipulation of patient records. To re-create input data, autoencoders are neural networks that have been trained to do so. Attacks can be uncovered by monitoring for anomalies in the input data that cause reconstruction mistakes. Autoencoders can help uncover attacks that involve tampering with or injecting new data. To begin, let us define what we mean by "generative adversarial networks" (GANs). The generator makes up numbers, while the discriminator sorts the real from the phony. Attacks that forge new data or alter current data can be uncovered with the use of GANs. These deep learning techniques can be taught to recognize aberrant patterns that may suggest an attack by studying vast collections of data gathered through IoMT.

11.4.1 Machine-learning-based IDS in IoMT

Our primary goal in this study is to evaluate and contrast the performance of several ML algorithms for intrusion detection in IoMT networks. Below is an overview of the ML algorithms under consideration.

11.4.2 Naive Bayes

Naive Bayes is a supervised machine learning technique used to determine whether or not some data points should be considered abnormal. Bayes' theorem asserts that given the presence of one event, the likelihood of a second event can be computed using the likelihood function, which forms the basis of the procedure. The Naive Bayes algorithm can be based on a dataset of normal network traffic in the framework of detection systems for intrusions to learn the confidence interval of parameters like packet size, source IP address, destination IP address, protocol type, and so on. The trained algorithm can then be used to categorize incoming network data as "normal" or "abnormal." The Naive Bayes method can be used in IoMT to identify unusual data flows that may indicate a cyberattack on healthcare infrastructure. Naive Bayes can detect unusual behavior, such as when medical equipment suddenly begins sending data to an unidentified IP address, and notify the appropriate parties.

Naive Bayes is predicated on the premise that certain features (such as source IP address, destination IP address, protocol type, etc.) can be used to determine the likelihood that a given network traffic is benign or malicious. Although this may not always be the case in practice, the algorithm operates under the assumption that the presence of one feature is not reliant on the presence of any other feature. However, this assumption streamlines math and generally holds up well in practice. In information retrieval systems, Naive Bayes can be written as an equation:

For any set X, the probability of malicious behavior is

$$P(\text{malicious} \mid X) = P(X \mid \text{malicious}) * \frac{P(\text{malicious})}{P(X)} \tag{11.1}$$

where:

The likelihood that network traffic is malicious, $P(\text{malicious} \mid X)$, is a function of the features that have been seen. If the traffic is malicious, then there is a probability $P(X \mid \text{malicious})$ that the attributes X will be observed. The probability that the traffic is malicious, denoted by $P(\text{malicious})$, is assumed to be high. The marginal probability of spotting feature X is denoted by $P(X)$. The program then uses these probabilities to place a new instance of network traffic into one of the two legitimate or harmful classifications.

11.4.3 K-nearest neighbor (KNN)

One common machine learning approach for IoMT intrusion detection is the K-nearest neighbor (KNN) method. To summarize, the KNN algorithm works by assigning each new data point to the same feature class as its nearest neighbors. When applied to IoMT intrusion detection, the KNN algorithm can be used to spot out-of-the-ordinary trends in the data produced by medical devices, thereby providing early warning of potential security breaches. This is a mathematical description of the KNN algorithm:

To begin, let us define a training dataset with m data points, each of which has a feature vector x_j and a class label $y_j : (x_1, y_1), (x_2, y_2), \cdots, (x_m, y_m)$. Whenever you have a new data point x, you may use a distance measure (such as Euclidean distance or cosine similarity) to locate its nearest k neighbors in the training dataset. Among the nearest k neighbors of x' assign it the majority class label. To calculate the Euclidean distance between two points x_j, x_k in a p-dimensional feature space, we can use the following formula:

$$d\left(x_j, x_k\right) = \sqrt{\left(x_{j1}, -x_{k1}\right)^2 + \left(x_{j2}, -x_{k2}\right)^2 + \ldots + \left(x_{jm}, -x_{km}\right)^2} \tag{11.2}$$

In the KNN algorithm, picking the right value for k is crucial. Overfitting, where the algorithm is very sensitive to noise in the training data, and underfitting, where meaningful patterns in the data are missed, are both possible when k is set too low or too high. The best choice of k will vary from application to application but can be found through cross-validation methods.

11.4.4 Support vector machine (SVM)

Support vector machines (SVMs) are a well-known machine learning approach employed by IoMT intrusion detection systems. SVMs function by locating the hyperplane in a high-dimensional space that optimally divides the space into distinct groups of data. The SVM algorithm can be used to detect intrusions by first learning the features of each class from a collection of labeled data (i.e., normal and abnormal network traffic) and then using those learned characteristics to classify new, unlabelled data. SVM can be expressed as an equation, which looks like this:

$$\text{Predicted result } = y(x) = w^T x + b \tag{11.3}$$

where x is the input vector, w is the weight vector, and b is the bias term. The purpose of SVM is to find the best possible settings for wb reducing classification errors. To put it another way, SVM looks for the hyperplane that creates the largest gap between the two groups. For intrusion detection in the IoMT, SVM can be trained on a dataset of network traffic to recognize both benign and malicious patterns. After training, the SVM model can use the features retrieved from network packets to make predictions about the nature of future network traffic.

11.4.5 Artificial neural network (ANN)

Artificial neural networks (ANNs) are a specific type of machine learning algorithm designed to capture complex nonlinear relationships present in raw data without making any prior assumptions about the data itself. They aim to replicate the analytical processes of the human brain. When compared to other ML algorithms, ANN has various advantages. The first is its quick learning and parameter adjustment for new types of data. Second, its generalization capacity is robust and consistent. Finally, it can enhance classification accuracy even when given data with arbitrary decision limits. Reducing sensitivity to changes in parameters and increasing fault tolerance is the fourth goal. Because of its useful features, ANN has been widely adopted as a potential ML method in a wide range of commercial and industrial settings in recent years. One of the most popular and useful ANN topologies, multilayer perceptron (MLP), has an input layer, an output layer, and a collection of hidden layers. The activation function is defined as follows, and it is used by the hidden layer (also known as the distillation layer) to understand the complicated correlations between features.

$$z_j = A\left(\sum_{M=1}^{n} W_{Ml} y_M\right) \tag{11.4}$$

In this case, n represents the input features and l represents the total number of neurons. You can also utilize alternative activation functions such as tanh, softmax, sigmoid, linear, rectified linear unit (ReLU), or others. During training an MLP network, the bias and weights are progressively adjusted at each epoch to minimize the output error obtained during training. As a result, the strategy contributes to an increase in the rate at which malicious acts are uncovered.

11.4.6 Deep-learning-based IDS in IoMT

Internet of Medical Things (IoMT) network and device security relies heavily on intrusion detection systems (IDS). The ability to recognize subtleties in data and extrapolate useful insights has increased the need for IDS models based on deep learning. Wearable sensors, medical imaging equipment, and implantable medical technology are just some of the sources of data used by IoMT deep-learning-based intrusion detection system models. The IDS model, which is based on deep learning, is trained using the processed and transformed data from these devices. Convolutional neural networks (CNNs), recurrent neural networks (RNNs), and autoencoders are only some of the deep-learning-based IDS models that can be applied in IoMT. Medical images can be analyzed with CNNs, while time series data from IoMT devices can be analyzed with RNNs to spot any irregularities. The model may be taught to rebuild the input data and spot abnormalities in the reconstruction mistakes, making autoencoders useful for unsupervised learning.

11.4.7 Convolutional neural network (CNN)

Obtaining sufficient labeled data to train deep-learning-based IDS models in IoMT takes a lot of work. This is because data produced by IoMT devices may contain private patient information and, hence, may not be easily accessible for training purposes. This problem can be solved by using synthetic data creation methods to generate labeled datasets that are statistically indistinguishable from real-world IoMT data. Improving the safety of IoMT (Internet of Medical Things) networks using a CNN-based IDS (intrusion detection system) is a viable option. Remote patient monitoring, telemedicine, and healthcare data management are just a few examples of the many uses of IoMT devices in today's healthcare system. Patients' safety and privacy may be in danger due to the rising prevalence of cyberattacks made possible by IoMT devices. In the realm of picture recognition and classification, CNN (convolutional neural network) is a deep learning technique that has proven to be highly effective. IoMT gadgets are able to spot suspicious network activity and identify potential cyberattacks thanks to IDS, which is based on convolutional neural networks.

In order to detect malicious behavior in network traffic, a neural network is trained using the CNN-based intrusion detection system. Figure 11.5 depicts the sample CNN architecture. The network is taught to differentiate between regular and aberrant network traffic by utilizing a dataset consisting of both types of traffic. After the CNN has been trained, it can be used to keep an eye on network activity in real time and raise red flags for system administrators if it spots something out of the ordinary. Using CNN-based IDS in IoMT has many advantages, such as the speed and precision with which cyberattacks can be identified and countered, hence reducing the likelihood of data breaches and increasing the likelihood of patient safety. The application of deep learning algorithms, in addition to standard signature-based IDS systems, can provide more robust and precise detection capabilities. The implementation of CNN-based IDS in IoMT is not without its difficulties. Collecting and labeling massive amounts of network traffic data is a major

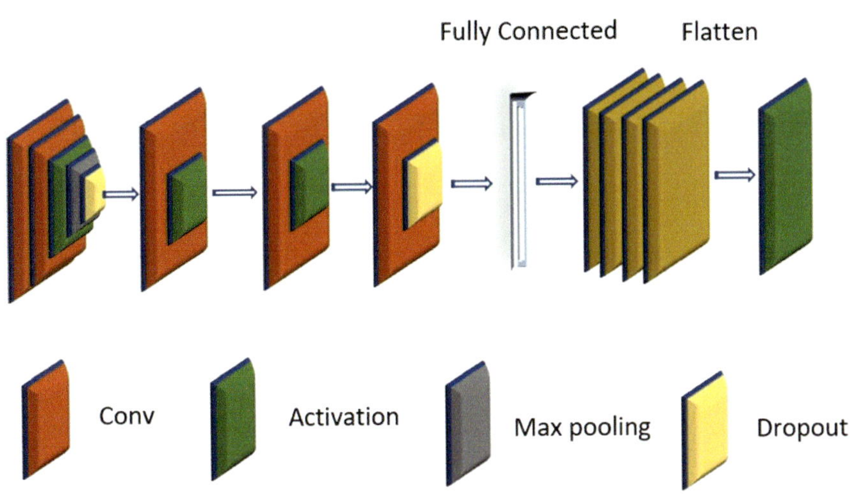

Figure 11.5 CNN-based architecture.

hurdle because it takes time and resources to do so. CNN-based IDS systems rely heavily on the quality and diversity of their training data, yet it might be challenging to include every conceivable attack scenario in the dataset. Identifying vulnerabilities in IoMT networks is possible with the use of a convolutional neural network (CNN) based intrusion detection system (IDS). A CNN-based IDS in IoMT can be roughly described as follows:

Data collection:

Network traffic and other relevant data, such as system logs, system calls, and file accesses, should be collected from the IoMT devices.

Pre-processing:

Extract useful features from the gathered data to use in training the CNN-based IDS. This stage includes data normalization, feature extraction, and data cleansing.

Training:

In order to train the CNN-based IDS, the preprocessed data must be used. The needs of the IoMT system can inform the development of the CNN architecture.

Validation:

Verify the effectiveness of the CNN-based IDS using a test dataset. Here, we check the IDS for precision, recall, accuracy, and $F1$ score.

Implementation:

Use a CNN-based intrusion detection system (IDS) in your IoMT network to spot potential security breaches as they happen. The IDS must be connected to the system's existing security infrastructure if the IoMT system is to effectively detect and mitigate threats.

11.4.8 Recurrent neural networks (RNNs)

To safeguard medical networks and equipment from cyber criminals, it is possible to create an intrusion detection system (IDS) based on recurrent neural networks (RNNs). Using labeled data, the RNN-based IDS may be trained to distinguish between benign and harmful input sequences. During training, the RNN's weights and biases are adjusted so that the discrepancy between the predicted and labeled outputs is as small as possible. Once the RNN-based IDS has been trained, it can be used to identify intrusions and abnormalities in real time by feeding in fresh input sequences and evaluating the result.

11.4.9 Long short-term memory (LSTM)

An IDS in IoMT can be built with a long short-term memory (LSTM) recurrent neural network (RNN). Training an LSTM model using data from IoMT network traffic allows for the creation of an LSTM-based IDS. The LSTM model may examine network traffic data for anomalies or assaults by analyzing the data's temporal dependencies. Using a network traffic analyzer that records data in real time allows for the collection of the necessary training data.

Using supervised learning, the LSTM model may be trained with network traffic data as input and a forecast of an attack or normal traffic as output. Training data can be annotated as either "normal" or "attack" data. Once the LSTM model has been trained, it can be used to monitor IoMT device network traffic for signs of intrusion. The LSTM model can either be installed locally or on a remote server that keeps tabs on all the IoMT gadgets' data transfers. LSTM has proven to be very effective, even though many other approaches can achieve this goal. This is because LSTM is designed to deal with the vanishing gradient issue that plagues most RNN designs, and it can learn both the local and global dependencies of the issue.

It is useful for modeling indoor temperatures because it takes into account both steady-state and transient processes. An LSTM primarily employs "cells" as its unit of information processing. These cells could be viewed as more advanced neurons in a typical MLP. Several gates within a cell work together to store and control the flow of information across a time-varying sequence. Due to this, LSTM can evaluate the usefulness of data and act accordingly. So, it is of great value for addressing issues of a sequential nature. The following is one possible definition of an LSTM cell:

$$I_t = \sigma\left(W_{jI} * X_t + b_{jI} + W_{HI} * H_{t-1} + b_{HI}\right) \tag{11.5}$$

$$F_t = \sigma\left(W_{jF} * X_t + b_{jF} + W_{HF} * H_{t-1} + b_{HF}\right) \tag{11.6}$$

$$G_t = \tanh\left(W_{jG} * X_t + b_{jG} + W_{HG} * H_{t-1} + b_{HG}\right) \tag{11.7}$$

$$O_t = \sigma\left(W_{jO} * X_t + b_{jO} + W_{HO} * H_{t-1} + b_{HO}\right) \tag{11.8}$$

$$MC_t = F \odot MC_{t-1} + I_t \odot G_t \tag{11.9}$$

$$H_t = O_t \odot \tanh\left(MC_t\right) \tag{11.10}$$

In this context, we use I_t to represent the input and H_t for the hidden state at the current time step t. All of f, i, o, and g are specific activation functions. f represents the forget gate, i stands for the input gate, o signifies the output gate, and g represents the production gate. Additionally, W and b denote the

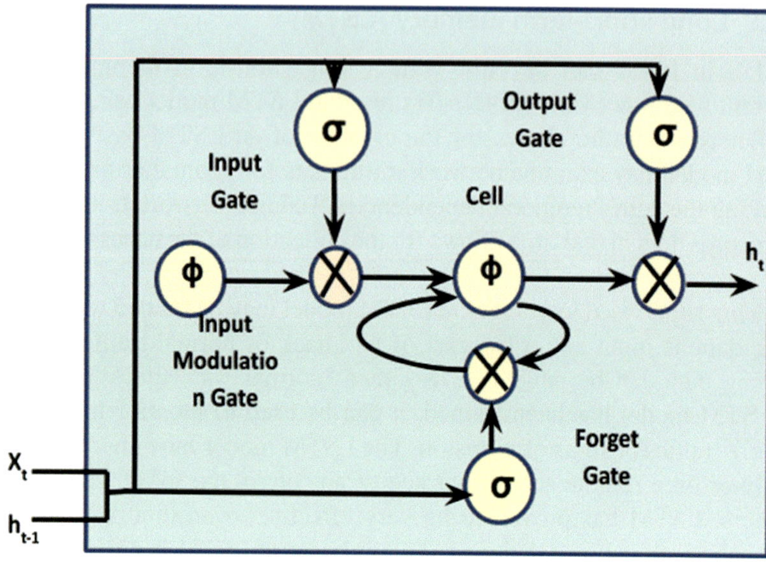

Figure 11.6 LSTM structure.

weights and bias terms that can be learned and applied between the gates. To gain an intuitive understanding of this process, you can refer to Figure 11.6, which offers a visual representation of the internal data flow within an LSTM cell. This schematic helps you grasp how information flows within an LSTM cell.

11.4.10 Hyperparameter tuning

In the process of creating an intrusion detection system (IDS) for the Internet of Medical Things, hyperparameter tuning plays a vital role (IoMT). Activation functions play a significant role in deep learning models and can have an impact on how well an IDS performs. The rectified linear unit (ReLU) function is often utilized as the activation function in the hidden layers of IoMT IDS models. Nevertheless, Sigmoid and Tanh activation functions are also viable alternatives. During training, the optimizer makes adjustments to the model's settings. It is usual practice to begin IoMT IDS with the Adam optimizer, which is widely utilized in deep learning models. While RMSProp and SGD are two popular alternatives, there are more to explore. The training step size is controlled by a hyperparameter known as the learning rate. The model may diverge if the learning rate is set too high, while it may converge

Table 11.3 Sample hyperparameter proposed for IDs in IoMT.

Hyperparameter	Values to try	Best value found
Number of layers	[1, 2, 3, 4]	2
Layer size	[32, 64, 128, 256]	128
Learning rate	[0.01, 0.001, 0.0001]	0.001
Activation function	[ReLU, Leaky ReLU, Sigmoid, Tanh]	Leaky ReLU
Batch size	[16, 32, 64, 128]	64
Dropout rate	[0.1, 0.2, 0.3, 0.4, 0.5]	0.3
L2 regularization	[0.01, 0.001, 0.0001]	0.001
Optimizer	[Adam, SGD, RMSprop]	Adam
Number of epochs	[50, 100, 150, 200]	150

slowly if it is set too low. Table 11.3 shows the sample parameter selection for the deep learning network for intrusion detection in IoMT.

To get the most out of your IoMT IDS model, it is best to begin with a low learning rate and progressively raise it. When a deep learning model does well on the training data but poorly on the test data, this phenomenon is known as overfitting. When the model's performance on the validation set plateaus during training, early stopping can be employed to terminate the training phase and prevent overfitting. Ultimately, it is critical to verify the model's accuracy using an independent test dataset. This will provide a reliable prediction of the model's efficiency under practical conditions.

11.4.11 Comparison of deep learning and machine learning techniques in IoMT IDS

Both machine learning (ML) and deep learning (DL) approaches can be employed in the context of IoMT (Internet of Medical Things) intrusion detection systems (IDS). Here is a comparison table between machine learning and deep learning for IDS in IoMT. Table 11.4 compares deep learning and machine learning techniques used to detect intrusion in IoMT.

Although machine learning models are easier and quicker to train, their effectiveness on complicated datasets is not guaranteed. Although deep learning models may be more accurate and generalizable, they are more difficult to implement and require more resources and data. Also, unlike machine learning models, deep learning models can automatically extract characteristics from data. Both machine learning and deep learning techniques have shown promise in IoMT IDS applications, albeit their utility depends on the nature of the problem at hand and the quality of the data at hand. With smaller datasets or when interpretability is paramount, machine learning methods

Table 11.4 Comparison of deep learning and machine learning techniques in IoMT IDS.

Category	**Machine learning**	**Deep learning**
Network architecture	Shallow and simple	Deep and complex
Feature extraction	Manually engineered features	Automatically learned features
Training data size	Smaller datasets are sufficient	Large datasets are required for better performance
Training time	Faster training time	Longer training time
Accuracy	Less accurate than deep learning models	More accurate than traditional machine learning
Interpretability	More interpretable	Less interpretable
Model size	Smaller model size	Larger model size
Generalization	Performs well on known features	Better at generalizing to new features
Hardware requirements	It can run on less powerful hardware	Requires powerful hardware for training and testing

may be preferable. If you have a large dataset and accuracy is paramount, deep learning methods may be the way to go. Ultimately, the needs of the application will dictate which of the two methods is used.

11.5 Conclusion

In conclusion, there are several ways in which the security and privacy of healthcare systems can be enhanced by the implementation of AI and ML in intrusion detection systems (IDS) for the Internet of Medical Things (IoMT). Cyberattacks have increased in tandem with the popularity of IoMT technologies; so it is crucial to set up reliable IDS that can detect and stop intrusions in real time. Intruder detection systems (IDS) powered by artificial intelligence and machine learning have shown impressive promise in each of these areas. Yet, problems like insufficient data, difficulty in interpretation, and lack of robustness must be solved. Consequently, more studies are required to overcome these obstacles and boost the trustworthiness of ML and AI-based IDS.

More sophisticated IDS will be needed in the future as IoMT technologies continue to expand. As the need to increase the accuracy and efficiency of IDS grows to ensure the safety and security of healthcare systems, the application of AI and ML will become even more important for the creation of IDS for IoMT. Overall, there is a bright future for the integration of AI- and ML-based IDS in health services, and these technologies have the potential to tackle the concerns of safety and confidentiality in IoMT. This research can serve as a jumping-off point for ML-based IDS researchers interested in expanding their knowledge of and improving the effectiveness of IDS against sophisticated, previously unknown threats. In fact, further research will focus on dissecting and contrasting ML and deep learning systems for IoMT network intrusion detection.

Furthermore, the trajectory of future research is anticipated to delve into the intricate realm of dissecting and contrasting various ML and deep learning systems for IoMT network intrusion detection. By comprehensively exploring the intricacies and nuances of these methodologies, researchers can uncover innovative approaches to fortify the security posture of IoMT ecosystems. This pursuit will likely encompass refining existing algorithms, devising novel techniques, and benchmarking the performance of diverse AI and ML models in tackling IoMT-specific security challenges.

References

[1] Fontanet A, Autran B, Lina B, Kieny M, Karim S, Sridhar D (2021) SARS-CoV-2 variants and ending the COVID-19 pandemic. Lancet 397:952–954

[2] Ravens-Sieberer U, Kaman A, Erhart M, Devine J, Schlack R et al. (2021) Impact of the COVID-19 pandemic on quality of life and mental health in children and adolescents in Germany. Eur Child Adolesc Psychiatry 30:1–11

[3] Siddiqui MF (2021) IoMT potential impact in COVID-19: combating a pandemic with innovation. Stud Comput Intell 923:349–361

[4] Udgata SK, Suryadevara NK (2021) COVID-19, sensors, and Internet of medical things (IoMT). In: SpringerBRiefs applied sciences and technology, vol 1, 1 edn. Springer, pp. 39–53

[5] Joyia G, Liaqat R, Farooq A, Rehman S (2017) Internet of medical things (IoMT): applications, benefts and future challenges in healthcare domain. J Commun 4:240–247

[6] Lu Y, Qi Y, Fu X (2019) A framework for intelligent analysis of digital cardiotocographic signals from IoMT-based fetal monitoring. Futur Gener Comput Syst 101:1130–1141

[7] I. Lokshina, C. Lanting, A qualitative evaluation of iot-driven ehealth: knowledge management, business models and opportunities, deployment and evolution, in: Data-Centric Business and Applications, Springer, 2019, pp. 23–52.

[8] E.K. Wang, C.-M. Chen, M.M. Hassan, A. Almogren, A deep learning based medical image segmentation technique in internet-of-medical-things domain, Future Gener. Comput. Syst. 108 (2020) 135–144.

[9] M. Sikarndar, W. Anwar, A. Almogren, I.U. Din, N. Guizani, Iomt-based association rule mining for the prediction of human protein complexes, IEEE Access 8 (2020) 6226–6237.

[10] W.H. Hassan, et al., Current research on Internet of things (iot) security: A survey, Comput. Netw. 148 (2019) 283–294.

[11] D. Gupta, S. Garg, A. Singh, S. Batra, N. Kumar, M.S. Obaidat, Proids: Probabilistic data structures based intrusion detection system for network traffic monitoring, in: GLOBECOM 2017-2017 IEEE Global Communications Conference, IEEE, 2017, pp. 1–6

[12] Yan L, Zhang Y, Yang LT, Ning H. The Internet of Things: From RFID to the NextGeneration Pervasive Networked Systems. CRC Press, 2008.

[13] Shih F, Zhang M. Towards supporting contextual privacy in body sensor networks for health. Monitoring service. In: W3C Workshop on Privacy and Data Usage Control, Cambridge, MA, 2010.

[14] Appari A, Johnson ME. Information security and privacy in healthcare: Current state of research. International Journal of Internet and Enterprise Management. 2010;6(4):279–314.

[15] Löhr H, Sadeghi AR, Winandy M. Securing the e-health cloud. In: Proceedings of the 1st ACM International Health Informatics Symposium, Arlington, Virginia, USA, 2010:220–229.

[16] Tsai FS. Security issues in e-healthcare. Journal of Medical and Biological Engineering. 2010;30(4):209–214.

[17] Wilkowska W, Ziefle M. Privacy and data security in E-health: Requirements from the user's perspective. Journal of Health Informatics. 2012;18(3):191–201.

[18] Agrawal V. Security and privacy issues in wireless sensor networks for healthcare. In: Internet of Things User Centric IoT, Rome, Italy, 2014:223–228.

[19] Kim JT. Privacy and security issues for healthcare system with embedded RFID system on Internet of things. Advanced Science and Technology Letters. 2014;7(2):109–112.

[20] Lake D, Milito R, Morrow M, Vargheese R. Internet of things: Architectural framework for eHealth security. Journal of ICT Standardization. 2014, River Publishing, vol 1, 301–328

[21] M. Z. Alom, T. M. Taha, C. Yakopcic et al., "The history began from alexnet: a comprehensive survey on deep learning approaches," 2018 pages, CoRR abs/1803.01164

[22] E. Aminanto and K. Kim, "Deep learning in intrusion detection system: an overview," in Proceedings of 2016 International Research Conference on Engineering and Technology (2016 IRCET), Higher Education Forum, Seoul, South Korea, January 2016

[23] L. Deng, "A tutorial survey of architectures, algorithms, and applications for deep learning," APSIPA Transactions on Signal and Information Processing, vol. 3, 2014

Index

About the Editors

Deepak Gupta is an eminent academicia who plays versatile roles and responsibilities juggling between lectures, research, publications, consultancy, community service, Ph.D. and post-doctorate supervision etc. With 16 years of rich expertise in teaching and two years in industry, he focuses on rational and practical learning. He has contributed massive literature in the fields of human–computer interaction, intelligent data analysis, nature-inspired computing, machine learning and soft computing. He is working as an assistant professor at Maharaja Agrasen Institute of Technology (GGSIPU), Delhi, India. He has served as Editor-in-Chief, Guest Editor, and Associate Editor in SCI and various other reputed journals (IEEE, Elsevier, Springer, Wiley, and MDPI). He has actively been an organizing end of various reputed international conferences. He has completed his Post-Doc from Internet of Things research group, National Institute of Telecommunications (Inatel), Brazil, in 2018 and eHealth and Telemedicine Group (GTe), University of Valladolid (UVA), Spain in 2019, Federal University of Piauí (UFPI), Teresina - Pi, Brazil in 2021 and Ph.D. from Dr. APJ Abdul Kalam Technical University, India in 2017. He has authored/edited 70 books with national/international level publishers (IEEE Press, Elsevier, Springer, Wiley, CRC, DeGruyter, etc.). He has published 330 scientific research publications in reputed international journals and conferences including 213 SCI indexed Journals of IEEE, Elsevier, Springer, Wiley and many more. He has also granted/published eight patents. He is the recipient of 2021 IEEE System Council Best Paper Award and Highly Cited Paper Award in *Applied Sciences Journal*. He has been featured in the list of top 2% scientist/researcher database in the world in 2019, 2020, and 2022 with Rank 51 in AI & Image Processing, Rank 423 in India overall and Rank 80604 in World overall.

Anuj Kumar Singh is working as Associate Professor in the Department of Computer Science and Engineering at Amity University Madhya Pradesh, India. He is also the Founding Head of Amity Center for Blockchain, Cybersecurity, and Digital Forensics. He has more than 20 years of teaching experience in technical education with institutions of repute. Dr. Singh also hold one year Post Doctoral Research Experience with South Ural State University, Russioan Federation in the area of Cryptography and Network Security. He holds a Ph.D degree in the field of Computer Science and Engineering from Dr. A.P.J. Abdul Kalam Technical University, Lucknow. Having published more than 50 research papers and articles in journals, conferences, and books including SCIE and Scopus, he has also authored one book and edited ten. He has also filed five patents. He is guiding several Ph.D Scholars and has also supervised more than ten dissertations at PG level. His areas of specialization include Intelligent Systems, Cryptography, Network and Information Security, Blockchain Technology, and Algorithm Design.

Yu-Dong (Eugene) Zhang serves as a Chair Professor at the School of Computing and Mathematical Sciences, University of Leicester, UK. His research interests include deep learning and medical image analysis. He is a Fellow of IET, Fellow of EAI, and Fellow of BCS. He is the Senior Member of IEEE, IES, and ACM. He is a Distinguished Speaker of ACM. He was included in the Most Cited Chinese Researchers (Computer Science) by Elsevier from 2014 to 2018. He was 2019, 2021 and 2022 recipient of Clarivate Highly Cited Researcher. He is included in World's Top 2% Scientist by Stanford University from 2020 to 2022. He won the Emerald Citation of Excellence 2017, MDPI Top 10 Most Cited Papers 2015, Information Fusion 2022 Best Paper Award, etc. His three papers are included in UK Research Excellence Framework (REF) 2021. Up to 2023 he has (co)authored over 400 peer-reviewed articles in journals: Ann Oncol, JACC, JAMA Psychiatry, IJIM, Inf Fus, IEEE TFS, etc. He has more than 60 ESI Highly Cited Papers and 6 ESI Hot Papers in his (co)authored publications. He is the editor of Neural Networks, IEEE TITS, IEEE TCSVT, IEEE JBHI, etc. He has conducted many successful industrial projects and academic grants from NIH, Royal Society, GCRF, EPSRC, MRC, BBSRC, Hope, British Council, Fight for Sight, and NSFC. He has given over 120 invited talks at international conferences, universities, and companies, including Harvard University, University of Birmingham, University of Sheffield, etc. He has served as (Co-)Chair for more than 60 international conferences and workshops (including more than 20 IEEE or ACM conferences).

For Product Safety Concerns and Information please contact our EU representative GPSR@taylorandfrancis.com Taylor & Francis Verlag GmbH, Kaufingerstraße 24, 80331 München, Germany